AF333147

Scrapy,
I salute the wild
spirit in you also.
Enjoy— Cartilages

Beyond the Edge

To Liz

Om mani padme hum

Namaste,

Mike Dennison

Beyond the Edge

A Backpacking Trip
Around the World

Mike Dennison

SAGARMATHA PRESS
SPARKS, NEVADA

Copyright 1999, Mike Dennison
All rights reserved.
This book may not be duplicated in any way without the express written consent of the author, except in the form of brief excerpts or quotations for the purposes of review. The information contained herein is for the personal use of the reader and may not be incorporated in any commercial programs or other books, databases, or any kind of software without the written consent of the publisher or author. Making copies of this book, or any portion of it, for any purpose other than your own, is a violation of United States copyright laws.

Published by:
Sagarmatha Press
225 Lillard Drive
Sparks, Nevada 89434
(801) 252-0983
Website: http://www.mikedennison.com
e-mail: beyondedge1@juno.com

PRINTED IN THE UNITED STATES OF AMERICA
BOOK PRODUCTION BY PHELPS & ASSOCIATES, LANCASTER, OHIO

Cover Photo—One of the world's highest handstands: 18,100 feet atop Kala Pattar. Everest is in the background.

Note: Foreign words throughout the text have been set in italics. The names of cities and towns, mountains, or other places— while often foreign—have not been italicized.

*Cataloging-in-Publication Data
(prepared by Quality Books, Inc.)*

Dennison, Mike.
    Beyond the edge : a backpacking trip around the
world / Mike Dennison. -- 1st ed.
    p. cm.
    LCCN: 99-73821
    ISBN: 0-9672582-1-9

    1. Dennsion, Mike. --Journeys. 2. Backpacking.
I. Title.

G440.D4A3 1999   910.4´1
                  QBI99-696

To my mother

Table of Contents

Opposite page: Everything you own is on your back, you are many thousands of miles from home, you're not sure exactly where you are going, no one could find you, and... it seems to be just fine.

*George Hery climbs Too Much of Nothing near
Carefree, Arizona*

Foreword

So many of us have said, "Been there, done that." But not this time! We could not have done that! Mike Dennison has outdone himself with this mountainous endeavor. He traveled around the world, filled his travels with impossible exploits, and remembered enough to write eloquently about his experiences—both physical and mental.

Many times I have nearly been worked to death attempting to keep up with Mike, one of the real monster physical fitness, weight training, hiking, biking, mountain climbing, running, trampoline, gymnastics fanatics of all time. The man with the "Dr. Pain" license plate gave up his job, sold all his belongings, traveled around the world, and experienced two lifetimes in fourteen months. He finally slowed down enough to think about it and, more importantly, has now told the rest of us about it. His experiences alone are worth twice the price of the book. He writes incredibly well and shares some very valuable insights about life and its meaning.

The book is a must read for all athletes, adventure seekers, and others who are interested in learning why and what we are seeking, whether it is adventure, adrenaline, perfection, the meaning of life, or any number of other searches for our real selves. This book is required reading for all of my friends.

–George Hery
gymnast, mountain climber, fitness consultant,
clinician for the President's Council on Physical Fitness and Sports, and
former World Trampoline Champion.

*There's a lot of friendship and training behind a 200-mile bike ride.
Two days before the Seattle to Portland trip, our Lake Ballinger Athletic Club
group posed for a relaxed picture.*

Acknowledgments

A number of friends and family read all or parts of the text and made significant contributions. Rich Morrisey, whose wife had made a similar trip long before they met, read and commented on the Africa sections and gave me valuable advice. My Aunt Celia, an author herself, was kind enough to spend a day reading the fifth revision and making notes about needed changes. She also drove from Los Angeles to Las Vegas to spend a weekend helping me select a publisher and finalizing much of the work that goes into finding someone to read and approve the manuscript.

I gave the Nepal and Europe chapters to Rick Stephenson. Since he had been there during the Europe tour and had subsequently been to Nepal, I knew that he could check the veracity of my descriptions and would know if I had left out anything important. His comments helped a great deal.

George Hery became my idol when I was 18, as I saw him win the World Professional Trampoline Championships in England. At that time I was switching sports from wrestling to gymnastics, and his four-year rise to the top of a difficult sport was just the encouragement I needed. Later, we did gymnastics clinics and camps for our respective gymnastics clubs and became good friends. In Thailand, I discovered the term for eternal optimism: *sanuk*. George was the first person I ever met who totally embodied this concept. His inspiration, before and during the writing of this book, was very helpful.

Jeff Lowe was kind enough to read my text while finishing his own book on ice climbing. He also offered to help me reach editors who had been interested in his literary efforts. If he knew that such help was invaluable, he never let on.

Stormy Eaton was my friend since we competed against each another in college in the late sixties. We met several times after my trip, and I explained why I visited places he couldn't pronounce the names of. He helped me focus on what my trip might mean to others who have unrealized dreams. After joining me in my running endeavors, he decided we should compete in triathlons. We had already water-skied, dived off cliffs, and coached gymnastics, and had become like brothers. His death in 1995 tore a hole in the hearts of the thousands he had inspired with his love of humor and life. He was the second person I knew who devoted his life to *sanuk*.

Janice Phelps was the first editor who replied via the Internet and the only editor who explained everything that needed to be done; then she helped me do it. Her advice and guidance were invaluable to this project. Working with Peter Bumpus on the editing was difficult because the task was immense, but easy because we shared a common goal. Without his help, this project could not have been done.

Special thanks to graphic artist Peri Poloni for her patience and creativity, to Mikel Vause for his encouragement and help, and to Diana Penny Sherpani for her support from England and Nepal. Julie and Bill disappeared from my life, but I owe them thanks for the encouragement to overcome my temerity. Subsequent traveling companions Penny and Nick Wood, David Blakeney, and Jennie Oliver made Asia even more special. Brad McCord, Evangelos Benetatos, and Charlie transformed Africa into a lifetime of adventure. And Ria Curtis was fearless and undaunted throughout the Ruwenzoris, the gorillas, and in Mombassa, and has remained a good friend. Liisa Frei, Dan Millman, and Bil Copp helped with advice and example and made me work harder.

This book is dedicated to my mother. She raised me alone, gave me a sense of values, and inspired a love of knowledge and adventure. Whenever I exhibited a fear of losing, such as when I tried to quit the wrestling team in my senior year of high school, she refused to allow it. She knew what I valued, and she knew what abandoning my goals would do to my later life. She was right, as are many moms. From her, I learned early on to take an intelligent and reasoned approach to even the most unlikely adventure. In her mid-seventies, she was still playing piano for hours each day, teaching astronomy at a nearby university, painting, and working in her garden.

I took this trip for myself. I knew that many among my friends and family would never be able to do what I was doing. The letters I wrote and this book that I have written came about because I thought that much of what I experienced would interest those who wanted to do it, too.

We've done part of it…. There is a lot that still remains.

p.s. When you discover the meaning of life, your life changes. When I returned from my trip I was somehow different. There was much more *sanuk* in my life and much more Buddhism in my character. And that was how I met

Jodi. In my adult gymnastics class, she exhibited humor, honesty, harmony, and happiness more than anyone I had ever known. During the first year of our friendship she ran the Rim to Rim Run at the Grand Canyon, learned guitar, became an avid mountain bicyclist, worked full time, and raised four sons. She was exactly what I would have created had someone asked me to write down the ingredients for friendship. After my return I knew that what she saw in me were changes from my trip and from my life. The trip was worth it by itself, but having opened the door to this special lady—I can't imagine a better ending. Just before the millenium, we'll line up at the starting line for the 1999 Everest Marathon.

For nearly twenty years, gymnastics was the adventure. Now, most of these young ladies have nearly grown families of their own.

On the way to Stormy Eaton's Super Camp for gymnastics in 1978, this was the handstand that led to the book's title.

HOW IT ALL BEGAN

My around-the-world trip began in the early spring in the early 1990s. Three weeks earlier, I would have wagered that it was going to be a great summer in the Pacific Northwest—and that I'd be part of it. But a summer dedicated to improving my bicycling, running, and climbing skills was suddenly underwritten with a huge question mark. Nothing could turn my world upside down like traveling around it would.

I had been managing the Lake Ballinger Athletic Club in Edmonds, Washington and working with some very interesting people. I had competed in wrestling, gymnastics, diving, and trampoline in college and had worked with the National Headquarters of the Amateur Athletic Union after graduation. Working at an athletic club was a good match for me. Part of my job was teaching personal fitness training, which gave me the enviable task of guiding some motivated people toward some attainable and life-enhancing goals. As the person in charge, I had put together a staff of six people who brought the joy of their own fitness to work every day. My job was going well enough; the real challenges of a new business were mostly behind us. I loved what I was doing and my job was suited to most of the skills I had acquired. The general manager, Dake Warren, was a friend with an enviable list of fitness credentials and athletic accomplishments. I worked every day in an environment that was nearly perfect, and there wasn't a "but" on the horizon. Or so I thought. I hadn't realized that I was teetering on the edge of an abyss until there was an earthquake. And that was created by friends Julie and Bill Wright.

For most of the 1980s I had lived in Arizona. Settled near the town of Carefree, I had almost unlimited biking, running, and climbing areas just out my front door. In 1988 I elected to see the rest of the state and entered the Almost Across Arizona Bike Ride. A large number of cyclists were going to spend eight or nine days riding from the Grand Canyon to Mexico. I met Bill as we were waiting in Phoenix for the bikes to be loaded onto tour buses. Julie read as he and I talked. They were from Colorado and had seen an ad for this ride in a magazine. We sat together on the bus and by the time we arrived at the south rim of the Grand Canyon, we were well on our way to being friends.

During the passing years, we got together for running, biking, and weight training workouts as well as for hiking and camping excursions. We wrote and talked by phone and shared our common interests.

While we were camped near the Colorado River at Tapeats Creek, I told them of my desire to someday travel around the world. As I rambled on in defense of an idea that many regarded as bizarre, I noticed that they were smiling—a lot. They were smiling not so much in amazement, but as though they shared a secret that I didn't yet suspect. Having seen that look from friends before, I cut the monologue short and smiled back. Their response to what I had said was to invite me to join them on their trip around the world. Mine was scheduled for "someday." Their trip was scheduled in two years. I listened as they talked about their planned schedule, savings program, travel gear purchases, and a lot more. We left the idea of my participation for my consideration.

As those two years passed, I did what most of us do: nothing. When I saw my friends, we invariably discussed the closeness of their impending journey and how their plans were shaping up. I had moved to Seattle from Carefree and was well into the struggle to help establish a truly service-oriented athletic club with Dake Warren and his family. I envied Julie and Bill and their commitment, but I had one of my own, and I had closed the door on the increasingly close adventure. Closed, as it turned out, but not locked.

When I said good-bye, it was an emotional time for us all. They were off to bicycle across New Zealand. I was off to run some sub-seven-minute miles with a training client. For the first time in my life, what I was doing didn't seem quite right. Rarely depressed, I met that emotion head on for the next several days. Julie and Bill wrote often during their trip and continued to invite me to join them. Finally, in a convincing letter from Australia, their entreaties swayed me. Ready or not—and I was decidedly not—I made up my mind to join them.

General managers of most businesses don't like employees who suddenly depart. Dake seemed surprised at my decision but was instantly supportive. He seemed to realize that this was something I needed to do. He offered me a chance to work at the club again when I returned, and that meant a lot to someone who was about to become "homeless."

I put an ad in the newspaper about the sale of everything I owned and passed the word among my training clients and the six trainers who worked for me. Strangely, the anticipated regret at seeing my possessions leave with others never emerged. Set against the goal of funding this once-in-a-lifetime trip, bicycles, stereos, and furniture became mere objects. I kept about eight hundred of my books and all of those items that would be meaningless or valueless to anyone else.

Included in what remained were my complete daily journals from May of 1974 to the present. Handwritten in spiral notebooks until 1985 and then recorded on computer disks, there were two huge boxes that I would store at my mom's house in Ogden, Utah. Along with the written word, there were hundreds of photographs. Like a small child asked to clean his room, every time I would start to sort through the pictures, I would get lost in memories and would scatter piles of organizational good intentions—until I realized I didn't have the time.

As I put them back in the various shoeboxes, I noticed one of my favorite pictures. In 1978 I had traveled to Arizona for a gymnastics camp at Mingus Mountain. On the way there, I had done a handstand on the edge of the view area overlooking the outflow of the dam. There was nothing but the thinnest of air between two hands on a concrete wall and the generators in a miniscule building below. Even on a windless day, it is a sufficient test of the adrenal cortex. I looked at the picture now and thought about what several people had said when they had first seen it: "What's beyond the edge?"

There isn't an easy answer to that particular question and all it implied: "Why take such a risk?" "What were you thinking?" "Why weren't you thinking?" "Are you crazy?"

Now, I was fielding the same questions about my latest venture. They were two different situations, but they seemed to create the same concern for my sanity. I didn't have an answer then, and I didn't have one as I sat in my bare living room. But the analogy struck me that this trip wasn't so different, in terms of risk, from that impulsive action taken years ago. There was a physical description of what was over the edge in that picture, just as there would be a physical description of each of the places I was going to visit on my trip. The major difference that I could see was that one lasted only a brief instant, but the other was going to take some considerable time. Both had some inherent risk. I hoped to find out just exactly what was beyond this particular edge.

–Mike Dennison
January, 1999

Gymnastics clinics were always fun. In Hawaii they offered running, biking and hiking opportunities unlike anywhere I had been. The run to the top of Diamond Head deserved a celebratory handstand.

CHAPTER 1
<u>SUDDEN DEPARTURE</u>

Well-adjusted people leading ordered and sensible lives have been known to wake up in the morning with inexplicable cravings. They want to move to Tuscany or Provence, or journey the length of South America by public bus. Others dream of rowing across the Atlantic in an open boat, or walking a thousand miles through the Himalayas...These visions usually pass and most people are fortunate to be able to roll over and go back to the safety of their dreams. But not everyone can resist the temptation to head for the horizon.
– Erik Hansen, from The Traveler

You're what?" Rick's voice crackled down the phone line. This was not the first time I'd heard that question.

"I'm finally going to travel around the world," I repeated. "There's an ad in the paper and a notice on the board at work. I'm selling everything and leaving in just over three weeks." There was a digestive pause and I could almost hear him thinking it over. Our friendship had started nearly twenty years ago; I found myself wondering if his response would be the same as that of so many others.

"Didn't we just talk last week about how much you are enjoying the athletic club and the Pacific Northwest?" he reminded me. "And aren't you enthusiastic about all the biking opportunities that are opening up?"

"Yes, and yes," I said. "I just started thinking about Julie and Bill and how much fun they were having, and I realized that the number of times in a lifetime that you find two friends who can go with you on a trip like this is probably just one, if you are lucky. And if I do make my trip—'someday'—I'll probably go alone and would have missed having friends to share the memories with."

"How much will all of this cost you and how long are you going to be gone?" The questions were getting harder to answer.

"I don't know. I figure that ten thousand dollars is the most I'll be able to raise before I leave. All my investments except my IRAs and the money from selling what I own should be just about that much. I'll probably be gone about fourteen months—or until the money runs out. Whichever comes first." Touchy subject, this.

"Where do you start?" he asked. His voice had started to sound like mine; some of the excitement had caught hold of him, too.

"I start with a flight from Seattle to Japan. Then I hope to try to hook up with Julie and Bill in Singapore." The last part about meeting my friends in Asia was a lot more crucial than it sounded. "I'm getting the shots this week and my passport should get here just before I leave. I'm going to drive what's left of my stuff to Mom's in Utah. The cheapest flight sends me back through Seattle before I go to Asia. Maybe that extra stop will allow me a bit of a window in case I'm cutting it too close on receiving my documentation."

"This is great!" he said. If I had a friend I expected to fully understand this adventure, it was Rick. We had climbed mountains, skied, camped, bicycled, and run together, And in the process, we had discovered that we were very similar in our likes and dislikes. Sometimes, when other friends had noticed our similarities, they called us "the twin sons of different mothers." That fit.

"So how do you know what to take?" Practical friend, too.

"Julie sent me a detailed list of what she and Bill had found essential. I thought I'd be limited to just what I could get into my new backpack, but I'm going with her suggestion that I buy an old duffel bag that will hold both my pack and a large gym bag. The idea is that the old duffel bag will hide the fancy new pack inside, and I can carry some non-trekking items in the gym bag. Really important items like credit cards, passport, verification of inoculation, and money will be carried in a fanny pack around my waist." I sounded a lot more confident than I felt about the issue of gear. I was pretty much just quoting Julie at that point. Whatever I took would have to last me for over a year. If it didn't, it would have to be replaced—or done without.

Rick knew that I spoke Spanish and a smattering of German and Japanese. "What language do they speak in Singapore?" he asked. We were both confident that it wasn't anything I was familiar with. He was trying to decide how prepared I was.

"Rick," I had said, "I didn't know until yesterday where Singapore was. I had to get out an atlas and look at China and Japan for a long time before I found out that Singapore borders Malaysia. I think it is a city, but I'm not sure what country it is in." I had answered his question about the language and had revealed my ignorance at the same time. We chatted about the health of his new daughter and the status of his two teenage daughters, and then I went to the army-navy store to work on Julie's list. Rick and I would talk again about this trip. Again turned out to be two days later when he called me at work.

"Now, how do you feel?" That was a good question. I hadn't been this excited about the unknown for a long time, but the fear of being woefully unprepared was tempering it somewhat.

"I'm not sleeping well," I answered. "Every day seems to be jammed full of work and lists. I'm getting a mailing list together and a 'last' letter to everyone. All of the mail drops were prearranged by Julie and Bill, and my letter explains when everyone should mail cards and letters. There looks to be about a month delay on delivery. I'm not training very hard—a little running is all. I don't plan on taking an exercise schedule with me. If I have a chance to work out while I'm traveling, I will. If not, it won't matter."

"Look," he said in a mock-serious tone I had learned to recognize, "when you get to the mountain, I want you to bring back the meaning of life."

"One word or two?" I shot back. "There may be a limit on what a guru will tell an American."

"One word. Something simple. Something that works for all people for any time period. You know, something profound."

We continued on in that vein, and kept it light. Rick and his wife, Anita, were a pretty empathetic couple. They had probably tried to picture themselves in a similar situation and could sense the terror that could arise from such a sudden decision.

I promised to call them from my mom's and to keep in touch throughout the journey. I knew that this trip was something Rick had always wanted to do, too, and I wanted to write often enough that he could sense what it was actually like. Marriage, children, and tenure at a good job blocked any chance of his actually making such a trip. In that sense, a lot of my friends were in the same position.

On a drive across Seattle, I thought about what I was doing. People in cars around me on the interstate were concentrating on their lives and on getting from point "A" to point "B." My life no longer had that type of focus, and I sensed that the difference from others I had felt in the past was going to increase. I smiled at that. The increase would probably be exponential.

I also spent some time reflecting on some questions several people had asked. "What's wrong?" summed up their approach. I don't consider myself stupid, and I know I have an unusual attitude toward life, but it took a little thought to discover what these various questions implied —that something very bad must be driving me to this. This wasn't true. From my viewpoint, I had been standing outside the candy shop with my nose pressed against the front window. Now, finally, I had quit staring so hard at the ultimate goal and had noticed that an open doorway was just a few steps away. All that remained was to walk through that open door….

I'd been in Seattle for three years. The bicycle training I had done had taken me all over the surrounding area. Friends and I had completed the 200-mile Seattle to Portland bike ride, the 157-mile RAMROD (Ride Around Mt. Ranier in One Day), and several "Chilly Hilly" rides on Bainbridge Island. As a result of the training for all these, I had come to know a lot of the countryside. Daily training rides had taken me on the Burke-Gilman trail from Lake Forest Park to Marymoor Park. And there had been weekend excursions to Snoqualmie Falls or through the Snohomish area. The Skykomish, Skookumchuk, Sammamish…they were once just features on a guidebook map. Now they were associated with sights and smells and memories of roads explored and wild berries eaten. There were a lot of strange sounding names on the map of Asia that I had pored over while looking for Singapore. How many of those names would one day have strong memories attached?

The days flew by, and I found that work was almost a distraction. Everyone knew that I was leaving and our conversations centered on both my preparations for the trip and what I expected to find. I could talk a lot more convincingly about the former. The latter was in the hands of Julie and Bill, and the really crucial part was that I meet them exactly when and where they had said. So I talked with the many fine people I had met at the athletic club and tried to answer their questions and explain my reasons. Very few seemed to understand why someone who was happy with his job and enjoying the Northwest life would throw it all over for a trip around the world. Some thought that someone in his mid-forties ought to be thinking more about security. Most thought it sounded exciting, but… There was always a list of reasons why they could not do something so strange.

Finally, there was the task of raising as much money as possible. A relatively disease-proof body, a brand-new passport, and a one-way ticket to Asia had been taken care of. I also had the beginnings of a considerable knot in my stomach. Two days before I was to leave, a letter arrived from Julie and Bill. They had taken more time at Ayers Rock and in Sydney than they had anticipated and the sale of their car was not going well. They might not be able to meet me at the agreed-upon time and on the agreed-upon day. Naturally, I could not reach them at this late date. Mrs. Douglas, my high school speech teacher, had often said: "Thorough preparation is the best fear remover." Thus, the knot.

In the last year I had read *Miles from Nowhere, The Man Who Walked through Time,* and *Adrift.* What stood out as common to all these adventures was the amount of preparation. Barbara Savage and her husband had ridden across the United States on their bicycles before their around-the-world bicycle tour. Colin Fletcher had researched and arranged food and water sites before he walked the length of the Grand Canyon. And Steven Callahan had already sailed the Atlantic in his 21-foot boat and had prepared for such excursions for years. When he got lost at sea on a life raft, he survived because of his knowledge.

I kept thinking back to my talks with Rick and other friends. I really knew nothing about what to expect. Singapore had been an unknown, but I couldn't even tell someone which countries bordered India.

On my last four days in the continental United States, I did not work. I packed my personal items in my Dodge Caravan and then spent two days meeting with those friends who meant the most to me. Some of them gave me a small trinket to take with me—something that they would like to have back when I returned. Two days passed in this emotional way.

And then it was time to drive to Utah. And then it was time to get on a plane to Japan.

Japan was a long flight. Going against the jet stream, it took about thirteen hours. I sat near the window and opened the money belt that was strapped to my waist. I took out a small, round, black, polished rock. My friend Missy Morrisey had given it to me. It had accompanied her on her worldwide trip when she was in her twenties. As I held it in my hand high over the Pacific, I knew it would remind me of the helpful talks we had shared before I left. She was nearly my age, but her trip had remained crystal clear to her. She and her husband, Rich, had become good friends in the two years I had known them. I set the stone on the tray table in front of me.

Two of my former gymnastics and trampoline students had married each other and their twin daughters, Brandi and Breelyn Whipple, had each given me a bright, shiny penny—I hoped that I could someday share tales of all of the places these coins had been. I set them beside the black rock.

One of my former fitness clients, Sherry, had given me a small gold cross. She joked that she wanted the Pope to bless it when I got to Italy. I hoped that by the time I reached Rome, I would be able to tell my story to someone at the Vatican and hoped to surprise her with some blessed success. The person sitting next to me openly stared at what I was doing.

Then I took out a small friendship ring given to me by Jelmina, one of the club members. She had been too shy to even talk to me during the year she had been a regular member of the athletic club. But with my impending trip, she was curious to know if I would be visiting her native Philippines. We had gone to lunch and her country sounded so interesting that I wished it had been on our itinerary, but it was not. More items on the tray and now some sideways glances from my seatmate.

Other than my passport and a sheaf of traveler's checks, that was everything in my money belt. In my pack in the cargo hold was one more gift. Rick had given me a Swiss Army knife. That would not only go everywhere with me; it would be a very important utensil. Yes, a practical friend.

There was something else in the money belt. A folded piece of paper had been inside my passport and had fallen out. I opened it and saw that it was a note; it said: "Remember Value Rigidity." As a psychology major in college I had been particularly impressed with an illustrative story used to define this concept. In one of the countries I was now approaching, monkeys were trapped by using a coconut. In this particular society in Asia, monkey brains were a delicacy. First, a hole smaller than the monkey's clenched fist was drilled into the fruit, and then enticing sweets were placed inside. When a monkey reached inside and discovered he couldn't remove his clenched hand, the owner of the trap would approach. Panic would overtake the monkey as he jerked at the anchored coconut with all of his strength. As the trapper got close enough to wield his club, the monkey would do everything except release the food in his hand. Value rigidity would cost him his life. As impartial observers, we can easily see what he should do. But the monkey couldn't. He valued food and was hungry; he should have valued his life and escaped. He could always eat later. Value rigidity guaranteed there would be no later. Presumably, the note had been written to remind me that I should look at the big picture, especially if the situation was getting desperate. I didn't recognize the handwriting; I hoped I understood the thought.

I put the items back in the belt and settled in to watch one of the four consecutive movies on the screen. Thoughts of those left behind and the willingly suspended disbelief of a movie kept me from worrying. Asia rushed to meet me. I knew exactly where I would discover the meaning of life; it was waiting just beyond the edge I was falling over.

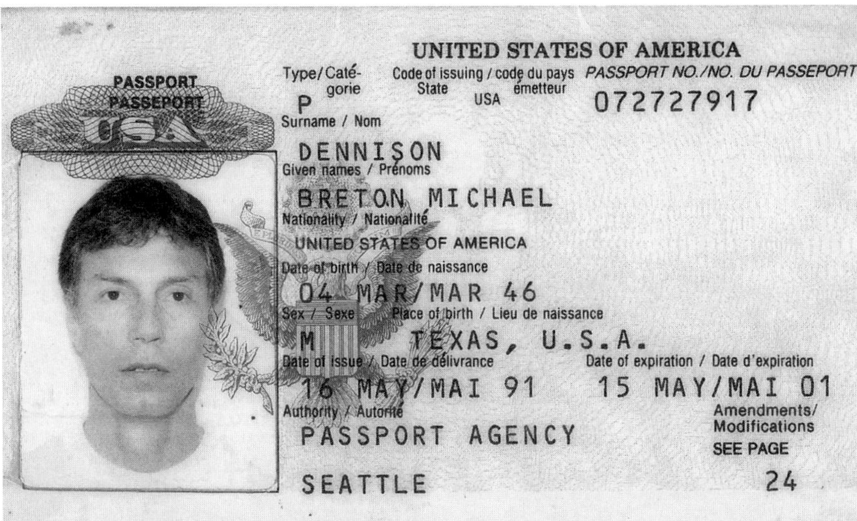

Top: If you look like your passport photo, you deserve the trip.
Above: The adult gymnastics class is introduced to mountain climbing at Lake Tahoe.

Mike Dennison and Stormy Eaton after a 10-mile run.

CHAPTER 2
<u>SINGAPORE</u>

Peculiar travel suggestions are dancing lessons from God.
– Kurt Vonnegut

All of my luggage was lost when my Northwest flight became a Japan Airlines flight—for the passengers, but not for our belongings.

We spent nearly thirteen in-flight movie hours flying to Narita, Japan; then our flight to Singapore was cancelled and we were shunted to another flight. We were still going to Changi Airport in Singapore, but later. I was focused on the little bit of information that I had: Julie and Bill would be at American Express at noon—sometime within the next six days. That was not much to go on, and it certainly didn't solve the problem of being left with just the contents of my fanny pack. The airline offered to deliver my things as soon as I had obtained lodging. I wondered when that might be.

It was one in the morning in Singapore and about six in the morning back home, but a day later. I needed to get some sleep. There was not so much fatigue that I didn't notice the beauty of this huge airport. It was open and tropical, much like Honolulu, and it was spacious and well lit. As I searched for a place to lie down, the lighting became a problem. Sensitive to light, I could find no place that was not illuminated like day. I hoped that I was tired enough to over-come this unusual condition, but it was a fitful few hours until 6:00 A.M.

Fresh red and white flowers were being placed on fifty tables by immacu-lately clad waiters. I had tried to sleep about fifty feet from a place to eat. The floor had been recently cleaned and waxed, and I could smell the rich aroma rising from the white tiles. The breakfast menu seemed very American although rice had replaced potatoes, and everything was offered in two languages. Fortunately, one was English. It was my first breakfast at McDonald's in ten years, and I came to Singapore for it. Waiters at McDonald's?

My waiter greeted me in flawless English, one arm placed behind his back as he handed me a menu. "Is this your first time in my country?" he asked. After

*Singapore is a beautiful island nation and rivals any large city in the world
for its friendly people and technological marvels.*

my affirmative, he took my order and offered to explain a few things while my
breakfast was being prepared.

"Singapore is both a country and a city," he explained, smiling. "There are
fifty-seven smaller islands surrounding the one you are now on. You have
noticed our signs in English?" I nodded. "You will find that courtesy throughout the country because of a very strong British influence when the city was
founded."

I was very pleased with this information. It answered one of the main concerns
I had. Perhaps language was not going to be the barrier that I had thought. "If
this city was founded, then where did most of the people come from?" I had
heard that there was a wide variety in physical appearance from country to
country in Asia and hoped to begin learning the differences as quickly as
possible. Perhaps I could begin here.

"About three fourths of our people are Chinese. Another fifteen percent are
from neighboring Malaysia. My ancestors were from China," he added. "But
there are a wide variety of dialects spoken here. My parents speak Cantonese
and Foochow. I have learned Teochew. Most people can get by if they speak
Chinese, Malay, Tamil, or English. There are many Indians here, too, and they

speak four or five dialects." He left for a moment, as my order was ready. Other patrons were beginning to file past the life-sized Ronald McDonald—standing to the left of the entrance.

"We have a literacy rate of nearly ninety percent," he said with obvious pride when he came back. "And we have a very interesting legal system—" He was interrupted and excused himself to wait on other tables. "Enjoy your stay in my country," he said smiling.

"Thank you," was about all I could muster in reply. His slight accent, obvious goodwill, and helpful comments made me feel most welcome, and I felt a sense of calm that I had not had for a number of weeks. I was in Asia and feeling safe. Now I sorted through my fanny pack for my travelers checks and a slip of paper that had the location of the American Express office on it. I'd be looking for Somerset Road. I paid with the few American dollars I had in one pocket.

After breakfast I took myself and my good mood to the door marked "Ground Transportation." Outside, there were taxi and bus stands. I didn't have any money that I could use. I stepped back through the automatic doors and retraced some steps to the official Money Exchange sign. I asked which method of travel was the least expensive and how much that expense would be. A smiling girl gave me the information and changed a ten-dollar travelers check. She handed me money that was different sizes and different colors. The currency was the Singapore dollar. I again stepped outside to wait for a bus. Somerset Road—that sounded decidedly British to me.

The bus driver took one of the colored bills out of my hand and replaced it with coins. He smiled at my look of puzzlement and said, "Welcome to our country." I thanked him and sat close to the front of the bus so that I could ask him about Somerset. "I will tell you when we are near it. It is a long way from here."

I settled in and anxiously awaited my ride to the city-state of Singapore. For the first eight to ten miles, the left side of the bus paralleled the East Coast Park. There were runners on many trails. Walkers, bike riders, and people sitting on benches were enjoying the early morning sea air. The port of Singapore was just beyond the park view, and the miles of ships were quite impressive. And then, so was Singapore.

As we entered the city, I had to immediately rethink my image of Asia. Huge buildings rose above wide streets. Every major European merchandiser seemed to have an outlet here. Mercedes were everywhere. Dior, Armani,

Rolex, Chanel... Then I saw some of American culture, too. Dunkin' Donuts, Burger King, Kentucky Fried Chicken. I didn't know Asian culture, but I was fairly certain that they would be sorry for these particular imports. As I marveled at this modern city, I shot an occasional glance toward the driver to see if he had forgotten me and my destination. He had not.

The bus stopped where there was no bus stop, and the driver motioned me toward the right rear of the bus saying, "Somerset is back there." I thanked him for his courtesy and stepped into the bustle of a modern Asian city. About every third person was speaking on a cellular phone. Those with no one to speak with all seemed to have phones at the ready. Was there more technology available than back home?

I quickly found that either Somerset was spelled Panang or I was in the wrong place. I found other spellings of Somerset: Oxford Street, Oxford Rise, and others. I asked a few passersby and found that Somerset was one block long and was, in fact, Panang on either end. Taking a chance that today might be the day I was to meet my friends, I put off the daunting task of finding accommodations and waited in the Burger King for noon to arrive. I read an English paper and wrote some journal notes on a borrowed piece of paper. I would certainly be glad to see all of my worldly possessions and someone who knew what was going on.

While I stared out the window and watched some bamboo scaffolding being raised for a construction crew, I realized that my lessened anxiety was due to the ability of nearly everyone to speak clear and fluent English. On the other side of the scale was my missing luggage, a foreign currency exchange, only a passport and a few credit cards, and a very foreign culture. And that was for starters. There was no doubt in my mind that this whole trip was a question mark driven by fear of the unknown.

Somewhere in the mix was the difference in driving customs. "Look right or die" had been the clarion call when I had been in England in 1984. When you exited a driveway and looked left, there was never anyone approaching. Of course not. Here, the British system was used, so I did what I had done in England: I always looked both directions. It could have been a lot shorter trip. I walked out the door, looked both ways, and headed for American Express.

Bill was fair skinned and had blue eyes and blond hair. About six feet tall, he weighed nearly 185 pounds and kept in good condition by running, bicycling and lifting weights a few times a week. He had a ready smile and never seemed daunted in any social situation. So far. Julie was also tall. About five feet ten inches tall, she had dark hair and a large, lean frame. A little over a year ago, I had helped her with her first marathon; she was a serious runner. She also liked to lift weights and did that nearly every day. She was not as openly funny and outgoing as Bill, but she had a devastating wit and liked to use it. Both were very bright and had traveled in Asia before. They were both in their late 30s; Bill would turn 40 during our trip. I hoped that their delay at Ayers Rock was not going to mean that I would be on my own for a week. At five minutes to noon, I leaned against the wall at American Express and stared at the entrance door. At exactly noon, my tall and smiling American friends strolled through the doorway.

Bill had lost a lot of weight. He looked healthy enough at 165 pounds— once I got used to the idea that he was feeling the effects of a vegetarian diet. Julie was always the one with the strict dietary regime. Now, Bill could hardly wait to tell me the details of his conversion. I could hardly wait to find some lodging and try to get some sleep. All of the energy had gone out of me when the safety net had been activated, and I was now very tired. And I was hungry. We rented one room for the three of us and ate in the hotel dining room. They explored while I slept.

The first full day in Asia was full of information and important lessons. The most important dent in my considerable ignorance came when Bill introduced me to The Lonely Planet series of guidebooks. There was one written for each country on our itinerary; these books covered customs, places of interest, basic language, historic overview, places to stay (for various budgets), and the approximate cost for lodging, food, and transportation. Usually, some sections were written by an American who had lived and traveled extensively in that country. I assumed that Germans, French, and others had similar books written by "ex pats," too. They were the perfect answer to all my problems from yesterday, except my luggage.

We started the morning with French toast. Food stalls across from our hotel offered Indian, Chinese, Thai, American, French, and Italian cuisine. The food emporium was a large concrete slab about the size of a football field. Food was both served and sold. We wandered around and were almost overcome by the smell of fish and other recent ocean dwellers. In other areas, food stalls contributed smells from spicy dishes. The French toast looked to be the best thing on our particular menu. Bread was dipped in eggs and chopped onions were added. We asked not to have the mutton included. Then a topping of sambol was spooned on. It was not syrup and it was very hot. As someone who followed the lead of his grandfather and added Tobasco to anything involving eggs, I was delighted. As we left, we passed several Vietnamese and Indonesian restaurants that we had not seen on the way in.

At first I was stupefied. Almost all of the conversations that swirled around us were in another language, or languages; I couldn't tell. Other than a few other Westerners, everyone was Asian. Singapore might look like New York City or London from a helicopter, but in the city it was nothing like anywhere I had ever been.

Our hotel manager reacted to my comments about the large volume of cellular phones. He told me that it was the latest rage. Gold or platinum credit cards were highly sought-after items, too. Almost everyone paid off the balance monthly, he said. It was the prestige of using them that was prized. He pointed to the building across from the Burger King that I had been in yesterday. The condos, which were under construction, were just over 1,500 square feet. He spared me a guess and told me that they started at a half-a-million U.S. dollars. This was quite a country. His last informational gem concerned the cars we were seeing. In a small and crowded city, huge taxes were assessed on those who wished to purchase a vehicle. The actual cost to own one could be double or triple what it would be anywhere else. I looked at a Rolls Royce Silver Shadow parked at a nearby curb. I didn't bother to do the math.

On our second night in Singapore, I tried to identify some of the more important changes that were going on. I sat on one of the three beds in our large and otherwise nearly bare room and made notes in my journal. The last thing I wrote was, "The city is draining and depressing for the disparity of class." I reread it several times, not because it was a profound observation, but because it represented my slanted American judgment. I could see that I would have to be more careful not to judge what I did not understand. At that very moment, bicycle-powered rickshaws raced past our open window as the drivers pedaled furiously in impromptu drag races. Their foreign passengers were also having a great time. I heard it and saw it, and observed that not many workers back home exhibited such joy while doing such physically demanding jobs. But I vowed to wait a bit before trying to write any "truths" about what I saw. I put a star next to that entry in the journal. Perhaps some of the meaning of life I sought might require forsaking judgments without foundation.

I did however know something about American problems, and this second night in a foreign land was about to give me a topic to write about that I under-stood. While the three of us wrote or read in our room, Bill cleared his throat and I looked up. He asked if I would mind leaving the room for a while so that Julie and he could have a private discussion. Something in his tone and look indicated that this was serious business and that I should do as asked. Bill told me that he would come and get me when they were through talking, which sounded even more ominous. I walked down the hall and read some tourist brochures in the second floor lounge. I read them all. It seemed strange to me; we were all laughing and joking after dinner, and we had settled into the room in the same lighthearted mood. I'm usually quite quick to pick up on tension between others, but nothing had been said in that room since Julie had started reading, and Bill and I had started writing.

Bill finally did make an appearance, but Julie preceded him, and she walked right on down the stairs and out of sight. I might not understand Asian body language, but I read her like a book. There was some serious trouble on deck. Bill confirmed this, but said that he couldn't discuss it, and he asked for my patience. I correctly guessed that I had nothing to do with the problem, and I offered to help in any way that I could. His look told me that he appreciated the gesture, but he didn't think anything I could do would pack much weight. Worried about Julie at this hour, I walked downstairs to see if she was still around. She was. Crying. This was definitely a night for firsts. It was the first serious difference of opinion I had seen in an otherwise exceptionally support-ive couple. And I had never seen Julie this emotionally distraught. Calm and serene, her best mood had always been one of elation. That and her fitness had been a large part of the basis for our initial friendship.

In the next two hours, I learned that Bill had received and kept a letter from a woman they had worked for in New Zealand. Julie found the letter in Bill's pack while looking for some writing materials. She had read it, held it up for Bill to see, and that had prompted my exit. The contents were fairly easy to guess. In their twelve years of marriage, this was the first severe threat to their relationship. Bill had never done anything like this before. Julie had been emotionally involved with her weight-training partner but had broken that off when it threatened to become more than platonic. Neither of them had any past experience to draw on in their attempts for dealing with all this raw emotion. I spent a few hours talking separately with each of them.

Before I went to sleep, both of them apologized for what this was going to do to my trip. At that moment, none of us could guess what that would be. All I knew for sure was that I was not going to be a neutral party in this no matter how hard I tried. Moreover, somewhere and somewhen, I was going to get some of the displaced anger. An uneasy truce was reached and the next few days in Singapore were tense at best. I began to feel much more comfortable when I was exploring on my own and I worried about that. After all, they had all the plans and the schedule. I had the enthusiasm and a backpack. I wondered if that would be enough. This was not the kind of adventure I had anticipated.

A few days passed and we were ready to leave Singapore. We knew a bit more about what my McDonald's waiter had started to tell me about the laws. Jaywalking was punishable by a S$50 fine (Singapore dollar). Littering was S$1,000; smoking was S$500; not flushing toilets was S$150; spitting was S$500. Even hogging the road carried a S$50 fine. If you were at a border crossing to Malaysia and you jumped queue, you were sent to the end of the line. There was more rejection and a fine if the gas gauge of a departing vehicle did not register a tank at least three quarters full. Obviously, Malaysia had less expensive gasoline. We commented on the two parts of all these societal rules: that they existed and that they were enforced. Someone was punished if he stepped on the rights of others. Singapore had our vote and I was still making judgments....

Bill smiled as we crossed the border. "Singapore is a fine city," he commented. Considering what he was going through at the time, he still had his sense of humor.

CHAPTER 3
<u>MALAYSIA</u>

*Douglas Adams defines flying as throwing yourself at the earth,
and, failing to hit it. Well, this type of travel seems to me to be
intentionally throwing yourself at the strangeness of the world,
and, failing to miss it.*
– Bret Varner

We hadn't the luxury of crossing the border from Singapore to Malaysia with our own vehicle; we were on a bus. We repeatedly noticed signs for the penalty of a gas tank less than three quarters full. There were also more signs regarding the penalty for jumping queue. A price must be paid for a society to be relatively free from crime. As far as I could see, this society was not much more restrictive in its rules than my own. What was different, clearly different, was that this society enforced the rules. For a few miles we discussed the meaning of the signs and what they represented. Then we noticed some changes outside our windows.

The Malaysian world that we sped through was much poorer than what we had experienced in Singapore. There were small huts throughout the countryside and people were walking everywhere. The clothing, construction of buildings, absence of private cars, absence of Western influence—the list of differences went on. For me, the Asia of the Third World was suddenly here. I watched the landscape change and the people with it. Julie and Bill seemed to have declared a truce and the hostility was on hold.

At a lunch stop, we changed some travelers checks and the last remaining Singapore dollars. The new currency was the *ringgit.* One U.S. dollar would buy just over M$2.00. That exchange rate would buy much more than we had anticipated, and we would be able to live within our daily backpacker budget of eight dollars each.

One of Bill's scheduled stops was the Taman Nagara National Park. The Wrights had done so much research into each area, that I took considerable delight in not asking anything about where we were going or what we would see. It was the response of a young child to a magical world. At least I hoped that was what it was. It might have just been that I was still in shock about being transported from "there" to "here." An Asian national park: I wondered how far we were from the park entrance.

If there had been a Yellowstone National Park in 1776, you would have reached it by one of several waterways. Taman Nagara was no different. We took a nearly four-hour boat ride in a very large dugout canoe with a small motor. There was no other access except the river. We settled in among a group of twenty other tourists and prepared for anything. What we got was an immediate cultural lesson.

Many people lived on the river. They fished in it, bathed in it, and used its waters for their irrigation systems and travel. We moved smoothly over the river's surface while many of the residents of the countryside took baths. The women we saw were very intent on not acknowledging our presence. The sound of the engine would alert them and by the time we came around the river bend; they were submerged up to their chins. And their faces were averted. Not one of the twenty or so women we encountered took a look at our boat. None. Our guide explained that shyness was only part of the explanation. He would not have thought of saying anything negative about the guests he was transporting, but we all understood that Westerners were held to be threats in many ways. The women were fully clothed, we were told. Their total immersion was just an additional precaution.

When we arrived at the landing dock, we were quite tired of hot jungle river travel. Now we needed some camping gear. The four-man tent we selected was made of heavy canvas and had only one small "window" at the back. When zippered closed, it was an inferno. We put it in the shade and where we hoped it would encounter a breeze. Then we started to explore. Taman Nagara had a fine lodge with overhead fans. Backpackers quickly learned to mimic the behavior of their wealthier Western counterparts. While we could not get away with such behavior in a posh hotel in New York, the Western Caucasian look we were sporting let us get away with more than we should. You could disagree with it; you just couldn't change it.

The picture on the opposite page shows me next to a typical plant in the jungle. Throughout the surrounding area there were trees that dwarfed all but the redwoods in California. As we wandered around, I had my first taste of isolation in a truly foreign country. Near the lodges, there were many people. Within a

In the national park of Taman Nagara, the plants all seemed like they were from another world.

Buddhist temple.

fifteen-minute walk, I could be completely alone. Bill had selected a good adventure—a gradual easing out of one way of life and into another. He was helping me to cope with the shock of being truly away from home. Tomorrow night we would camp in a blind.

My morning omelet ruined my day and threatened to ruin everyone's night. Cooked in rancid oil, it had made me violently ill—all day. I hiked to the "hide" (blind) with my body shaking from illness. Once there, I tried to rally but could only climb to the shelter built in the large tree and lie there in one of the beds. I felt weak and hoped that it wasn't anything more serious than bad food. It certainly felt worse. By dark, I was shaking in earnest. My companions and four others were perched in front of the open-air "window" and had flashlights to "spotlight" the salt lick, which was one hundred yards away. None of us had sleeping bags; it was 85 degrees with 80 percent humidity. As my chills got worse, I found an emergency sleeping bag tucked in one of the pockets of my daypack. It weighed only a few ounces and was intended only for an emergency situation where no other bag was available—in Nepal. The downside was that these bags were much like giant pieces of extra strength tinfoil and just as quiet. They were especially annoying when the person using them suffered from chills and was shaking from head to foot. Who knew how far the rustling sounds were carrying? Fortunately, my companions were a good-natured lot, and the noise didn't seem to scare away a *civet* (large cat) or several deer. I saw nothing during the night.

As we prepared to return to our tent in the morning, I was feeling much better. Weak but better. And the deer came back, so I saw wildlife after all. I felt like living was a good option. I crossed fried foods off my list. Just the thought turned my stomach and I thought of more soothing foodstuffs. I actually felt well enough to try a solo run along a side trail and was rewarded with an end-of-trail cave. Poised at the entrance, I remembered that the nearest medical help was at least four hours of dugout canoe and a number of bus hours away. I contented myself with watching bats leave through a small hole in the rock near the base of a tree. I was hungry, anyway. At the conclusion of two days of nearly no food, my appetite came roaring back, but now I craved rice and mild vegetables.

Julie and Bill had convinced me that local potions for protection from biting insects were a must. I had ignored that idea at the tent site and had been the lone victim of a concerted attack. Whatever feasted on me while I slept, its bite had an unusual effect: the area didn't heal. I had read that the leech bite includes an anti-coagulant so that blood continued to flow. This mystery insect produced a bite that did not scab over. And it itched. That combination was difficult to combat during the waking hours; when I was asleep, I scratched off the semi-scabs before I realized it. As a result, my legs had upward of thirty such sores and looked terrible. Even in the heat and humidity, I was tempted to wear a pair of light cotton pants. After the first try at that remedy, I gave it up. The pants easily rubbed against the sore areas and kept them open. Pus formed. This was not good.

The answer, of course, had been staring at me for the three weeks I suffered. If it was a local potion that would have prevented this, perhaps I should have consulted a local doctor for a solution. So steeped was I in Western medical ways that I assigned all other forms of medicine to the "witch doctor" school. My attempts at becoming thoroughly neutral regarding culture again brought me up short. During the cure, there was time for some humor.

One day Julie and I were wandering around an ancient city and visiting some of the old ceremonial sites. We had been nearly a month away from the national park, and I had only been taking the medicine for a week. The legs looked as bad as ever. Maybe they looked worse. As we walked toward a place where we could take a picture, two young men walked by. Noticing my legs, one of them asked solicitously, "What's wrong?"

I pointed at the infected areas and said, "Insects." The look on his face was the same as though he had just heard me say "bubonic plague." He looked terrified and ready to run.

He looked at me and said, "Sex?" Julie broke up laughing. She had made the connection. Our word for the kingdom of bugs sounded like I had contracted my problem in sex. I was never going to get out of this; Julie knew it, but I didn't.

"No, no," I said, "not in sex—insects." Now that I knew what the boys were thinking, it sounded pretty weak to me, too. Here before these young men from the countryside of Malay existence was one of those libertine Westerners that they had been cautioned about. And here he was, wandering in their village area and in the company of a scantily clad woman. (Julie was, of course, scantily clad in knee length shorts and a three-quarter-sleeve shirt. Racy attire for this part of the world that wouldn't get noticed in the West).

Having only opened my mouth to change feet, I started to explain that Julie was not my wife. As I stated that fact, I could see Julie in my peripheral vision. She was shaking her head in what appeared to be a bemused "no." I plunged on. It was my hope that they would understand that she and I were not involved and that, therefore, this was not the result of sex. They looked at me as though my unmarried status with this "woman of questionable virtue" was a foregone conclusion.

Thinking that I could salvage something from this encounter, I looked earthward and sadly mumbled, "Sex." I thought that this would, perhaps, be a "scared straight" encounter. Julie seemed to be rethinking her oft-stated premise that I was brighter than average. She looked like she wanted to tell me a great many things, but at the moment, she was incapable of speech. She was capable of laughter. Considering my miserable appearance, Julie's mirth was also misinterpreted by the young men. I could only wonder what Malay stories would be circulated about a woman who thought that a debilitating sexual disease was funny. As we walked away, Julie was able to control her laughter—as long as she didn't look at my legs—or me.

In another week, the medications had healed everything and only a few scars remained. Julie was still easily amused. Singapore and Malaysia had been very enjoyable. And, there had been a tremendous amount of learning going on. Now, as we prepared for Thailand, I was already aware of the need to go to the tourism office for visa approval and the payment of a fee. And I found a copy of *The Lonely Planet Guide Book* and worked on some of the phrases for basic courtesy. I was still ignorant of almost all that Thailand could offer, but I was relaxed with the knowledge that surprises of the organizational kind were going to be fewer and farther between. We eagerly headed for the border.

I hadn't seen anything that resembled an answer to the meaning of life, but I had learned that withholding judgement was important to traveling well. Neutrality combined with curiosity was the best combination for enjoyment. Learn everything you can and then wait for understanding. The longer I was in Asia, the more profound this notion seemed. Maybe something that important would help me answer Rick's question.

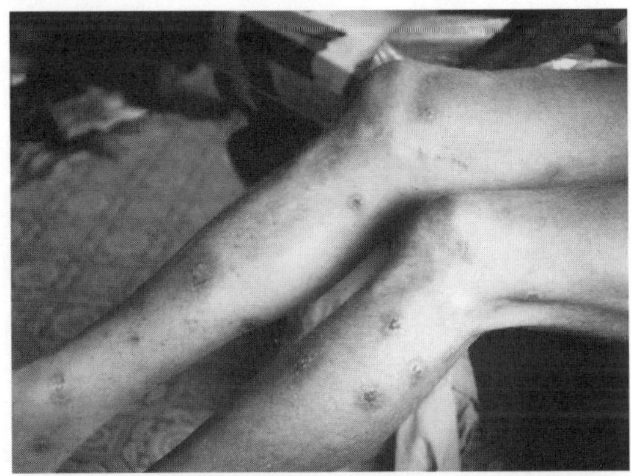

A cultural lesson does not always have to be an intellectual exercise. And, legs like these aren't without their humorous story.

Thailand's wats, *like this one at Sukhothai, are reminders of ancient Siam.*

CHAPTER 4
<u>THAILAND</u>

Om Mani Padme Hum: I salute the jewel in the lotus

There had been far too many arguments going on between my companions. Some of it had spilled over into my friendship with each of them. That was expected. I couldn't imagine how any third party wouldn't appear to favor one or the other of the combatants. Since Julie was the one who had been "wronged," she was the one who was granted the most leeway in her behavior. She took all of it. And she had the most clout, which she also used. There was a tightrope in the friendship, but I couldn't step on it—not to mention trying to walk on it. I was punished often enough that the trip started to be less fun.

I offered to run with both of them and train them with a fitness session of resistance exercises that would simulate weight training. Julie wouldn't do the exercises because Bill did them; Bill wouldn't run because Julie did. Sometimes, neither of them would join me. Soon, that lack of participation started to be a blessing and I found that training alone or with strangers from other countries was much more pleasant. This was early in my trip and already there were gale warnings on a rapidly approaching horizon.

When we applied for our visas for Thailand, Julie delayed the procedure while she searched for her passport. It was not the first time we'd had to wait. This would be the third country on our trip together and the sixth on her trip with Bill. The idea that she had not kept her passport in her fanny pack and had not memorized her passport number was surprisingly annoying. Was she doing it to create problems? I didn't know. What interested me the most was my reaction. Why was I suddenly so concerned over a few five-minute delays on a trip where a schedule was rarely important? If a stranger had joked about his failure to keep his passport handy, I would have laughed with him. A stranger shouldn't get better treatment than a friend. That wasn't such a good sign. We moved onward.

We were almost three months into traveling together. Two months before, we had left Singapore. Now we were leaving Malaysia. I waited outside our hotel and began talking with some children who were waiting for the *bas sekolah* (school bus). The children were mostly Muslim and were therefore mostly boys. They were all dressed in blue pants and white shirts—obviously a school uniform. The girls hung back and watched. While not all of the girls had their faces covered, their faces and hands were the only unclothed areas. They waved and left and I spent the remaining few minutes talking with a local taxi driver. His car was called a Proton and he told me that it cost about $12,000. It was made in Malaysia and the radio was made by Blaupunkt. That's a fine radio for a taxi.

We rode on the bus from Kota Bharu to Hat Yai. From the Malaysia–Thailand border, it was three hours. The entire trip into Thailand was spent with the noisy accompaniment of a television set mounted from the ceiling near the front of the bus. The speakers were clearly not made by Blaupunkt. They were on full blast, but it was obvious from the reaction of our seatmates that the bass and treble rendered the sound track equally mysterious to all. Loud seemed to be good. All around us people were chatting and reading and looking out the windows. No one watched the television and no one seemed disturbed by its intrusion on what they were doing. The motto for tourists seemed to be: "Attenuate or die."

From Hat Yai, we had another four-hour ride to the coastal town of Krabi. There was more of the same noise. We sat farther back in this bus. We could see less of the countryside, but we could hear each other and those around us. Just in front of us was a very nice middle-aged woman who turned to us and began asking questions. Her English was so flawless that we were stunned. She was also the proud owner of a smile that was magnificent, and we saw it often as we complimented her on her language skills and her country. She was an English teacher and she loved to talk with strangers. That, too, was obvious.

She asked if we had noticed the groups of women standing along train and bus routes in the morning. In answer to our affirmative, she stated that it was unsafe for children and women to venture alone in the morning darkness. Groups gathered together in the relative safety of the town neighborhoods and walked together to the train and bus stops. Sometimes, she explained, neighbors or family members joined the group and returned after sunrise. From the pastoral look of what we had been seeing so far, the idea of robbers and rapists seemed hard to believe. It was, we told her, an assumption that foreigners made when they colored appearances with their ignorance. We would no longer stroll casually toward a station of transportation.

We hadn't realized it then, but we had just been given our first lesson in safety. It had been done in an indirect manner that we would eventually realize characterized a shy and tactful culture. In fact, she was explaining the dangers to her own people, but the topic was selected because of its potential importance to us.

Our trip was made more delightful as we talked and received our first language lesson. The happiness that we had noted at the bus park, in both the ticket agents and our fellow travelers, was called *sanuk.* Enjoyment of life—at work and play—seemed to make the two indistinguishable from each other. Anything one truly liked to do was *sanuk.* In America there is often a wide gulf between work and a party. In Thailand the two are represented by the same word: *ngan. Pai-tio,* we were told, means "wandering around." It was a broad concept and not to be confused with *pai de lan,* which means "to wander around town." We whiled away some worry-free miles listening to a discourse on the difference. Our entire trip would be defined as *pai tio;* we were wandering around the world.

Jai yen means "cool heart," and it also seemed basic to the Thai concept of not displaying anger. We were getting a lesson in much more than language here and we rarely interrupted with questions. The conversation was allowed to flow freely in whatever direction our teacher wished. We saw how old the culture was as we passed by miles of ancient ruins; we were learning just how different it was, too. We focused on all that she said. Perhaps we were attenuating the noise from the television.

I asked for and received a brief introduction to Thai civilities. *Sawadt di khrap* means "hello" or "good-bye." It sounded to me like "sawa de cop," and I remembered it phonetically that way. In many Asian languages, there is a polite and respectful addition to almost all conversation, and it was that way with this greeting. For that reason, the "cop" portion of a greeting occurred in nearly all phrases spoken to strangers, elders, and others of importance. Women added *kah* to create their polite form of address.

"Thank you" is phonetically *kapoon cop.* "How are you?" is *Sue bye deh roo?* and is answered by repeating the first words, *sue bye.* With the addition of this much dialogue and the previous words and definitions, I was ready to prey upon unsuspecting Thais at our next destination.

I was just getting to like this easy introduction to a new country when we arrived in Krabi. We had to sort out our evening lodging and make some non-bus travel arrangements. Bill worked through an agitated crush of touts and finally selected one to take us to a "fine, beautiful, and inexpensive" lodge. Until this trip, the word "tout" had no defined meaning for me. After the trip it would always conjure up a gathering of shouting and gesticulating young men who were trying to make a living selling a night's lodging. "In your face" took on a new meaning. As for our fine, beautiful, and inexpensive hotel, I was learning that the last of the three criteria often precluded the first two. Still, we were ushered into a barely lit room with three beds and a ceiling fan. It was clean, had only one small window high on a wall, and was about fifteen by eighteen feet. There was an eight-foot long metal rod for us to hang our clothes on; it was attached to the two walls in the corner and seemed sturdy enough to trust. That was it. There was a communal bathroom down the hall, a very primitive shower a bit farther, and a small restaurant next door. Less than two dollars each had secured adequate lodging for us.

This sort of accommodation was exactly right for those who did not have much money or who had to budget for a long trip. During the many months of travel, we would stay in such rooms most of the time. A room with a shower

The beaches in Thailand are not always full of tourists. There are remote places where the accomodations are not developed but where the views are spectacular.

and bathroom attached was a luxury. Only when it was not much more money or when we were all willing to share a room was it feasible. Clean was the important thing. With a sturdy lock. Disease and theft would be very bad situations for us; many decisions about where we stayed and what we ate were made to prevent either from happening. We slept well and were up before dawn for a breakfast of eggs, fruit, and vegetables.

That morning we booked a boat crossing to the island of Koh Phi Phi (Pee Pee). After about an hour of sitting in the sun on the bow of the boat, I realized that the *déjà vu* I was feeling was actually quite real. I was living the daydream I had been having for years. The breeze of the boat's forward movement, the flying fish, the deep green vegetation on every island we passed…this was where I had often been before. It didn't come as any surprise when we rounded a spit of land and saw a lagoon with almost unnatural blues and greens in the water. Tourmaline came to mind. And the water was crystal clear. The beach had huts, and over where the rich people would be staying, there appeared to be a golf course. I didn't know the Thai word for paradise, but I knew I would know it about twenty minutes after our boat was beached.

We had been given a free night of lodging at Long Beach as part of a package from last night's hostel. This was not to be confused with what most Americans think of as a way to charge tourists for something more expensive than they want. This was not an up-sell. A little cash had changed hands between the people in Krabi and the people on the island. Most of it was a family business anyway. We were backpacker-class tourists and we didn't spend much. But we did spend, and the rule seemed to be that there would be a package available for any level of travel. It worked. The huts we stayed in were simple and adequate: a door, a window, and a sleeping mat. The food was very, delicious, with American dishes on the menu. There was also pizza and we especially enjoyed that.

The "Julie and Bill Show" had come to paradise. They were still battling over some issues. In our third month of travel, there wasn't much sign of a truce. Most of the time it was not too bad. But at mealtimes it was unusually bad. At first, their comments about the surliness of the waiters and waitresses seemed pretty apt. Meals were slow and sometimes an order was not exactly what we had asked for. Or, perhaps the two were related—they were so slow that we couldn't remember exactly what we had ordered. There didn't seem to be much *sanuk* here. Then I noticed something. When I went for my predawn morning run on the beach trail, the crew was sweeping and cleaning the open-walled dining area. I returned, showered, and had a leisurely breakfast. Then we caught the midmorning sun and did some reading or writing. We had lunch for an hour or two and then walked a couple of miles to "town" for some shopping. We returned for dinner and then relaxed on the beach before we had a final drink and went to sleep. And the same people who served us breakfast served us that last Coca-Cola.

A few inquiries later and I discovered that except for religious holidays and the rainy season, the workday was from just before first light until just after dark. That was seven days a week. That was a stunning testament. At least I was stunned. It was what once went on in my own country, and while I had read about it in every American history class, it was much more forceful to bump into it in the real world. If this was my first experience with that type of work schedule, it would not be my last. I continued to watch the staff and to spend some time talking to them.

Bon worked for 1,500 *baht* per month. The *baht* was the Thai currency we were now using to replace the *ringitt* of Malaysia. His pay was equal to approximately sixty U.S. dollars a month. He had a family, and his wife did some work when she was able. Once the thin veneer separating a tourist and a waiter had been dispensed with, Bon and I found each other very interesting. He knew nearly nothing about the world outside a hundred-mile radius. It was soon apparent that his interest in me didn't extend to facts he could not comprehend. He was fascinated with our stories of our journey and how we could afford it, but much of it was beyond his understanding. We found that within that 100-mile radius, Bon was a professor. His most important lesson for me when we first met was the phrase *mai pen rai.* It was *mañana* without an attitude. Whatever was not done might not have needed to be done. And if it needed to be done, but wasn't? Well, *mai pen rai.*

Bon seemed pleased with my morning running. As long as it was my morning running. He had seen tourists do it before. He couldn't conceive of ten thousand non-Thais running for 26.2 miles, so it was useless to try to explain my occasional marathon. He was pleased to listen, but it was clear that he didn't understand. Add health to the list of things he didn't understand. Health either was, or it wasn't. Usually, it was. When it wasn't, your family and neighbors would take care of you. Health insurance wasn't going to make much sense, either. I showed him a handstand and he became truly animated and not so *mai pen rai-ish.* It was clear that he was the only Thai in his island circle that knew a *ferang* ("long nose" or foreigner) who could stand on his hands. He didn't understand my handstand either, but here was something that not everyone could do and he wanted to be the first person on his block to learn it.

We practiced the many progressions for the safe learning of being upside-down. The lead-up skills involved various types of headstands. There was growing concern among Bon's family that he was damaging his head and brains with all the practice. He would not be denied. Finally, I had to caution him that the skin on his forehead and the hair on his head did not have a lifetime guarantee and he was in danger of losing both. He explained that whenever someone asked why his forehead was bruised he would demonstrate each of the practice skills. Upon further discussion, it was clear that the demonstration often involved the hardwood surface of the floor at work or the abrasive sand of the beach.

There was, of course, another aspect of Bon's new fitness craze. Most young Thai men do hard physical labor and play rigorous games. Bon had settled into his middle-aged family status with a job, which although tedious was not physically demanding. Small wonder that the morning after he had done three hours of upper body practice, extreme soreness put him in danger of missing one day of his seven-day workweek. As much as he wanted another lesson the next day, it was all he could do to bring us porridge and fruit. As with most Thais, he had a naturally sunny disposition and he soon had us laughing with his description of bathing, dressing, and trying to eat his own first meal of the day. I promised to stay for a few more days and continue the lessons. It wasn't a hard decision to make.

On the way back to the huts, Julie found a bottled water container that had been discarded along the pathway. It was labeled "Pee Pee Drinking Water." It was a souvenir destined for home and I made it a goal to fill it with the small seashells that were everywhere along the beach.

Two weeks went by.

On our last morning at Long Beach, I was again running on the jungle trail from one beach to another. There were a series of footlocker-size boulders to negotiate and then I was racing across the as yet untrammeled sand. Down the beach I saw one fishing boat that had recently come in with the night's catch. As I drew nearer, a lone fisherman stepped from the water and started to run toward me. His face had a look of seriousness. Then he started sprinting toward me. The look was now ferocious. I increased my speed, too. In another country, I might have worried. In Thailand, it seemed I didn't need to. He suddenly broke off the charge and sprinted around me a couple of times—laughing wildly. By that time we were both laughing. A lot of communication goes on

The Royal Palace in Bangkok is famous for its intricate tilework.

when spoken language is not involved. Here was another person who did not understand the running for exercise that Westerners do. But, it was all right to mock that and the size difference between us, and the fact that we look so serious while we do something we say we enjoy. We waved to each other as I moved on down the beach. There was a decided improvement in my *sanuk*.

Bon treated us to a free dinner. He was nearing a headstand of some consistency and had already received a great deal of notice for his practice exercises. Now he reviewed some of the customs of his land for us. First he explained a practice we had noticed many times. Many Buddhists we had met had told us things that clearly were not true. We remembered each instance because the questions we had asked all involved the location of something. Having been given "wrong" directions on many occasions, we were quite keen to hear a rational explanation. Bon told us that the fourth noble truth of Buddhism concerned Nirvana and the eight-fold path. The third part of the eightfold path was "right speech," which precluded saying anything that might be displeasing to others—even though it might be completely true. For this reason foreigners were told what they wanted to hear. Instead of asking, "Does this road go to Sukhothai?" we should just say the name Sukhothai and look neutrally at both choices. Our phrasing had forced several Buddhist Thais to smile and agree that the proposed destination was, indeed, down a particular path, when in fact it was not! This was a worthwhile dinner and we were glad it had come early in the trip.

Taking life was the most serious offense to the Buddhist Thais. Bon hastened to explain that this didn't always stop Thais from eating meat. In Bon's village, fish were not killed. They were put on the bank, and if they died?...it was a shame to waste food. Bon was smiling his mischievous smile. I liked Buddhism already. I wondered if Rick's question about the meaning of life could be answered this early in my adventure. It certainly seemed that Buddhism led to a serenity and peacefulness rarely encountered back home.

Because of the Thais' belief in reincarnation, anything that prolongs existence is not highly valued. Buddhists believe that through desire or craving existence is prolonged. So, the cultural pattern is to refrain from those thoughts. To be hard-working, ambitious, or energetic is to invite additional reincarnations. The inactivity we had often observed could have been due to laziness, lethargy, indifference, climatic changes, diet, disease, or a valid belief in the ethics of the Buddha. To their credit, Julie and Bill seemed willing to rethink their initial evaluations of the Thai people.

Bon had been a monk. Our surprise was muted as he explained that nearly all rural males spent as much as three months as a monk. Even the current king was a monk for a period of time. Every day we saw saffron robes throughout the villages or descending the hillside trails. Monks were everywhere. The monks we saw were not allowed to refuse any food offered to them. We saw them every morning with their begging bowls, as they walked through the streets of town or the lanes of the countryside. Bon enlightened us about the begging. The monks could not refuse the offerings, but they also did not thank or respond emotionally to the person who was donating. In fact, the gift of food brings merit to the giver, so that gratitude is actually due the monk for providing an opportunity for merit to a member of the laity. That was the opposite of what we had concluded. The joy of giving opened the heart.

Sometimes monks were given long and pointless work projects to frustrate their attachment to tranquility. Having always wanted to be attached to tranquility, I thought back on much of my life before this trip. There were many lessons in my ensuing thoughts.

The dinner we ate with Bon was at his place of employment and at his expense. He explained why we were not at his home—a closer location. In

Upper left: The motor is on the back of the boat, but the propeller is very far back, which makes the boat very easy to turn and also able to venture into shallow waters. Upper right: The main village is just out of this picture.
Lower left: This is typical lodging—thatched huts with generator power from about dusk to 10:30. The water is shallow and coral gives it some very unusual colors—from blue to aquamarine, to green.
Lower right: This photo looks like the ideal beach—anywhere, any beach...

Running in Thailand

Thailand, invitations to dinner were reserved for intimate friends or immediate family. He had been uninterested in our offer to take his family to dinner. The financial strain of returning a foreigner's hospitality at home would be too much. A Thai might decline such an invitation. But, Bon pointed out, that would be too confrontational. A more likely scenario would be that the Thai citizen would simply not show up at the appointed time. In Thailand such a response would be considered a graceful solution to a difficult situation.

Thai culture made sense now that we had a guide to some of the subtleties. We had been removing our shoes, sometimes. Bon explained why Thais were more careful than we. It is mandatory at temples, and signs and officials politely enforce the practice. Such enforcement is necessary for foreigners; Thais need no such cautioning. To have worn shoes in a home such as Bon's would have been interpreted as an expression of superiority to the host. It is also very impolite to raise one's voice toward a superior or elder. To lose one's temper and scream and shout is extremely ill-mannered. To look someone directly in the face is both improper and rude.

If Bon was trying to attack the typical American on vacation, he didn't need to be this subtle. His three American friends took a few minutes to put together a mental picture of a tourist who violated some or all of the rules we had just heard. Two very different societies were at work here and we were fascinated.

Bon wanted to know if he should continue, and we assured him that it would give us great pleasure to learn more. We heard about thresholds and doorways. There were ten household spirits believed to inhabit the threshold. The proper procedure was to step over it and not on it. Sometimes, to assist tourists, a building was not consecrated, so the rule would not apply.

Julie asked how Americans were perceived. Bon seemed not to know what she was asking. She asked again in a different way. Again, he seemed confused. It dawned on us that he was being obtuse because the answer might have offended us. We weren't put off by what he had already told us and we told him to continue. When he did mention that loud chatter and quick hurried movements were associated with monkeys, we understood the occasional wince we saw near tourist centers. The perfect lady, we were assured, was cool, trim, unassertive—yet gracious and quick to smile. Bon seemed to sense that we had absorbed about all we could, so he explained one more important belief: The head is sacred.

If you accidentally touch a person's head, you should ask his pardon. We were told to never pat a child on the head. The foot, by contrast, was lowly. You should not point with it, slide something toward someone with it, or have someone step over your outstretched legs. Raising your feet above someone's head was offensive. I had an image of a bunk bead and when I explained it to Bon, he told me that my example was a good one. Then I remembered the handstands. What had I been doing? Bon assured me that it was not offensive, but he seemed relieved that I had figured out the nature of my possible insult. He suggested that I might explain what I wanted to do and to seek approval before doing it. That was, of course, if I wanted to continue to do handstands and to observe local customs.

As an afterthought, he added a couple of miscellaneous comments as we concluded our meal: Use your chin to point and not a finger. Do not point directly at someone. Do not eat standing up or while walking around. And eat and present gifts with the right hand. We had already heard about public displays of affection and knew that hand holding was about the limit of what was proper.

From another source, we had learned that it was considered polite to always leave some food on a serving platter or on our plates. It was an insult to clean your plate. The more food that was left, the more generous the host appeared. We did that at Bon's meal. Bon appreciated our decidedly non-*ferang* gesture. We all shared a deeply felt *wai,* and Bon was demonstrative enough to gently hug each of us. We thanked him for the excellent meal, his hospitality, and his friendship, and we left paradise by boat for a place called Ao Pra Nang.

Bill handled all of the planning for each of our destinations. It was something he liked to do, and he was very good at it. Sometimes it seemed like he spent a lot of time planning for the next stop, and I found myself wondering how much he got out of actually being at one of the destinations. It was becoming increasingly clear that the three of us wouldn't travel together much longer, and I supposed I'd find out how much planning was involved. In the meantime, he did an excellent job and rarely asked Julie or me to help.

As a result, I was not sure whether Ao Pra Nang was an island or a peninsula. I did know that it was still in Thailand. We got there by boat, but the landmass we paralleled never seemed to give way to water. It was, of course, not important. The huts there were quite nice and the beach was very small. A walkway led from where we were staying to another beach. When we explored the walkway, we passed a huge resort area that was closed for the season. There was a very forbidding fence on one side of the walkway and huge limestone cliffs on the other. After a mile, a new beach came into view, deserted and spectacular. The limestone cliffs looked like a freshly cooled lava formation and rose for hundreds of feet directly above us. There were even a few caves, which we explored after running for a while.

The phrase, "ignorance is bliss," might have been invented for me. Certainly, at times, Julie and Bill fell happily into that state. After the run, I discovered that the first grotto-like cave was filled with a shrine. There was a pile of wood around a decorated area. Flowers and even photos were found. We correctly deduced that this shrine had something to do with the well being of local fishermen. That was about as correct as we were going to be for a while. The pieces of wood seemed to be somehow out of place and we couldn't quite understand why. They didn't look like ordinary driftwood stacked up for a religious pyre. Although the pieces of wood were a variety of sizes, they appeared to be similar in shape, and all were carved.

About that time, the significance of the wood became abundantly clear to all of us. They were called *lingams* and they were carved as a phallic symbol. When we returned to the huts and the dining area, we found brochures about the area and about the caves. Any of the Thai employees, all young men, were quite willing to discuss our find—especially with Julie. In less time than it took to tell, she refused to go anywhere without one of us. Cultural differences were constantly making an appearance.

What wasn't making an appearance was an adventure. We had been doing typical tourist activities, and it was just great. But it reminded us of the busloads of people who stopped at the Grand Canyon, snapped a few pictures, walked to a couple of viewpoints and bought a trinket as they left. If it was all you could do, then it was better than nothing. But it was *not* all that I could do. I wanted to explore a few places that were not part of the typical tourist agenda. I had seen a division in that walkway toward the other beach, and I decided to take the path less traveled. My companions were going to beach it, and read and relax. I promised to report back to them about where the trail led, and I was off.

The boardwalk ended twenty yards after I made the turn. And it ended right at the base of one of the limestone cliffs. I could see a bit of a trail moving from right to left through the detritus at the base. The path appeared to be worn enough; quite a few people had been that way. I added one more to the list. A hundred yards later I heard voices above me. Around the base of a limestone column I saw a beautiful blonde girl sitting on a log. The log, however, was balanced between two rock outcroppings and was twenty feet above me. It was clear that she was not going to ascend much farther. Her companion was twenty feet above her and hanging onto a knotted rope while resting his feet on a narrow ledge. The rope disappeared some forty feet above his head. He, too, seemed not to like the predicament they were in.

Having climbed mountains since I was eleven, I had little fear of a pitch this easy to climb. However, I couldn't go up until they got down. And they couldn't get down unless they got some help. It was a lot easier to climb up some rock faces than it was to climb down them—a fact they had just realized. She seemed to be quite glad to accept some help that would actually get her to terra firma without free fall. He was another matter. He seemed intent on making it appear that the only thing stopping him from continuing up was her descent. They had been together long enough for her to nip that idea before it gained momentum. When I finally succeeded in getting her to the ground, she thanked me and offered to stay and wait for him. The look that she cast his way spoke volumes. He was the last to understand the nature of his own fear. Her refusal to accept the blame was soon understood by all three of us. That did it and he soon joined her. They thanked me and disappeared back toward the boardwalk.

About the time that I reached the point where he had been, I had a problem. Drilled into me from the early days of my climbing was the idea of never trusting any climbing aids that you or your friends hadn't put in—that day. Don't climb without inspecting the rope. Don't climb without inspecting the anchoring piton or bolt. Don't climb alone if the danger exceeds any possible benefits. I remembered the opening line in a book called *Belaying the Leader:* "The leader must not fall." Well, that was twice as true in the case of a solo climb. Don't fall. Don't, don't, don't. The list kept you alive; ignoring it could get you killed. Suddenly, I was as full of adrenaline as the couple who were now safely on their way to a meal and a tan. Of course, I could have gone back...

It took almost no time to climb the rope and reach the ledge above. Thinking about it took far longer. The rope and its anchor bolt were quite secure and very trustworthy. It was a good thing, too, since there was another rope and another vertical face to negotiate, another ninety feet of up before I could see what was at the top. There were tracks on this ledge; others had at least been this far. I climbed up without incident. Now I hoped the fun would begin.

Last night it had rained. I had slept the sleep of the dead and didn't hear it. Here, in the jungle growth above the cliffs, there was mud everywhere. I was in shorts and tennis shoes and within minutes I was in shorts, tennis shoes, and a coating of thick red mud. I assured myself at the crest of the hill I was climbing that I might fall again, but I wouldn't ever get up this slowly.

I rested at the top and looked down the other side. The trail wandered down through some rock outcroppings and vines and disappeared over an edge. Falling going uphill was less of a hazard than falling while going down. I didn't have a fear of heights I could see; the unknown frightened me silly. That might not explain why I started down the trail anyway.

I only fell once. I started sliding and only a series of limestone rocks slowed me down. There was a bit of a gash on my calf and some blood, but I had expected worse and was pleased just to have come to rest at nearly the same elevation at which I had started. I also had the answer to what was beyond this particular edge: a fifty-foot drop to a jungle pool. The climb down was very easy, the limestone was sharp but solid, and hand- and footholds were easy to reach. It was eerily quiet—not at all what I had expected from the jungle. It was also beautiful. The circular basin that held the water continued on up to the sky. Cobalt blue and green and gray were everywhere. I stayed a few hours and then started back up.

Just at the base where I had seen the couple, two German men were moving up the trail.

"The most important thing," said one of the Germans, "is to stay alive."

"I know," I said smiling my mud caked smile, my left calf bleeding. "I'm working on it."

I traded one aphorism for another: "It's not the fall that hurts," I called back to them. "It's the sudden stop." I had found my adventure, as they would find theirs.

It wasn't enough in the way of adventure, but it did remind me that tourism was as simple as you let it be. Active participation made a very large difference. Perhaps that was part of what Rick had sent me after. Participation. I filed it away next to the withholding of judgment. It was time to explore the jungles of Thailand.

CHAPTER 5
<u>NORTHERN THAILAND:</u>
Trekking the Jungle

Ever tried. Ever failed. No matter. Try again. Fail again. Fail better.
— Samuel Beckett

Bill had already scheduled a trip north from Bangkok. We would take another bus and perhaps make it as far as Mae Hong Son, near the border of Burma. Bus rides were entertaining and enlightening, but they were getting to be very draining. Nothing we did in the way of travel seemed to involve less than every waking minute of the day. And there was often a second day piled on top of the first.

Generally, we bought tickets a day or two in advance. Not being familiar with each country, we visited only official sales offices. This had the added advantage of giving us the exact route for the day of travel. We would usually eat at one of the curbside stands that surrounded the bus park. Being early was always a good idea, and waiting to eat until we had confirmed our bus seating seemed wise.

Meals were being mentioned more and more often in my journal. Julie had decided that my food choices were not the healthiest. She pointed out that my affinity for the Coca-Cola company was just one such example. By this time in my trip, my body weight had dropped almost twenty pounds and my percentage of body fat seemed to be at about my normal marathon level—roughly eight percent. I started my day earlier than my companions and exercised much more frequently. And, I didn't take afternoon naps, as both of them did.

At the athletic club in Seattle, I had conducted hundreds of body composition tests and had read at least two books a month on nutrition and cardiovascular fitness. Julie had even worked for me for a few weeks to obtain some money before their trip had begun. I knew two things about her very pointed comments: they had nothing to do with what I ate or what I knew about fitness, and they were making meals very uncomfortable for Bill and me. The latter seemed the most important.

I was probably being forced out of the nest in a process that even Julie might not have recognized. In the meantime, there was the travel by bus to contend with. And that had nothing to do with Julie or her ideas about my choices.

There were always people to help us throw our aged duffel bags on top of the bus. The first time or two, we had thrown the bags up to waiting hands and had secured seats on the bus. Once under way, someone had walked down the aisle and had collected for the service. Inasmuch as the service had been provided for all travelers, but the Westerners seemed to be the only ones paying, we elected to load and unload our own luggage.

Bus stops were usually for meals. Meals were cheap and quick, and there was rarely much variety. There was a lot of rice and cooked vegetables. The choices seemed to be with or without meat, and all three of us were vegetarians for a variety of reasons. Mine was that I had only been sick for one day—as a result of that rancid cooking oil. I was hoping that there would be no other days like that one. So, we ate quickly, bought lots of sugar-free cookies and bottled drinks, and watched the people and the countryside drift by. The stereo was finally reduced to mere background noise, but it was never silent unless it was broken. I could see how to break it, but there were always too many eyes cast in that general direction.

Every stop that was not a meal stop was either a breakdown or a pick-up. It wasn't so much that the stop brought vendors from out of nowhere—it brought vendors from everywhere. The Asian version of fast-food restaurants paraded outside our windows or up and down the aisle of the bus. Fruit, drinks, hot food; it was all there. And the chants were repeated over and over, often in a native tongue, and when they saw us, in English. Sometimes, a vendor would be caught mid-bus and be hard pressed to move through the standing crush of humanity. When the bus horn sounded to announce imminent departure the first few times, we fully expected the vendors to start a mad scramble for either exit door. We did not yet understand *sanuk*. Instead of debusing, the vendor would simply continue to ply his wares and would make it back to the door at the next town. There, we were told, he would simply find the bus park and ride the next bus back to his home town—selling all the while.

Bus drivers did not take fares, which hadn't been true in Singapore. The extreme crowding in Malaysia and Thailand made it necessary for people to enter at either door. The bus driver had enough to do just to negotiate the heavy traffic of cars, trucks, bicycles, motor scooters, and pedestrians—and, other buses. Fare collection was left to a very athletic and aggressive young man. He had to have a great memory, too, since he had to note all of the new people who forced their way into the doorways at each stop. Very adept at moving through the crush, he would arrive at the new passenger, ask the destination, and collect the appropriate fare. It was easy to see how the three of us were singled out. We were the ones who badly mangled the pronunciation of our destination and who held out a handful of money because we didn't know how to compute the fare. The local people cooperated with both his movements from one end of the vehicle to the other and with his smiling collection of fares. The element of danger happened when the bus was too crowded and the fare collector had to leave the bus to stop some people from clinging to the handrails. After that was accomplished, he would often have to run at full speed and leap for those same rails. Each toll taker seemed very good at what he did.

The Asian buses never seemed to change. Except for Singapore, most of the vehicles we rode in were quite old and decorated in accordance with customs we could only partially understand. Horns were used for everything. In the U.S., a Thai bus driver wouldn't last three minutes. They honked, tailgated, almost never signaled a lane change or a turn, and sped at every opportunity. The stereotype of a New York cabby would describe the driving well; Thai drivers, however, meant absolutely no offense by anything they did behind the wheel. On the back of many vehicles, especially the slow, there was a sign that said, "Please Honk." While we were happy to know that the constant horn honking was producing no ulcers or road rage, it was a huge annoyance and ranked above the television on our list.

From a mid-bus position, we could almost never see the object of the horn blasts until we swung into the passing lane (usually the oncoming traffic lane). There were enough close calls that we never fully relaxed and enjoyed the serenity of the passing countryside. I wasn't a Zen master, barely a neophyte, but even I could see how fatalism was built into the system. How many years of such travel would it take before I just left it all up to God and The Great Plan and slept from one town to the next?

Arrival was a signal for the touts. No matter how poor and ragged our clothing, or how unkempt our appearance, we were fair game and rich—not necessarily in that order. Bon had explained it to me once. Many Thais in the towns and villages had a rough idea of what it cost to travel internationally. It was easy to convert dollars to *baht* and calculate how many years salary it would take to accumulate that much wealth. I had, for example, spent thirty

The Thai people take exceptional care of public and private buildings and grounds.

months of Bon's wages on airfare alone. To continue to travel for over a year—I was rich, indeed.

The perspectives Bon offered had gone right to the heart of most matters, and this had been no exception. It was a point of view I had not considered. So the touts descended on the "rich" tourists and we tried to be good-natured and kept our bags close by. Gymnastics was a great icebreaker, with the occasional handstand. Even better was the agility to get out of and on top of the bus quickly. I let Julie and Bill fight for the opportunity to give a commission to one of the hordes.

And so, we were again bus-bound. We went slowly up the switchbacks of some beautiful low mountains. The three of us collectively made an unspoken decision: We were tired of travel by bus. Recognizing that look in each other, we made a spoken decision: The next town of any consequence would be home for a couple of days—at least. The next town was Pai (pie). It would be home for a longer time than we had anticipated.

I could have lived in Pai. The small hotel where we found accommodations was owned and operated by a wonderful couple who were both employed in the local education system. As a result of my interest in their language, I was encouraged to join them during study sessions with their children. It was clearly no use to communicate with their twelve-year-old. She was fluent in English and four or five northern Thailand dialects. She knew idioms, slang, and the names of some of our politicians and almost all of our entertainers. This was not the last time that I would hear "M. C. Hammer" uttered by someone who had never been more than twenty miles from the remote place of their birth. I studied with the four-year-old.

Actually, for the hour of my study time, there seemed to be a lot of laughter and almost too much *sanuk*. Evidently, the family's mynah bird in the cage out front had less of an accent than I did and slightly more vocabulary. The only reason I wasn't studying next to the caged bird was that I had a longer attention span. Or so I was told. We had a great time and I filled up page after page with notes and words and phonetics. For the vocabulary base I wanted to establish, I was drawing pictures and filling in the names. In that way, while traveling on the bus, I could name the various things I was likely to see. It had worked well with Spanish and no doubt would work well here, too.

It was through my adopted family that I found a bicycle. Although elderly and heavy, and with only four of its original ten speeds, it was mine and it had air in brand-new tires. Having averaged over four hundred miles a week of bicycling before the Seattle-to-Portland ride last year, the four months of bikeless travel had left me with some considerable withdrawal. Now I was once again mobile and under my own power. I still had to worry about the bus, but now all I had to do was to avoid being hit by it. I rode out of town each day and practiced my language skills on unsuspecting farm folk along more of that road less traveled.

In Thailand I discovered that the United States might be committing troops in the Middle East. I learned it at lunch, and I learned it in German. At least I heard it in German. The owner of a restaurant was married to a German girl, and they also spoke French fluently. He had been discussing the paper with a couple from Frankfort and I moved closer to listen. Without missing a beat, the three of them switched to English; they had assumed my nationality from the "Who Is John Galt?" tee shirt that I wore. They were considerate and very informative. I asked to read the paper when the discussion broke up.

I found another article that interested me a great deal. It concerned the crime of *lèse majesté*. I had read about it in school but could get no farther with my memory than something to do with a king. The article explained that a foreigner had just been sentenced to seven years in prison for making disparaging remarks about the king. In Bangkok, every morning at eight, the national anthem was played. Everyone stood; most Thais sang along. Religion, politics, and philosophy were taken very seriously here. Another article discussed a politician found guilty of being unusually rich. At first I thought it was funny. After I had time to think about it, it seemed an apt description of a political crime that was all too common.

One day I returned from biking to find that Bill had again succeeded in finding us something interesting to do. We had been looking for a trek that did not involve a lot of other tourists, went to out-of-the-way places, was vegetarian, and had a guide who was fit. That was a lot of criteria, but Bill was smiling when he told me that we would be traveling with the No Mercy Trekking Company. My smile matched Bill's. That was more like it.

Our guide's name was "Toy." His real name, he assured us, was unpronounceable. He was in his early twenties, exceptionally fit, and knew a lot about the USA. The lot that he knew included every song that The Eagles ever recorded and most of the Bee Gees greatest hits. We were signed up and ready to go within a day. It was our first trek and the four days promised to be very educational.

Our packs were very light. We would stay in a different village each night and Toy would provide our meals. Other than personal effects, we would need only some rain gear and a few changes of clothes. Julie couldn't find an umbrella that she liked in the local shops, and Bill had left his waterproof gear in storage in Bangkok. We all knew that this was the time for me to point out that the jungle was lush because of the rain, and it was time to spend some money on prevention. We also knew that I wasn't going to say anything as confrontational as that, not with the personal battles being waged between this increasingly unhappy couple. There was nothing like marital problems to alter friendships of all kinds. I had a waterproof poncho and an umbrella; my friends refused to spend any money on what they would surely need.

The Jeep ride to the trailhead was short and scenic—another welcome change from tedious bus-dom. We trekked for a no-mercy four hours through the jungle and thoroughly expected to see Franz Kafka emerge around each bend. Toy was busy singing many songs I had listened to as I grew up. I mentally sang with Toy as we blazed up and down hill and dale. And he definitely got more words right than I did. He also sang a song called *Sow Doy*, which he said meant "mountain girl." It was beautiful, even though none of his charges understood the words.

Toy's woodcraft skills were outstanding. We would stop near a waterfall in the most dense jungle area and he would cut down a few bamboo shoots. He would also cut a large section of bamboo and use a machete near each of the joints.

A fifteen-foot-high Yaksha *stands guard at The Royal Palace.*

Out of the resulting cut, he would fashion each of us a drinking cup. Out of the long piece between joints would come a rough eating utensil—rounded like a spoon, but with three finger-like tines in the shape of a fork. And it was all done quickly. He patiently answered our questions and explained much of what we hadn't noticed around us. Just as Bon's explanations of culture had opened our eyes to social differences, Toy would have to instruct us about surviving in the jungle.

The villages to which we would be going were primarily agricultural. Whatever animals they raised for food or trade helped the economy. Our first stop was a Lisu Village. Toy's phonetic translation of hello sounded like *akku bon mwa.* Their beliefs were largely animist and the spirits were found in trees and in water. When they heard thunder, for example, they believed that a spirit was in a nearby tree, and they would leave food near it and would not cut it down. Animals had no spirits and were hunted by men with small-bore rifles. The women did almost all of the work; most of the Lisu villages had been here for thirty to thirty-five years. Toy told us that these people originally came from China when Mao took over. They were the richest of the hill tribes because of opium sales.

Opposite page— Above: Kinnaras *are half man and half bird, and also stand guard on The Royal Palace grounds.* Left: *An open air market offers almost anything imaginable, from fresh vegetables, fruit and fish to exotic spices.*

Above: A handstand in a Lisu village in northern Thailand. Permission was always requested before such actions, to comply with local beliefs in the sacredness of right-side-upness.

Marriage could be within the tribe or between villages. In January, young men of fourteen to sixteen years old often traveled to the next village where they drank rice whiskey and smoked opium derivatives. They also looked for a prospective bride. Within the next year, the young man would decide whether he wanted to pursue a marriage, and his parents would begin negotiations if his answer was yes. Girls moved to the husband's village. Toy said that when marriages did not work, the husband usually committed suicide in the mountains. Buddhists cremate their dead, but the Lisu do it only for accidental death. When there was a long and peaceful life, they buried their dead in the ground. Without knowing about this aspect of his American charges' culture, he commented that it was a rather primitive custom—and perhaps a bit barbaric.

The local school was quite nice, but appearances continued to deceive us. The teacher was paid by the government and did not live in the village. As a result of the difficult terrain and lack of government scrutiny, the teacher did not often put in an appearance. Paychecks, however, continued to be sent. English was not taught. The children were not in school during our visit. They learned our names and mimicked everything we said. They liked my handstands and a water bottle that collapsed, accordion style, and they laughed at every attempt to say something in their language.

The next morning started well before sunrise as the pigs, chickens, and dogs started a litany that would not stop all day. Toy, on the other hand, did not start until nearly ten—the result of far too much rice whiskey with our host last night. When we did leave town, the entire village turned out to wave good-bye. The pace was slow for a "mercy, please" half hour, until Toy figured out the answers to questions like "What?" and "Why?"

After an hour and a half of trekking, we took a slight detour to a magnificent seventy-five-foot waterfall. We had been passing through beautiful fields of corn, cucumbers, tomatoes, and beans. While we were still two hours from our next destination, we were all in need of cooling off. The waterfall proved to be the right answer. As we were bathing, clouds began to rapidly form over the mountains. At about the time we finished dressing, the skies opened up, and rain began to fall in earnest. Toy led us to a small house nestled at the farthest edges of the fields.

There were only two people at home: a young girl and a baby. The girl looked like she was about twelve. Toy's greeting sounded like *a boot aya,* and he told us that this family was originally from a Lahu village. We used this chance to speak to someone that had never seen a white person and asked Toy to be our interpreter. People in this tribe did not know their ages. However, this girl would be married next year and would be moving to the village toward which we were going. She repeated one phrase several times during the course of our conversation, and it seemed to be directed at Julie. When we asked for a translation of *dot chot lao,* we were told that the girl was commenting on how beautiful Julie looked. We all knew that Julie looked better when she was not muddy and wet, with her hair plastered to her head. Julie was allowed, however, to be the only one to bring that up. Of further interest to us was the fact that this young girl had heard that all white people were from the same country. Not for the last time did our efforts to explain oceans and airplanes fail to cross a huge gap in understanding. In this case, although airplanes had been seen high overhead, what they were had remained a mystery. And for someone who had only seen a waterfall with a pool at its base, an ocean was far too much to understand. Or, perhaps, believe. After a quick lunch and in less of a downpour, we moved on to the Lahu Village.

In this village, the house we stayed in was one that Toy had helped build. This village had only been here for four or five years. The walls and floor were bamboo and the support wood was hard, heavy, and termite resistant. All vegetation had been cleared from the village area and, because of frequent rains, there was deep mud everywhere. The Lahu yelled their gossip to avoid extra trips through the mud.

The owner of the home was twenty-seven and had three children. His oldest was a daughter and she was thirteen. This tribe loved animals and children—accounting for a lot of both. We settled in for a dinner of rice, chili peppers, omelets, vegetable soup, and bamboo shoots. It was very filling and very healthy. At each of the villages, Toy would cook a great deal of food for his charges; he would also cook a great deal of extra food for the family. He loved to cook and was very good at it.

Number one daughter was up as early as this village's animal farm. Cradling a flashlight under her chin, she started the fire, made tea, did last night's dishes in hot water, cleaned the kitchen area, and went out to the cornfield to get food for the animals. She returned to clean the rest of the house and then joined her mother to begin the trek to work. Clearly, this village required a lot of work from its women. Toy confirmed that when he and his friend finally awoke from sleep inspired by more rice whiskey. The women, he said, would often travel for hours to work in distant farm fields. Younger girls, perhaps as young as seven, would baby-sit by strapping infants to their backs as they worked in fields closer to home. Toy told us that these people were originally from Tibet—more people escaping Chinese occupation. We started late again, but we were told that it was only about four hours to the Karin village.

The greeting sounded like *da blute*. It might have sounded that way because we had only heard it used in the pouring rain. Torrential rain. During several log crossings over swollen streams there were few worries about falling—there was no way to get much wetter. My poncho was partially protecting Bill, and Julie was using my umbrella. Toy had a towel over his head. I had Mother Nature—with a vengeance. Toy pointed out some pine trees and banana stands. The bananas were not edible, except by animals, but the banana pod was quite prized as an ingredient in curry. Toy did not need to point out that we were trekking on clay for most of the hike. He was having far fewer footing problems than we were, and the downhill sections threatened to give Thailand its first four-person luge team. The domino theory of Asia acquired new meaning as we tried to find something substantial to grab before we could pick up any real speed. We heard some gibbon-like sounds as we crossed a particularly open area of jungle. Then there was just the steady beat of the rain on the leafy floor.

The Karin were from Burma, Toy said. They were the most recent arrivals. The night's lodging was on a covered deck area outside the house. The owner was also the "mayor" and quite well respected in the community. The children were not shy and one young boy was quite proud to show us his pet—a large rhinoceros beetle. The huge insect was attached to a four-inch, pencil-thick stick by means of a twine noose fitted over his large pincers. When the five-year-old was through playing, he would simply jam the stick into the bamboo wall and wander off to do something else. The pet wasn't as dangerous as it looked, but none of us accepted the offer to hold the stick and let it crawl on us.

Toy again fixed an amazing meal from the things collected during the trek. The curry from the banana pod was spicy and very good. I was beginning to think that the food back home was going to be fairly bland. I had always liked Mexican food and one of the reasons had been the wide variety of spices used. Asia was turning out some equally wonderful treats, and meeting our high carbohydrate trekking needs at the same time. Evening dropped a curtain of soft blues and greens as we sat around the fire and talked with Toy and our host. Tomorrow, we would start back. I, for one, didn't want to return, even to the relatively isolated town of Pai. If this was a sample of what trekking was going to be like, I was willing to sign up for more on the spot. We were in Pai the next evening.

A phone call to the Indian Embassy in Bangkok confirmed that our visas to India had finally been processed. We could return, do some final paper work, and within three days be ready to leave Thailand. Upon returning from our trek, we had been "forced" to stay in Pai for almost five days while our documents were processed. We had made calls every day and always with a negative result. Finally, it was done. Rural versus city; it had not been a difficult decision. Now it was time to move on again.

We returned to Bangkok, which we had begun to call by its Thai name of Krungthep (City of the Angels). Our lodging was not far from the Royal Palace and it was this huge compound of buildings that made our time in the city so tolerable. Here, we were able to get some of the history of Siam. As usual, I was most interested in the rules and regulations that had been shaped by this country. There was plenty of fascinating information.

Since we were now seeing historical sights in Bangkok and the ancient capital of Ayutthaya, the stories we were told made it even more interesting. For one thing, the ancient city of Krungthep was like Venice, and the transportation had been most often by boat. Travel along the *klongs* (canals) occurred in other parts of the country, too. Kings Rama V traveled for weeks with a fleet of up to six hundred boats and a retinue of four thousand people. Now that made an interesting picture. Even more fascinating was what we learned from our hostel's host: Royal barges in ancient times were carved in the shape of dragons or sea monsters and were very ornate. There were over thirty miles of waterways to negotiate in Krungthep. The king had to be elevated above his subjects. No house could be built more than one story high and the king wanted nothing to interrupt his glide through his kingdom. Therefore, royal musicians announced his pending arrival and all of the populace had to be hidden from his view. Doors and windows were closed, and those who were outdoors had to hide behind hedges or canebrakes until he had passed. For all intents and purposes, he had a kingdom without subjects.

Royal rules and a hierarchical society, strict protocol—much of it was still in place today. But even as late as the mid-nineteenth century some of the rules had disastrous results. No commoner could touch a member of the royal family. If a boat capsized, there were rules governing rescue: "If a boat founders, the boatmen must swim away; if they remain near the boat, they are to be executed. If they lay hold of him (the royal person) to rescue him, they are to be executed. If the barge sinks and someone else sees the coconuts (life preservers) thrown and goes to save the royal person, the punishment is double and all his family is to be exterminated. If the barge founders and someone throws the coconuts so that they float toward the shore (away from the royal person), his throat is to be cut and his home confiscated."

Such regulations for nonswimming royalty must inevitably result in tragedy. In 1881, a boat capsized with the favorite wife of Rama V and his daughter. She was twenty-one and expecting a second child. Attendants stood by helplessly as she drowned. That incident helped to change the law—as it should have.

Day after day we were able to explore an entirely different history and culture. There were no shortages of teachers and we loved to listen to their stories. I spent an entire day at the Royal Palace—drawing and writing and trying to take it all in. Outside the Pantheon building at the Royal Palace stood *kinnaras.* Gilded, they were half man and half bird. Nearby were *yakshas,* fifteen-foot-tall guardians armored in brilliantly painted stucco. By spending the day, I was trying to imagine this place and these guardian figures as they would appear to the poorer people who came here on pilgrimages from the countryside. It certainly must have reinforced their faith in the divinity of their king and the superiority of their culture. Even with no more understanding than my Western eyes provided, I was amazed.

Jasmine and sandalwood joss sticks, wind chimes hanging from the upturned eaves—it was all very impressive. An elderly Thai gentleman sat down to observe some of my sketches and told me a story I was not likely to hear or read. It was about the harem quarters of the Grand Palace. At least indirectly, his story explained why the movie *The King and I* was not shown in this country. The harem, I was told, was a separate town. Under the direction of women, it was composed entirely of women. Courts, laws, and other institutions existed quite apart from "normal" Thai society. There were shops, gardens, and lawns—an entire city devoted to the king. More than three thousand women lived here. Each queen had between two and three hundred servants in her household. Others would also wait on those servants highest in station. Once married to the king, there was no divorce. Provided that a woman bore a royal child, she could never be banished. While she could never remarry after the death of the king, she and her children would always be part of the hierarchy of royal society. It was a secret city. I couldn't wait to write down what he had told me and to tell my friends.

Thailand: the trekking, the islands, the largest city, and the people; it had been wonderful beyond my expectations. We have a lot of *sanuk* in the United

States, but sometimes we need to remind ourselves that *sanuk* is much more important than a "successful" lifestyle without it. I didn't have the answer to the meaning of life, but I knew that I was closer to it because of what I had learned in this magical country. I didn't want to leave.

Mail drops and the expectation of more letters from friends kept us thinking about the next country. Julie and Bill had reminded me that they had received letters in each country via the American Express office; I had not. Four months into this trip and I hadn't heard anything from the world I had left behind.

Our next country was going to be a real change: India. My first surprise was that it was in Asia. The second surprise was that we were going to have to fly. Burma was unsafe except for very expensive chartered trips. And, even then, there were no guarantees. We washed all of our clothes, spent a lot of time getting clean and looking like it, and headed for the airport.

Top: India's culture is a bit different. Here, many animals are celebrated with unique ornamentation. Left: A pet trained to steal sun glasses. Right: Au Pra Nang's limestone cliffs tower over a lovely beach and caves.

CHAPTER 6
<u>HEMKUND LAKE:</u>
The Sacred Shrine

*If we do not find anything very pleasant,
at least we shall find something new.*
– Voltaire, while journeying downstream into unknown country

We were in India. We had landed in Delhi and once again found ourselves in a beautiful airport. The processing of tourists continued to go smoothly, but we had arrived late and were told that there was not any safe transportation into town. Outside, there were hundreds of people on the pavement. It was cool inside and hot outside and we hoped to stay indoors as long as possible. Sleeping on the tile floor in temperate comfort seemed quite desirable. Julie and Bill elected me to approach a guard near an exit.

"What do you require from this place for your well beings?" It was beautiful, lilting English, and before I could mutter so much as a "huh?" he asked more questions.

"Your good name, please?" I assured him that my good name was Michael and when asked, "What is your native place?" I told him, "USA."

"I am knowing you all in my country and am enjoying conversing with you." He was grinning broadly, proud that he had left me awed by his command of etiquette and English. I assured him that I enjoyed my conversation with him, too, and proceeded to try to hold up my end of the bargain by relating our circumstances.

As my traveling companions approached, so did other airport functionaries. Everyone, it seemed, was attracted to a group of happy and smiling conversationalists. The guard listened to the interjections of a coworker and placed a linguistic arm of protection around "his" tourists. "Please," he said, "you must be careful with his speaking. He is having very strong accents and sometimes he is being difficult to hear with correctness."

As tired as we were, this introduction to India was proving to be a delightful experience. We were allowed some space in a corner and arranged our packs for pillows. The nearest bathroom was on another floor and almost outside the building. To get there required stepping over at least twenty sleeping bodies and traversing a long and dark hallway. This had been a safe trip so far, but it was always prudent to be a bit cautious until you had your bearings. Or sleep, whichever came first.

All we could manage before our eyes slammed shut was to exchange a small amount of money at the official airport bank. The Indian *rupee* was divided into one hundred *paisa*. Many countries with struggling economies did not use coins at all. Before we were through with the trip, we expected pockets full of treasures for the people back home.

In the morning we exited the airport and were met with touts from hell. It was, after all, a tough living for them. We selected a bus instead of a *tuk tuk* (a motorized three-wheel vehicle about the size of a rickshaw). The bus would take us to a *tuk tuk* stand, and we would find the Anoop Hotel from there. Because we had only four hours of sleep, it would be good to finally have a room with a bed and a bath.

There was no doubt that we rode on an exceptionally elderly bus. There were holes in the floorboard and that general level of condition was found throughout. Still, there were a lot of parks near the airport and everything was green and lovely. People walked along the roadsides, and I found myself missing the Asian faces I had seen for the last five months. Bill pointed out, for the second time, that India was part of Asia. We tried to decide if "oriental faces" was politically correct. Evidently none of us had been gone long enough. Had it only been five months? We remarked that this hardly seemed like the overcrowded India we had heard about. We had to learn to watch comments like that.

The bus driver assured us that the hotel we had selected was drug-infested and unsafe. He knew of a better one. We had been advised to stand firm and to judge for ourselves. The concept he was touting was called *baksheesh* and the country ran on it. What he was really saying was that our hotel was not paying him a commission. When we selected a *tuk tuk* driver for the last leg of our trip, he was also dismayed at our selection of hotels. Ours was "drug-infested" and "unsafe." He knew of a better one. Again, we stood firm. Around us were large homes and grassy lawns and wide sidewalks with only a few strolling people. We were a mile from the hotel.

At about three blocks from the hotel, the landscape changed. There were few analogies in an American's vocabulary for what we experienced. Suddenly, there were hundreds of very rundown buildings with streets just wide enough to drive an elephant down. Hundreds of shops crowded each block and people were everywhere. As we walked up the steps to the Anoop Hotel, an elephant *did* walk by. It was being ridden and had its entire face painted in bright colors. Several Brahma bulls grazed on hay bales a half block away. They had decorative headgear and blankets of beads. Strange noises came from everywhere and were deafening. Our hotel looked like it could be drug infested and unsafe. Perhaps ignorance wasn't bliss, after all.

Inside, it was a different story. The walls were of gray marble and the rooms were quite spacious. While it wasn't completely quiet, it was decidedly better, and the overhead fans kept it cool. There was a restaurant on the roof, and we had breakfast and watched hawks swoop down to snatch food from unsuspecting people. Tourists and children were the only ones not wise to this practice, and the birds would go for anything on the assumption that it might be good to eat. None of the birds looked malnourished.

We went to American Express to collect our mail, and I received five letters! It was only September, but Christmas had come early. I changed some money, bought a chess book, and a copy of *Atlas Shrugged* at a very good bookstore and returned to the room. One thing I noted at the bookstore was the children's book section. And what caught my attention was the equivalent of a Dick and Jane book. I had opened it and read the following: "Run Lak and Nit. Run to the tree. Run to the sun." Opening another book on Little Red Riding Hood, I discovered that her basket had contained: "Cakes, oranges, and *mangosteens.*"

In addition to my letters and the bookstore, there was more good news: The tourist guidebooks suggested that visitors drink only bottled liquids. Julie wouldn't like this, but the Coca-Cola Company and I continued to support each other.

We were all tired of being poor and traveling at the bottom of the tourist pecking order. It was crowded too much of the time, and the travel was exhausting. We knew that in the Third World our complaints fell on deaf ears, but we were only visiting these places and not living our lives in them. The strain had been telling. Someone must have been listening.

Julie and Bill had been given the names of some friends of a friend who were with the British Embassy in Delhi. To find out what to do and see, Julie called them. They suggested that what we should do was to come to the embassy to see them. There didn't need to be a second invitation.

We were invited to spend a week—with our own apartment, a swimming pool, a restaurant, and a pub. We went into shock at the prospect. They offered us a car and driver to take us to Agra to see the Taj Mahal. That kind of hospitality was very touching, and we used the time to recover and to ready ourselves for our trip to Northern India.

I decided to go for a run at Nehru Park, not far from the embassy. So that I could come and go as I pleased, I had been issued a visitor card. As I approached one of the gates, I felt a great sense of elation. No one had told me, but the very somber looking guards had to be Gurkha soldiers. I was sure that the unusual hats and uniforms were those awarded to these famous soldiers. I had heard about them for most of my life, and they were unexpected here. They looked at the card and snapped a swift salute. Their devotion to duty was so legendary that I knew they could salute or take my life, depending entirely upon an order.

I asked our friends at the embassy about them when the run was over. Their brief history lesson was instructive. The British had won a major battle in the mid-eighteenth century that had given them control in India. A decade later, there were problems on the northern borders. Disputes over boundary lines and incursions by the fierce Nepali people resulted in a war between the British and the Nepalese. It took two years of "no quarter" fighting before a truce was signed. The Gurkha Brigade came about as the vanquished Nepalese were allowed to volunteer for regiments under the command of the East India Company's army. They are still fierce fighters, today, and serve fifteen years or more. I did not know it at the time, but I would learn much more about these modern warriors when I reached the mountains of Nepal.

The Gurkhas and the Sherpas: I had hoped to meet some of each. India had gone well so far.

Our new friends also gave us some information on just how different India was. There were more than fifteen major languages and over seventeen hundred dialects. Even Hindi, the language that we had assumed was the most commonly spoken, was not spoken by a majority of the people. It seemed to the three of us that the term "India" was much the same as the term "South America"—except that South America was not considered one country. With so many differences, we started to see why there had been so many problems. We listened closely to the embassy personnel to see if we could detect how they felt about their stay

Opposite page: A Sikh pilgrim tolerates a handstand at the edge of Hemkundt Lake, sacred to his faith. Sikhs bathe in the frigid waters and smiled at a brief attempt to join them.

in India. Over the next week, it seemed evident that they enjoyed it very much and thought that the diversity made the society better.

We enjoyed the trip to Agra to see the Taj Mahal. Our driver had worked for the embassy for most of his adult life and knew many stories that would entertain tourists. Driving in a luxury car past oxcarts, old bicycles, and pedestrians was a unique feeling. A week ago, we would have been walking or riding in a bus. The buildings and the views lived up to all we had ever heard about this world famous monument. Still, our guide told us of two other attractions that we should not miss, and both proved to be as spectacular as the Taj Mahal. We had never heard of either of them.

Fatepuhr Sikri was an abandoned fort and city of huge dimensions and great beauty. It sat atop a large hill and had huge elephant-proof gates, a bank, internal watercourses for gardens and stables, and beautiful "apartments." It was built and abandoned. Some told us it was because there was not enough water to sustain the city. Others told us that the builder had a vision and was instructed to leave. The work that had gone into it was as impressive as anything we had seen.

We also took an afternoon to visit the Jama Masjid, a beautiful and functioning mosque. We took pictures and talked with some of the Muslims about their city and about this beautiful monument to their faith. Not far away was another large compound that we had not heard about. Many of the Muslims suggested that our trip would not be complete without knowing more of Shah Jahan and the Red Fort. They were right and after our visit I knew I would remember this famous architect forever.

The Red Fort was built by Shah Jahan between 1639 and 1648. The moat, which surrounded it, was thirty feet deep. We entered through the Lahore Gate and were told that elephants were needed to open and close the giant doors. Just inside the gate was a covered bazaar of two stories. The upper level, we discovered, housed Indian army families. In the distant past, they sold silk, brocade, velvet, gold, jewelry, and gems in that area. We paused and tried to picture the tourist trinkets replaced with the wealth of kings.

The Drum House was a music gallery above the gateway, and kettledrums, *hautboys* (oboes), and cymbals were used during the Emperor's morning meeting in The Hall of Public Audience. Some of the four layers of painted plaster were still there today. The last layer used paint containing pure gold. All of the inlaid flowers, stems, and leaves on the Drum House were of pure gold.

The Hall of Public Audience used sandstone covered with white plaster and was polished to shine like white marble. It was then decorated with gold stucco. The marble throne canopy inside the hall had a gold railing and then a silver railing. The courtyard was covered by a canopy of silk that was held up by massive silver-plated poles. The canopy could shade a thousand people. The third railing, following the gold and silver, was of sandstone. The sandstone throughout the many buildings had all been hauled in over two hundred kilometers. The flagstone floor was covered with silk carpets. Heavy curtains hung from the outside of the building and ropes were used to raise and lower them. The marble canopy enclosed a throne called The Seat of the Shadow of God. The central figure on the inlaid panels behind the throne was of Orpheus, legendary Greek hero, and son of Apollo. In this hall the famous inscription can be found: "If there is a Paradise on earth—it is here, it is here, it is here."

The center of the inlaid flowers was lapis lazuli. Jasper was used for the mustard-yellow petals. Agate and carmelian formed the outer red petals. Jade was used in the green stems and leaves, and mother-of-pearl in the fine veins of the leaves. The Peacock Throne was six feet by four feet and was like a single bed on sturdy gold gem-studded legs. From the base, twelve gold-studded columns rose to a gold canopy lined with diamonds and pearls and fringed with more pearls. On top of the canopy was a peacock with a sapphire-studded tail. On each side of the peacock were gold flowers inlaid with precious stones. The estimated cost was 10 billion rupees in the 1630s. It was his best throne; he had six others.

The Life Giving Garden consisted of two similar marble pavilions opposite one another. Water flowed from the back wall. The water cascaded over a marble shelf that held gold and silver pots of flowers. At night the niches behind the water veil held candles. Water flowed between the pavilions and into a square pool at the center. In Shah Jahan's time, there were 218 fountains around the pool, 49 around the pavilion, 112 lining the tank, and 30 in each of the channels flowing toward the square tank. Flowers and fruit trees were everywhere.

The Royal Tower had the Stream of Paradise issuing from it as a small canal. It led to the Royal Baths. Inside the baths there had been hot and cold water in areas made of marble. These were not tubs, but there was a fountain scented with rosewater in the dressing rooms.

I made many more notations in my journal. Fortunately for those who would never travel to see any of the wonders created by Shah Jahan, there are many library books with brilliant pictures and more detailed descriptions.

It was soon the end of our week. We were out of the embassy grounds and soon out of town.

It was hot in Delhi. And it had been hot in Thailand, Malaysia, and Singapore. We traveled out of Delhi to one of the British hill stations at Mussoorie. Cool and mountainous, it was a wonderful break from the heat and humidity. My large hotel room had an eight-foot by eight-foot window with shutters instead of glass. The base of the window was only three feet off the floor and it offered a place to sit and write while looking down a hundred vertical feet to the sloping hills below. I have a clear picture in my mind of coming back from having a vegetarian pizza at a café, opening the door, and finding clouds literally rolling into my room. I sat on the window ledge and enjoyed the cool moisture and the fresh breeze. This was not the India I had imagined—ever.

I ran on back roads and up the trails leading to decomposing mansions. The temperatures were ideal, and the hill stations had become favorite getaways for the wealthy, and that included wealthy Indians. I wandered around town at the conclusion of a run, returned to the hotel for a bath, and then sat on a veranda overlooking a major street and wrote about what I saw. Most of what I did, I was doing alone.

At various places in all of the cities we had visited in India there were handmade signs. Some were on walls, others on fences. Many were about four feet by six feet. I copied one that was just across the street from the hotel:

Know God before you worship God
Know that all your belongings are a gift from God
Know that you belong to the whole of humanity and not
A particular religion, sect, or nationality
Know that you must not hate others for differences in diet and dress
Know that you should not renounce the world that
God has bestowed on us to live in
Know Nirankari Mission, Mussoorie, India

We were going north to Uttar Pradesh and hoped to do our first trekking since Thailand. Our path would take us through Rishikesh where the Beatles had come to seek enlightenment. Ashrams abounded as a result; there were well over one hundred. The Maharishi Mahesh Yogi's Transcendental Meditation Center is there and is quite popular for tourists.

Enlightenment must have been a truly remarkable thing and certainly was not dependent upon location. Charlatans abounded. We were adopted by one named Jerry, but the local police adopted him back and we parted with neither money nor karma. Tomorrow we would leave Rishikesh for a place called Joshimath. At that moment it was just another hard-to-remember name. After a twelve-hour bus ride, we would have been happy to call it home. None of us wanted to face the return trip. From there we planned to do two treks.

I was ready to find a Hindi language lesson. I had learned nothing of the local language in Singapore, a bit in Malaysia, and quite a bit in Thailand. Julie and Bill had given up. Other than some Malaysian, they seemed content to rely on the English language, which was everywhere. In a bookstore in Rishikesh, I found someone with enough time to assist me.

Namaste is the greeting and a farewell. It is generally accompanied with a *wai:* hands placed together as in prayer and a slight bow forward with the body. "Thank you" is *dhan ya vaad,* and it took a few tries before I associated it with "donny bought." "Yes" is *jee haan,* and "no" is *jee na heen.* Oh good, nothing simple there. *Kit-naa* is "how much?" "I don't know" is *main reheen simja.* And, since I often didn't understand, this got most of the rote attention. The definition of *achchaa* eluded me. The language guides said it meant "all right" or "very good," but I was assured by most of the Hindus I talked with that it covered a wide variety of subtleties. The bookstore manager who patiently helped me confirmed this and smiled at my confusion. Nodding my head as though I understood and repeating it several times seemed to get the job done. As a reward for my successful completion of my lesson, the bookseller gave me a term invested in a great deal of mystery. He prefaced the word by telling me that it would cause the street sellers to leave me alone. I envisioned a curse so vile that I might get myself in a very bad situation just to be free of a vendor. He assured me that it was a powerful word, or two.

The words were *bhaag jaa-o* and were pronounced exactly the same as a very picturesque town in the Philippines (*Baguio*). It was easy to remember that all vendors who spoke Hindi were afraid of a Filipino town, and I couldn't wait to tell Julie and Bill that we could now wander the streets with impunity. Funny, they seemed to focus more on the idea that my new phrase might get us a lot more than goods and services. We were going to wander around the streets after lunch, and I was elected to see how effective it would be.

As the requisite horde of ware sellers approached, we started by focusing on *jee na heen* (no) and *main naheen simjaa* (I don't understand). That worked for most of them. Two continued to follow us. Their English was very good. Julie and Bill moved a few feet away and looked ready to bolt into the nearest cab if the incantation and its aftermath turned ugly. I looked at two men who had just called me "uncle," and I told them in all seriousness that if they didn't quit trying to sell us their wares, I would be forced to say something very bad. They stopped walking and so did I. It looked like I didn't have any other alternative but to try this powerful means of starting an international incident. At the last second, I thought I saw a possible way out. "You wouldn't want me to become angry and have to say *bhaag jaa-o,* would you?" I said, smiling. They smiled hugely in return. Perhaps they had thought that my threat was some white magic of which they were unaware. Instead, it had been just some nuisance words pronounced in an accent that made them almost unintelligible. They bowed and said *namaste* and hurried away before I could do something else to convulse them with laughter. That was some threat. Julie and Bill moved closer—friends again.

AAAARRRGGGHHHH! For true risk and adventure, we had taken the exceptionally elderly bus from Rishikesh to Joshimath. We did it during the day and we sat on the window seats nearest the front of the bus. Not a muscle relaxed because there were very few places en route where the bus was not cornering on a narrow one-lane road. Julie and Bill sat on the right side of this mobile terror and I sat on the left. When we compared notes, they had been thinking the same thing: At the first sign of trouble, get out. Depending on which way we thought we were going to tip, each of us had an open window or doorway planned for our exit. If we didn't get too exhausted from pulling up on the armrests around each corner, we thought we could make it. The road had been literally carved from the vertical cliffs above a nearly unending series of deep canyons.

There were no guardrails on the road and the turnout spots would barely allow passage. If you were on the bus that backed onto one of these while another attempted to creep past, you felt that one slip by the other driver was going to bump you into space. And there was plenty of that. Anywhere from one hundred to nearly one thousand feet of sheer rock wall was below our tires at every moment of the twelve-hour trip. If I leaned out my open window when the drop-off was on my side, it was much like the view from an airplane. The wheels often had less than six inches of clearance.

We had heard in Delhi that the papers no longer published any information about bus accidents. Feeling that it was bad for tourism, they decided to omit any reference. Just outside Rishikesh, we had seen a bus being pulled out of a river after only a twenty-foot fall. It hadn't been a recent accident, but it was obvious from the condition of the remains that the passengers had been dealt with harshly. After that point the drop-offs became so severe that there would be no need to attempt a rescue or retrieval. For twelve hours our bus driver turned the wheel or shifted the gears and kept a watchful eye out for oncoming traffic. He took three short rests. At least three passengers needed the rest more than he did. I, for one, found no fault in those stops and thanked him for his effort when we finally arrived in Joshimath.

Finding a hotel was no problem; the touts were there to greet our bus. The theme seemed to be price or amenities. It was difficult to judge. We didn't know whether they were being honest or not. We did know that they were all very earnest—very. We finally settled on a room with most of the necessities and with a reasonable price. We knew that whichever hotel tout we selected, it would be a hilly trip from the pile of luggage to our quarters. We were right. The room was large, spacious, and had three large beds. And, it had a balcony. In no time, we had our packs emptied and our possessions organized. It was time to explore.

I walked around this quaint little mountain town and searched for a restaurant. I still wanted rice and the first two places didn't serve it. No rice? This couldn't really be Asia. The third place was a very small doorway between two buildings and only four tables were available. Such shops were called dhabas. The owner said, "*Namaste.*" I said, "*Namascar.*" He said, "*dal baht*" (rice and lentils), and I nodded just before I took a seat at an empty table. He said, "*pani*" (water), and I said, "Coke." He understood immediately that I could not drink the water. Dinner was served. All the other patrons ate with their right hand, as was the custom. I was given a spoon. That was followed by a huge plate of rice and lentils, and a plate of chapatis, which were much like thin tortillas. It took a while, but I ate it all. Without missing a beat, one of the cooks gave me a second helping as large as the first. As I watched the others, I noted that this was the custom. The bill came to seven *rupees* for the food (28¢). The two drinks were twelve *rupees* (48¢). Dinner had been an all-you-could-eat 76¢ meal. I knew where I would have lunch and dinner. There was no menu, but that didn't matter. The food was delicious.

It was time to trek, and we spent the next day sorting out a company to take us. On the following morning, we had our packs filled with basic items and were on our way to the bus park. And we found ourselves on a bus with no other Westerners. When we stopped, after only an hour and a half, we were ready to hike to the village of Govindghat. Bill had scheduled this trip as he had most of our excursions, and here he outdid himself. We were now part of a large group of Sikh devotees on their way to Hemkund Lake and the Valley of Flowers. Sikh men do not cut their hair and, therefore, wear traditional turbans and have full beards.

Each of the turbaned Sikhs was friendly and curious. Evidently, not many non-Sikhs made this trip. They were more than happy to ask us about "USA" and to tell us about themselves. Most of them were from the Punjab. Their particular belief system had begun with Guru (Divine Teacher) Nanak. This had been in the late fifteenth and sixteenth centuries. There had been nine gurus who had succeeded Nanak, and they were revered by all Sikhs as divine teachers. Guru Nanak welcomed all disciples to his faith, according to our new friends. Men and women, all castes and creeds—all were welcome. Meals were eaten in common and all were welcome—strangers and family alike. They worshiped God, we were told, through repetition of the name of God, by hard labor, and by sharing earnings with others of equal spiritual importance. Everyone seemed steeped in knowledge about each of the gurus and could quote much of their scripture. I wrote down a quote: "There is no Hindu, there is no Muslim. There is only One Being Who is the Creator and the uncaused Cause of all…. God is One." I couldn't write fast enough or remember well enough, and their conversational good intentions washed over us during the bus ride and at each meal at campsites. During the next three days, the only non-Sikhs we saw were each other.

Paralleling the Alakananda River, the trail was very well maintained. But these pilgrims were not here because they were fit and seeking a shrine. Many struggled mightily to negotiate the steep sections and the miles of elevated terrain. Some had to be carried on a litter. Because many small cooking stalls were available along the way, it was only necessary to carry clothing. With that type of arrangement, I was able to walk more quickly than I had anticipated and the pace and resulting fatigue felt very welcome. I was still trying to recover from the bus ride from Rishikesh.

There had been some severe storms in the area during the previous year's monsoons, and repairs to the trails were under way. I stopped to watch the Herculean efforts of some of the workers. Two men were using one shovel. A rope was attached near the shovel's blade and that extra leverage allowed for a lot of consistent effort. One would dig and the other would pull on the rope to allow more dirt to be moved. No one paused to even glance back at me; each person had a job and worked very hard to complete it.

Not much farther along, the trail was blocked by a Himalayan "truck." Twelve men carried a huge concrete pipe with a diameter that looked to be four feet or more. They were arranged six on a side and used two stout poles connected by rope slings. The load was considerable. They moved at an incredible pace and I walked quickly behind them amazed at the coordination of effort it took to keep everything from crashing to earth. It took no imagination at all to see what stumbling would do to the delicate balance they had achieved. Those near the back could not even see the upcoming terrain. I suspected that each man was supporting a shifting weight of nearly seventy-five pounds as the trail and the load constantly changed. Somewhere up the trail, the government was planning on moving a lot of water and there were a great many of these pipe sections being transported.

After I exchanged greetings and explored the four or five Hindi phrases I knew, the trail was again mine. This was the first group that seemed quite happy not to have to entertain a lengthy discussion. When I could say no more, neither did they. My early start on the trail had let me pass all of today's hikers from our bus. For a change, I almost regretted that; this trip had been a fascinating cultural experience so far and this particular excursion promised to be even better.

Near a small community, the trail branched and I was almost past several people who were talking when the bicycle registered. Bicycle? I stopped and stared and then walked over to the talkers. It was clear who owned the bike. He was a young Hindu and was promoting peace in India and harmony in the world. The vehicle he had chosen for this task was an amazingly heavy and overly laden relic. For my sake, he briefly reviewed his book of clippings from newspapers: crossing the world's highest motor roadway pass, visiting every province in India, visiting places holy to various factions throughout the country. He had passed the 3,000-kilometer mark in his travels and today he hoped to reach the village at the base of the climb to Hemkund Lake. I did, too, but this terrain could not be ridden on his bicycle, and he would have to push or carry it and all his belongings. When I arrived at the village, I took out a book that my friends at the British Embassy had loaned me and I found a passage that seemed appropriate.

Here is the excerpt that the young cyclist reminded me of. It was taken from Alex Thompson's *Ram Ram India* (a bike ride across India from north to south by two Britons):

> Rossiter's [the author's traveling companion] gaze is fixed on a
> man rolling over and over along the road, tumbling steadily in our
> direction. As he rolls head over heels, his companion walks beside

him with the luggage, a brass pot four inches high.

He is a Sadhu—a type of Hindu Holy Man who has decided to give up his job, and begin a series of penances on a massive scale, believing his earthly business has reached its maturity. To do this has meant leaving his wife, his eight children and his house; but he tells us between rolls that this is the only way to improve his karma—a kind of Hindu law of cause and effect relating to one's good or bad actions to types of possible reincarnation.

The Sadhu measures his progress at the end of each roll by sitting upright and carefully placing a small marker pebble he carries on the broken up tarmac of the road. Rossiter is transfixed…hit between the eyes with the fact of another human being completely outstripping both of us in terms of physical endurance and, if the expression on his face is anything to go by, enjoyment. The Sadhu sits up and smiles at us…much of his torso and chest is grazed and cut up from the rigors of rolling. He tells us he's come all the way from Kanpur and is now on his way back there—two hundred and fifty miles to the north, at least.

There was a passion burning in all facets of this society that was easy to appreciate but difficult to understand.

I rented a small room at the small village of Govindghat and ate while waiting for Julie and Bill. When they arrived two hours later, I welcomed the diversion. A great many Sikh men had been discussing America, religion, politics, how I liked India, and how much I knew about Sikhs. The intensity was so pervasive that I wondered whether a discussion about what time it was would be met with that same intent gaze. Everyone was friendly, and they seemed pleased that I was enjoying their country very much. They were especially interested in the small trinkets I carried with me. For some reason, they were delighted with the friendships represented by the items and by the fact that I carried them with me everywhere. The pennies and the cross were particularly impressive.

Julie and Bill arrived and announced that they did not have to rent a room since some of the people they had met on the trail had offered to let them share the free rooms across the trail. The next morning they offered to pay half of the cost of my room if they could have a place where 130 other people were not sleeping. And not sleeping seemed to be what many of them were doing. Religious fervor seemed to cause many loud discussions and nightfall didn't seem to inhibit them. Julie and Bill hadn't been able to sleep.

In Govindghat I experienced the most primitive conditions of my entire trip. The stairs up to my room were barely holding together and a great deal of ground could be seen through absent or broken boards. That was important to me because the bathroom was downstairs, and this route had to be negotiated in complete darkness. The room itself was about eight feet by ten feet and was poorly poured concrete. Only one window allowed air into the room. It had bars on it but no pane. We had no mattresses on the floor and there was a thick coating of dust. Most prison cells in the United States don't offer this primitive a facility. I consoled myself with the thought that I could leave here whenever I wanted to. Or, considering the bathroom trips at night, when I had to.

I have loved early mornings for as long as I can remember. Still, I waited until after breakfast before starting my trek in the cold morning air. The area was truly beautiful—in many ways it looked like parts of Montana or the area around the Tetons in Wyoming. On this day, only a light daypack was needed so I decided to push the pace just for the exercise. About a mile into the hike and just at the start of a series of rocky switchbacks, I passed a couple of soldiers wearing their green non-combat uniforms. They said "good morning," but like most elite soldiers, they did not appreciate being left behind. After another mile I cast a quick look over my shoulder and noticed that they were only sixty feet back and smiling at my obvious surprise. From there to the top of the ridge and the lakeside, no one did much smiling and we arrived about twenty feet apart. Well, I had wanted exercise.

At 15,000 feet, it was brutally cold. The large lodge, which had been built lakeside, was not heated—as far as I could tell. I had been sweating profusely and everything I wore was drenched. I was shaking, even after I changed into a dry top. I walked to the lake to see if an outsider could feel any of the sacred shrine's magic. My chilled condition was forgotten immediately as I watched Sikh men of all ages and sizes strip to loincloths and immerse themselves in the waters of Hemkund Lake. Ice was on the rocks from last night's sub-zero temperatures and water was frozen along the edges. Some pilgrims stayed in for ten minutes in the rapture of something I couldn't feel. Some of those I had talked with the night before decided that while I couldn't feel it all, I could feel some of it. They had hiked here at first light and encouraged me to join them in the sacred waters. I stayed in the water for as long as I could and even today I can still see the smile of a gray-haired Sikh who was there as I disrobed and still immersed to his beard as I tried to dry off. And he smiled the smile of the truly blessed.

Now I was truly cold. Julie and Bill were almost two hours behind and I was in danger of being the Birds Eye quick-frozen non-pilgrim. In a move of great kindness, two Sikhs asked me if I would be their guest in a cooking shelter. I hadn't known there was one, but when I looked around for the largest gathering of people, I knew I wasn't the only one who was cold. They were serving hot tea. I was soon inside a large lean-to where several fires were being tended and water was being boiled. We were well above timberline and wood was an understandably precious commodity.

I received several cups of hot tea and had a chance to practice my Hindi with the Sikhs who tended the fire. It was a common observance among the nearly frozen that a full cup of something warm presented a dilemma: Did you drink it and warm the inside, or did you cradle it between frozen fingers and hope to lessen the shaking? Bill, too, succumbed to the request to immerse and then welcomed the chance to help tend the fires. After a few hours we were all warm enough to descend to the village. Before we left, I went to a sacred area near the lake and spent some time holding each of the special gifts I had carried in the fanny pack. I thought of each of the friends who had written, of those who had asked me to carry a reminder of our friendship, and of my mother, who patiently awaited word of my safety. Another piece in the puzzle of life's meaning: the importance of family and friends.

On the evening before the descent to the trailhead, Bill had a bout with stomach problems. His ailment seemed to be the result of a bad samosa, which were deep-fried pastry triangles. The oil they were fried in was often the culprit. Rancid oil continued to be my main reason for avoiding fried foods. Having always wanted to see what it was like to carry a heavy load like the Sherpas in Nepal, I was happy to try to carry both his pack and mine. At first, the novelty made the packs feel reasonable. After a few miles, that feeling almost totally eroded. Porters who struggled uphill with their huge loads reminded me that I struggled equally on a descent.

Smiling pilgrims kept my spirits up, and I stopped a few times to pose with various groups and their cameras. Many times the greetings were in English: "Hello, my dear." After pictures and pleasantries, we would bow to one another— hands pressed together in a *wai*. "Enjoy your pleasant journey" replaced "have a nice day." Several times I was allowed to look at the *kirtipanis* (Sikh swords that are religious symbols) being carried to the lake. Finally, my sore shoulders and aching legs reached their goal: the trailhead. Never was a bus terminal such a welcome sight. I was already in awe of the porters here in India. What, I wondered, would Nepal be like?

CHAPTER 7
KUARI PASS AND
THE HIMALAYAS

…If one advances confidently in the direction of his dreams
and endeavors to live the life which he has imagined,
he will meet with success unexpected in common hours.
– Thoreau

Back in Joshimath, Bill spent a couple of days trying to recover from his stomach problems. I tried to catch up on journal entries that were too brief or illegible because of frozen finger penmanship. During his recovery I continued my chess lessons, and we talked about his marriage. He wasn't sure if it was going to continue or not; Julie had made some threats to travel on her own. He seemed resigned to endure daily punishment for the remainder of the trip.

Just above our hotel I had noticed a large flat area about twice the size of a football field. I chose to write on a waist-high stone fence up there because there was always something happening.

Children on their way to or from school would often gather as close as they dared to peer at the tall Westerner's scribbles. One day, a young boy approached me and timidly asked to show me a sample of his writing in English. The ice had been broken, and that was a signal for the rest to join in. They all signed their names and then ran off giggling. They would have their own version of this encounter with a Westerner who was apparently trying to speak Hindi.

On the second day of Bill's recovery, my "person from Porlock" was a bicyclist. He wasn't a bicyclist when he started, but he was a bicyclist two hours later. I gave up trying to write something profound, leaned against the wall, and openly stared. Two teenage boys had found an old bicycle with nearly flat tires. Neither knew how to ride it, but both were determined to learn. Each attempt involved one boy holding the bike while the other sat on the seat, held the handlebars, and put a sandaled foot on each pedal. The holder began to push and the rider began to scream. At one point, they discovered that the bike was easier to keep upright at higher speeds. After that, each push and ride was an all-out attempt to achieve lift-off. Another discovery came hard on the heels of the first one: It was easier to survive the fall at lower speeds. Fortunately, they were two athletic boys and their falls amounted to more dust than pain. When one finally succeeded in riding until he wanted to dismount, it was cause for great celebration. I joined in an appreciative round of cheers and applause.

Not long after the boys had gone, I heard a great deal of noise off to my left. Ignoring it to finish part of a drawing, I noticed that it was getting closer— fast. Someone had confused the narrow streets of Joshimath and this large open area with Pamplona, Spain, and four young men had just chased some bulls out of one of the side streets. It took a very short time to take a firm stand on the outside of the stone wall until they had gone past. These weren't the wild bulls of Spain, but the degree of their tameness around an American was not going to be tested that day. Not by this American it wasn't.

Before the bicycle and before the bulls, I had been writing about what I had learned so far. At this point in my trip, I had recognized at least three attitudes that went hand in hand with the best of my experiences. One was the idea of participating in the adventure of life, which I had noted during my first mini-adventure at Ao Pra Nang in Thailand. The next was *sanuk*: the idea that work and play should be enjoyed and interchangeable. Last, my friends and family had grown in importance. Possibly that was due to homesickness, but I thought that there might be more to it. I suspected that I needed to think about what friendship and kinship really meant. I hadn't reached a decision about where these fit into any grand answer, but I was paying a lot more attention to the events that brought these elements to mind.

Julie and Bill, meanwhile, were anxious to do more adventurous things. Another trek would be just the ticket.

At the end of our first week, we prepared our gear for a hike to Kuari Pass— a 15,000-foot ascent. Julie and Bill wanted to hire a porter to carry their gear. That made sense since neither felt particularly well at this stage of our trip. They selected a guide–porter combination and that was sensible. We certainly needed a guide. Unfortunately, the guide they selected spoke no English and that promised to be a problem later on. The outfitters that we were dealing with said that he was Nepali, and that although he was quite old, he was also quite fit.

They also told us that his name was Pram Singhe (a decidedly non-Nepalese name). He was to carry all of the food for four days, the tent for Julie and Bill, a makeshift tent for himself, a stove, two blankets, a sleeping bag, and various odds and ends. We were told that the weight limit was forty-five pounds for what he would carry and his pack seemed to be all of that.

Pram Singhe proved that he was fit as we started for the ski resort town of Auli the next morning. There was a dirt road of switchbacks up the mountain, but it was too costly to travel by automobile. Our guide knew several trails that traveled straight up the mountain and cut across every switchback. He and I were "sweat" in no time. By not resting, I was able to reach Auli and stretch out for a while on some recently cut logs. My pack weighed about thirty pounds and I marveled at Pram Singhe's ability to negotiate the terrain with bare feet and a heavier load. What was impressive about Auli were the support structures for a tram. We had paralleled the towers all the way from Joshimath. Workers who were eating near where I was resting told me that the tram project had been underway for ten years or more. Considering our isolation and the trip from Rishikesh, I was amazed that it hadn't been a hundred years. As the rest of the group arrived, they startled a group of very large monkeys who were feeding beneath the trees. That wasn't something I had connected with India and certainly not at this altitude. Snow covered the ground for six months of the year. I tried to imagine troops of monkeys summering at Telluride or Snowbird, and I rethought my concept of jungles and monkeys.

Our day finished with a second long ascent above the resort. There were a few farmhouses during the steep portions of the hike, and we paused to enjoy the view that they saw all year. I started wondering: If you had never known another place or another way of life, could you appreciate the beauty of what you were seeing? The other point of view seemed somehow important, so I wrote it down in my journal. For a moment, understanding and point of view related in a new way, but I didn't have time to consider how, just then. Across from us the peak turned golden and then fiery red as the sun sank over our first night's camp. Clouds rolled in.

The next day was a beautiful trek through high pastures and forests. We commented on what looked like Spanish moss hanging from the overhead branches. At this elevation, it seemed strange that the trees would be this large and that there would be moss in this quantity. I hiked ahead, again, so that when I found something worthwhile I could write about it and rest in the process. Not knowing where to turn and not having English as a medium, I was careful to stop wherever there was a definite choice in trails. By early afternoon I saw Nanda Devi (25,650 feet) for the first time. While still a long way off, it was my first well-known Himalayan peak and I sat on a rock and took the view in; I forgot to write anything down. In this case, I knew it wasn't necessary.

We had made good progress and now we were on the edge of a meadow. The guide had confirmed the word *pani* for water. Pram Singhe seemed confused as to where to establish camp; Bill was exhausted and said he could go no farther. With additional comments from all three of us, Pram Singhe was even more unsure. *Pani* was mentioned, but our guide didn't seem to know where there was any. *Pani* might be one of those words with more than one meaning. From his facial expressions and gestures, the other meaning might be "idiot." He would eventually find a steady supply of *pani* and would make frequent trips in what appeared to be good-natured resignation. The tent was set up and Julie and Bill would sleep there for the night. I elected to find a place outdoors. My sleeping bag had been hauled throughout the heat of Singapore, Malaysia, Thailand, and parts of India. During these two treks it had made up for that inconvenience. It was rated to twenty degrees below zero and would allow me to be comfortable here. Because of last night's rain, I chose to sleep under the overhang of a large boulder.

I arranged a rock border and flattened the sleeping area by adding fresh dirt and leaves that I transported from under the nearby trees. Using my Swiss Army knife, I cut some pine bough ends for extra comfort. Food was hung on a line just over my head in a small daypack so rodents wouldn't turn this trip into a fast. The nearness of the line and food to my head ensured that even an acrobatic creature would not dine with impunity. I was a light sleeper and hoped that tonight wouldn't be an exception.

Good luck had placed me on the leeward side of the boulder and neither the rain nor chilly wind had any effect. Our guide slept near the tent with his clothing and a thick sleeping blanket as his only protection from the mountain storm. The next morning it was clear that he understood my sign language as to whether he was cold or not. He said not. Today he would be able to relax and enjoy the day without his charges. We were going to hike to a place called Kuari Pass.

After a discussion about how Julie and Bill felt, they elected to sleep in. I left at first light and climbed the hill above our meadow. Across from the peak we were on was another of slightly more height. About three miles of narrow ridge connected the two, and with the morning sun behind me, I could see a group of people standing at the pass across the canyon. Though there was no chance that they would still be there when I arrived, I started briskly along the ridge. I paused once to write down some thoughts on the beauty of this place and this day, but after several tries I gave up. Those were deep blue skies and the air seemed the cleanest I had ever breathed. The rocks were a stark contrast to the greens of the vegetation, and the flowers were small but of brilliant hues. I used common words in my attempts because I couldn't find anything that fit. All my senses worked at the limit of their capabilities and that heightened the experience.

I even found enough ecstasy to run the last mile of the mostly level meadows. When I arrived at the point where the trail crested and started down the other side, there was no sign of anyone. It was a steep and rocky trail that plunged off this side of the mountain, and I was glad not to be coming up it with a heavy pack. I could see most of the trail behind me toward camp, and no one moved along its track. Perhaps Julie and Bill were feeling worse than they had anticipated. The altitude and their illness were not a good combination. This was the fourth or fifth time that they had complained of illness or of not feeling well. Perhaps it was the strain of their relationship. The lines had been drawn and my solo sojourns were happening more and more frequently. The friendship was clearly dying.

I found a house-sized grassy area with some jutting rocks on either side that acted as a windbreak. I was literally on top of the ridge and only ten feet from the point where the trail started down the cliffs. It was warm. At 15,000 feet it must have been at least seventy degrees. I took off my shirt and used my daypack and windbreaker for a pillow and ground cover. I fell into a light sleep.

I awoke to the sound of horses' hooves not twenty feet away. And they were closing. As I sat up I remembered that there was something wrong with horses and here. Before I could figure out what that something was, I was almost struck in the face by the talons of one of two very large eagles. They were flapping their enormous wings in order to climb just high enough to crest the ridge and to find the thermals on the other side. In a light dream state, I had confused the sound of their beating wings with that of galloping horses. I awoke to the reality of two very surprised birds. Their adrenaline and mine were probably a match; they had come within inches of colliding with something that wasn't supposed to be there. Within ten seconds they were a hundred feet above me on the strong currents rising up from the deep canyons below. I was still warm, but no longer sleepy.

After several hours of relaxation, I was on my way back. Julie and Bill waved from a large outcropping that they had scaled. They had been able to get about halfway to the pass and had selected a magnificent area from which to view Nanda Devi and the mountains surrounding Joshimath. I waved back and returned to camp for a much-needed meal.

Returning to Joshimath for a day's rest brought an increase in our anxiety level. Either we would have to take residence here and write friends for money, or we were going to have to take a bus back down the mountain. We didn't need to return all the way to Rishikesh, but we would have to go to the juncture of two rivers that formed the Ganges at a place called Hardwar. From there, we would make our way to another hill station called Almora. The narrow and winding road proved no better as a descent and we were sweaty-palmed for another six hours.

When we arrived at Hardwar, I recognized it right away. That was a shock until I was able to remember where I had seen it before. There had been a documentary on Sir Edmund and Peter Hillary on PBS. They had taken powerboats from the Bay of Bengal and had gone past Hardwar and up a gorge to the Shivalik Mountains. Finally forced to stop in increasingly steep canyons, they had abandoned the boats and had staged ascents on various Himalayan peaks. Hardwar, I remembered, was a sacred city of pilgrimage. No alcohol was allowed and it was a strictly vegetarian existence there. Bathing in the sacred water of the Ganges was very meaningful. It had been years since I had seen the show and that was all I could remember.

From the last hill station of our trip, Almora, we would travel to Gorakpuhr in India, our jumping off point for Nepal. We would arrive by train in Gorakpuhr and take a bus from there. Nepal had always been the focus of my reading about the climbers and the challenges they had faced in the mountains: the tough and hardy Sherpas, Tenzing Norgay and his book *Tiger of the Snows*, and the first ascent of Everest. And, there were the Gurkhas and the legend of their fighting zeal. As much as I wanted to stay in India and explore, I couldn't wait for Nepal.

CHAPTER 8
<u>KALA PATTAR AND</u>
<u>EVEREST BASE CAMP</u>

*History illustrates the special place mountains have held in the past.
Is it any surprise that humans naturally look to mountains as sources
of inspiration? Mountains represent places for renewal, of rebirth
which draw humans toward them. This desire to visit and climb
mountains will always be alive in humanity regardless of the efforts of
technology to make humans soft; their minds, their memories
will pull them toward the pearls.*
– Professor Mikel Vause, mountaineer

Julie, Bill, and I survived the bus ride from Gorakpuhr to the Nepalese capital of Kathmandu. In a book about travel through Third World countries, there was always a lot of narrative about comfort, speed, and safety—or the lack thereof. However, when you were making your own pilgrimage to the Himalayas, you could put up with a lot. A thirteen-hour bus trip on a dirt road was a lot.

We changed buses as the countries changed. The bus from the Nepal border had a different style of taking tickets. Unlike in Malaysia and Thailand, here, people rode on the roof. There were too few cars and too many people for it to have been otherwise. Safety seemed to be a concern only in that women and children remained inside. The three of us were just trying to preserve enough space on our predawn bus and didn't realize that our luggage had become seats. We got an important clue however about fifteen minutes into the ride when the ticket taker opened the window next to me and crawled out and up. We were doing about thirty miles an hour when he opened the window, and I was about to politely object that a lot of cold air was not what I wanted. When he easily scampered out, I had no idea what he was doing. I closed the window and shared a quizzical look with Julie.

He returned in another fifteen minutes, opened a window next to Bill on the other side of the bus, and climbed back into the aisle. It seemed fitting that

Nepal and its villages are beautiful but often offer the unexpected.

a Nepali would "climb" the bus. Bill stuck his head out the open window and reported that there were many legs hanging down from the luggage rack. Every bus we took in Nepal used this system. We wondered how many ticket takers retired from old age. Our crowded bus rolled on into the light of our first day in Nepal.

The road we were on would eventually be paved. On this day it was under a kind of construction that was hard to comprehend. As we rode in the dust and over the bumps, we looked out over beautiful valleys that always seemed to have a river running through them. We looked closely and could see people down among the river rocks with large wicker baskets. A line of struggling Nepalis could be seen moving from the rocks of the riverbed up trails that led to the roadbed. From where we were, the trails were not visible, but it took little imagination to see that "down there" and "up here" were separated by a lot of steep. What we could see were a large number of sweat-soaked people pouring river rock out of their baskets and starting back down the trail.

The rock was for gravel. Without rock-crushing machinery, converting large rocks to small rocks was a huge endeavor. Gravel was made with a regular size hammer and a seated Nepali. Thousands of them lined the roadway in the sun and worked until the hammer needed to be replaced. On roadways where this process had been completed, tar was poured. The method was extremely labor intensive. Men with poles across their shoulders and a bucket of hot tar on each end struggled from the pouring site to the next area of road to be done. Others smoothed it around to cover the gravel.

It was the kind of activity that I would have associated with the building of the pyramids, had I thought deeply about large-scale projects in terms of pure human toil. But this was not going to produce a comparable monument, just another paved road. I told Julie and Bill a quick story about the first expedition to successfully climb Nepal's Annapurna.

In the early 1950s, Maurice Herzog and some other world-class climbers attempted and reached Annapurna's summit—the ninth highest peak in the world. Theirs was a tragic tale of success—many of the climbers suffered frostbite severe enough to prevent them from ever climbing again. Even finding the mountain and a way to gain access to its base was difficult and threatened to turn the expedition back. Still, after they had succeeded and had been treated for their injuries, they were invited by the king of Nepal to a ceremony in Kathmandu.

Herzog and his team had traveled from Gorakhpur, as we were doing now. They had been carried by porters or on horseback and they spent many days on their journey. Eventually, they were told that they would soon arrive at a carriage road and would be taken by car to Kathmandu. Naturally, they could not conceive of a car anywhere in a country where there were no roads. The answer, of course, was that the cars had been brought in by porters. Herzog had been incredulous at this bit of information—especially since some parts of the trail were barely wide enough for two men to walk abreast. A metal bridge that they had crossed had been barely five feet wide.

His guides informed him that both cars and trucks had been carried to Kathmandu—over two passes that were over 6,000 feet high. The vehicles, minus their tires, were lashed to huge platforms, which were carried by fifty to seventy-five porters. Following riverbeds instead of the trails Herzog's party had used; the barefoot porters carried the vehicles all the way to Kathmandu. There, one hundred vehicles used twelve miles of roadway. Of course, gasoline had to be carried in, too.

Herzog's *Annapurna* had amazed me when I had first read it at age twelve. Now, seeing what I had once only imagined made me realize how little I had understood. As we swung around the curves leading up to Kathmandu, we could see the impossibility of what the Nepalese had done. And, what they were still doing. In some places reinforced walls of stone stood over one hundred feet high. And there were often two or more at every curve. I guessed that perhaps as many as four thousand large river rock were used in each of those walls. The observations didn't eliminate the fatigue of a thirteen-hour journey, but they did put it in perspective. It was something Nepal did to me many times over the next two months.

During the bus ride, we picked up snippets of information from other Westerners. For example, from 1881 until 1921, fewer than sixty-five Europeans had visited Kathmandu. Nepal had always been a very poor and a very isolated country, and climbing, more than anything else, had opened it up to the world. Of the 19 million residents, we overheard that over fifty percent were under age twenty-one. Of immediate importance was the fact that the Nepali rupee was currently exchanged at a rate of thirty-four for every American dollar. We hoped that was good.

Julie and Bill had decided that, after we arrived, they would go their own way. Their marital problems would have to be worked out by a method they had yet to discover. I had no doubt that they would be better off doing that on their own and at their own pace. The same would also apply to the trek to Everest Base Camp that we had scheduled. They wanted a guide and porter again; I wanted to see what it would be like to carry my own pack to the very base of Everest. I also looked forward to dinners where the issue of nutrition wasn't being beaten into an untimely death. The parting of the ways would be good for all of us, and we were fortunate to understand it when we arrived. For some reason, I thought back to First Interstate Bank's slogan that appeared on the ATM screen back home whenever I used my card: "We want to make you a loan." Reading it was one thing; saying it had always amused me. Now I would get to see how amusing being alone would be.

I had no idea whether English was spoken by people in Nepal not associated with trekking. Gone were two travel-experienced friends who had certainly eased the burden of my indoctrination to Asia. As far as organization went, I had only the approximate dates and locations of mail drops for the next year. That schedule could be changed if I wanted to write to everyone and let them know that things were now different, but if I wanted to do that, it would have to be done now. Had I learned enough to be able to take care of myself? I didn't have the guidebooks that my friends had traded for. Bill had the camera and the film. If teetering on an edge ever became popular, I had a very big start.

A Nepali truck stop. Heavy packs can be set down and lifted up only from walls such as these. Most tea houses have such walls for their patrons.

What relaxed me about my new single status was the high intensity of the trip so far. We had never failed to meet other Westerners wherever we had gone. People were friendly and conversational in every place we visited. We had yet to meet another Westerner who didn't speak some English. We had met almost no Americans, thus far, but English among travelers was either the mother tongue or a fluent second. Fluency among local residents in a second language was almost universal. If the past was any clue, being alone would be by choice. Because the three of us had usually been doing tourist things, we were always hearing from others about how to do them better. Or, sometimes, why not to do them at all. Others at the lodges were often coming back from someplace we had been getting ready to go. That, too, wouldn't change. As far as wandering into areas that should be avoided because of disease or other dangers, both Westerners and natives were quick to give protective advice. Even as we obtained our visas for a new country, the American Embassy would provide such information when needed. I had learned all this from the travel we had done. Whatever our other differences might be, Julie and Bill had certainly made me into a more confident voyager.

Thamel was a small enclave within the city of Kathmandu. It was our destination, and the destination of thousands of others. Many had come to simply enjoy Nepal's capital and wander the city and surrounding country. Some had come for the river rafting. Nepal had the Asian single horn rhino and over eight hundred species of birds. Climbers, trekkers, white water canoeists—the active and the inactive were everywhere. On the bus, I had been told that over 60,000 people trek in the Himalayas in Nepal each year. I checked into the Dreamland Hotel and prepared to begin the adventure of Nepal and the Himalayas. I was alone for the first time.

I walked to my room and thought about my own changes. I spoke two more languages than I had in Seattle and I knew that Asia and its cultures had made me much more respectful of others. Worried that I might not be treated well because of my "foreign-ness," I had found just the opposite. Respect, religion, and philosophy were woven into every aspect of the societies I had seen so far. It was humbling. And the effects often showed up months later. Even other travelers were adapting. I organized my belongings and returned to the front desk of the hotel and found more examples of what I had just been thinking about.

I asked the time so that I could adjust my shock resistant sports watch. Nepal was five hours and forty minutes ahead of Greenwich Mean Time. And forty minutes? I hadn't thought that was possible. It certainly didn't seem as tidy as the system I had grown up with. Not only that, but the year was different, too. The year 1995 was 2051 in Nepal—fifty-six years ahead of the Gregorian calendar. New Year's was in mid-April. While there were twelve months, they occurred in the middle of each of ours. Baisaakh, the first month, was from mid-April to mid-May. It was what it was—but I had to smile. Alice had only been to Wonderland. The watch wasn't the only thing that needed to be shockproof.

The Dreamland Hotel was very low budget but was staffed with people as kind as those in Thailand or India. I knew that there would be a Nepali word for *sanuk* and that I was seeing its expression here. Two young men took care of the front desk, full-time. They ate meals at the restaurant as did all the staff, and they slept on the couches in the small lounge when the office closed at night. After they prepared the lobby and desk area each morning, they assisted the guests and showed prospective tout-directed foreigners the premises. They were happy to help me with language lessons.

In Nepal, the greeting is the same as in India: *namaste. Tapailai kasto chaa?* means "How are you?" There are a number of correct replies, such as *malai sanchai chha* or just *sanchai*—both of which more or less mean "Fine, thank you." My instructors told me that *ram rossa* was a reply for excellence of being. That brought back memories of the book, *Ram Ram India. Dinuhos* means "please" and generally implies "give me some." "Thank you" was the same as in India, and my old friend *dhanyabhad* was back. *Kana* is "food," and I already knew that *pani* meant "water." *Umaalako pani* is boiled water—a must unless I was going to drink only bottled water or soft drinks. My first language lesson got me through a fine dinner in the restaurant. I tried out my new words and the waiter was pleased to understand. Or said he was.

In the process of a language lesson and dinner, I learned that Nepal was ninety percent Hindu and there was a caste system here, like that in India. In the caste system, *Brahmins* are the priests, *chhetris* are the warriors, *vaishyas* are the merchants and farmers, and *sudras* are the artisans and menials. This system, I was told, was accepted by nearly all of those affected. I asked if it was outlawed as in India and received the reply that it was not something that could be altered by the laws of man. It was a nebulous answer, but clear in its application. Both of my new friends at the Dreamland Hotel were *chhetris*. They were not, however, wealthy, so they couldn't marry until they had established themselves. Spending almost twenty-four hours a day in a hotel couldn't offer much of a social life. They explained that marriages were arranged within castes. Hindus were born as Hindus. They couldn't change that fact. Since it was not a system that you could join, there was no proselytizing. This was another fascinating culture and I told them how much their explanations were appreciated.

It was a disappointment to discover that I could not see the Himalayas from Thamel. What could be seen, I was told, was the Ganesh Himal. To see that spectacular view, you could take a bus or a car or a bike and travel to a far away and small hotel at a place called Kakani. I wouldn't take a bus anywhere I didn't have to and I didn't have enough money to hire a private car. There was no problem. Mountain bikes, some surprisingly new and lightweight, rented for about $0.75 per day. For a bicyclist that fact closed the deal and I was soon the proud renter of a 12-speed yellow bicycle that weighed in at a respectable 25 pounds.

There was a ring road surrounding the city and the instructions for the proper exit for my ride were quite good. From there, I was rewarded with a steady and steep climb on a very nice paved road. I left early in the morning, knowing that the morning chill would be offset by the climb. I was the only one commuting in that particular direction. Cows, women, children, and men walked toward town with various and sundry wares. Bicyclists also descended the steep hills, and the riders were well wrapped against the cold and the imminent collapse of their vehicles. Their bikes were heavy and old and the weight of the rider and goods threatened to crush the wheels at any turn. Especially brave were the men who carried large canisters of metal that contained liquid. They seemed to know how brave they were, and their shouts of greeting and smiles of pure joy reflected off my look of obvious concern.

The climb paralleled a wall that ran for at least three miles. Inside the confines of all that brick was land owned by the king. I wrote in my journal about the parallel between this area and the story of Sherwood forest. At this point in my trip, I wasn't concerned that this land might be put to better use. I was learning that appearances colored by my Western outlook were nearly always deceiving. The first valley opened up about the time I realized just how long it had been since I had done a hard uphill ride. The sun was just rising over the tops of the steep hills and people were starting to work the fields.

I was not the first Westerner on this road—not even close to it. Children saw my yellow bicycle from half a valley away and the day's chores were history. Yelling "good-bye, good-bye," they raced to a point that intersected my passage. It wasn't a greeting they repeated endlessly, so it must have had more to do with a need for some assurance that I didn't intend to stay for long. But until I was gone, I was content to wave, smile, and say good-bye, too.

Rice fields were everywhere. Nepal had 19 million people and only about 800,000 were in the Kathmandu valley. That meant that almost every available space below 12,000 feet was going to be as cultivated as possible. Beautiful green terraces stretched away on both sides of the road. Up or down, steep slope or gentle, farms were everywhere. Mostly women worked in the fields. Young children tended the animals when they weren't chasing after lone bicycle riders. Those not in school might start working as young as four. By age eight, many would be working full time. To me, school seemed to offer an easier time as well as the opportunity to break the cycle of poverty.

After an hour of uphill riding I heard the first motorized sound. Twenty switchbacks below me, a bus was climbing, too. If sound was a good indicator of gear, this overloaded transport was not going much faster than I was. More surely, perhaps, but not much faster. In twenty minutes I had been caught. The inside of the bus was a sardine can to some exponential level. The top was a mass of clinging Nepalis. Arms waved from everywhere. Teeth shone in a sea of grins. It was all friendly. Some of the younger rooftop riders adjusted the wave to resemble a beckon. I smiled back at that. All of us had just started up an even steeper grade and the bus had slowed accordingly. I was able to stay just behind but was unable to pass. Now, encouragement was combined with friendliness as both vehicles struggled on.

After a mile of climbing I realized that my headache was going to be around for a while. The catalytic converter had not yet been mandated in Nepal, and certainly none of their buses had ever been equipped with one. I couldn't see if my skin was blue yet, but I was sure everyone else could. I stopped and waved to the smiles as they moved upward and out of sight. After twenty more minutes of bus-free climbing, I reached the turnoff to the hotel.

It was colder here on the ridge and the clouds were above and below me. This wasn't a storm, just clouds periodically crossing the ridge from the valley below to one above. The main road snaked off to my left and the absence of any sign at this juncture led me to believe that this might be an area known only to locals. I turned to the right, taking a chance that this was the road to Kakani. Still ascending on a paved road, I was surprised to round corners and find girls and boys sitting on the tarmac and weaving or assembling something. They, too, seemed surprised at my sudden appearance. Evidently, not many vehicles traveled this way. These older children were quite shy. They responded to my greeting of *namaste* with polite civility, but they were obviously whelmed by my presence.

Finally, I saw a huge hotel-like building. It turned out to be a military head-quarters—which explained all the rifles and uniforms. The soldiers' pointed fingers were directed up the road and I continued on in that direction. Two young barefoot boys discovered me and raced alongside my bicycle. One had a two-foot long broom handle with a bent piece of wire on one end. He used that to tap an old bicycle tire that he rolled ahead of him. Both boys kept pace with me for the half mile to the hotel. Then, laughing and smiling, they raced back to tell someone.

The hotel was perfect. It was very neat and clean and unoccupied. I ordered a breakfast of oatmeal and pancakes and looked over the prices for lodging. I could see why there was no one here. It was very expensive and owned by the government. Wealthy tourists might stay here, but I was one backpacker who could not afford much more than the price of this meal. After eating in the warmth of the sun that filtered through a large window, I walked outside to see what the clouds were doing.

Ama Dablam rises majestically behind a stupa. *For good luck, people pass to the left of such structures—or make a complete circle of them. Here, Alex Paulos pauses for a brief rest.*

A quarter acre of lawn and a few tables and chairs occupied the only flat area before the hotel grounds dropped off on two sides. I had reached the chairs before I realized that the white clouds across the valley were not all white clouds. Huge peaks loomed above me. I basked in the warm morning sun and watched the protean clouds and the snow-covered peaks of the Himalayas. The bike ride had done what I had wanted; I was ready for the bus ride to a place called Jiri and the twenty-eight-day trek to Everest and back.

My extra gear was stored in a locked room at the Dreamland Hotel. Bidur and Bupendra, my two new friends, assured me that no one would go into that room unless one of them was also present. And each person in that room would have to identify his own luggage and the nametag would have to match. I had to be comfortable with the precautions since I was leaving most of my money behind. On the night before I left Kathmandu, Bidur explained a couple of cultural items that might help me. He knew that I enjoyed participating in local culture and that I might stay with a local family for an evening. He cautioned me not to touch food or utensils that local people used. Most Hindus will not eat food that a non-Hindu has touched. In the public teahouses or among the Sherpas this did not apply. Also, he told me not to throw anything into the fire in any house. The household gods live in the hearths. He knew that I didn't have a camera with me, but he told me that many Nepalis worry that their picture will be burned or destroyed in some manner that will do them harm. Perhaps I would pass that information on to those with cameras? Asking permission would be more than a polite gesture. I thanked both of these young men for the language lessons, the hospitality, and for ensuring enough water for a brief shower each morning. Civilization was about to change.

Jiri was another twelve hours on an old bus. You would think that continued exposure to the marathon bus sessions would make for a seasoned traveler. Not for me. However, this bus ride had a difference that I had not yet experienced. It was so overcrowded that people clung to the open window frames from the outside of the bus, their feet braced against the metal sides. Even a very tough Nepali could not expect to ride like that for more than ten or twenty minutes. Even if that estimate was wildly wrong, twelve hours was impossible. And there was no more room inside for anything larger than a rodent. Just outside of town, nearly twenty minutes from the bus park, we stopped at a roadside turnout and a scramble was made for the roof.

A Canadian couple were the only other Westerners, and we sat together atop piles of strapped-on luggage. We had been closest to the front door and had been propelled outside by the crush. It was definitely better on the roof, but on top of a bus? I remembered the bus ride from the border and Bill's comments about the legs dangling from the top; now I was actually doing it myself. The ride was slow as we negotiated the narrow and steep roadways. It was warm and the views were spectacular. There were no guardrails on any corner of the road.

We were fortunate to be sitting near a *sirdar* who was on his way to join an expedition. The ultimate Sherpa organizer of a major expedition, a *sirdar* was at the top of the Nepalese trekking and climbing hierarchy. His command of English was excellent and so was his ability to teach Nepali. For about half of the journey we learned more about proper greetings, where trails led, how to ask for boiled water, and the names of various trekking sites. We learned the words for pretty woman, how to say thank you, excuse me, and other polite phrases. With practice on our part and patience on his, we were conversational on a two-year-old level by the time we arrived in the trailhead town of Jiri. Our hotel owner for that night was delighted with our accents and our attempts to learn his language. He, too, added a few words for us to try. One of those was the word *didi.* Its literal translation is "elder sister," but it was used as a respectful address to women at the various teahouses along the way. You didn't have to travel for long to understand that in Nepal, *didis* ruled.

At six o'clock the next morning, the Canadian trekkers and I were out the door and looking for the trail. We had some verbal directions but were justifiably nervous about the possibility of hiking for hours in the wrong direction. Perhaps Julie and Bill had been right in choosing travel guides. A guide could be an inexpensive solution to the problem of wandering off course for days. Porters cost about three dollars per day, and a guide was not much more than that. We walked for about fifteen minutes and struck a trailhead that looked as though ten thousand people had recently been by. This was definitely the place and we started up optimistically. Who needed a guide or a porter?

The agreement with these new friends was to go at our own pace and I soon found that the elation of being in the Himalayas and the sporadic running I had been doing were making this relatively easy. Soon, I was alone on the trail. And then I wasn't. There were huts and homes on all sides of the trail and porters appeared from everywhere. They were much tougher than I had ever imagined. Herzog and members of his party had been carried down from the mountains by people just like these. Men who weighed 140 pounds had carried men of 160 pounds over the worst terrain imaginable. Here, porters struggled with loads that ranged from 60 to 180 pounds.

Last night's host had cautioned us about *chortens, stupas,* and *mani* walls. All three were religious structures we would see on the trails. A *stupa,* we had been told, was a large hemisphere of earth that was topped with a brick square that faced the four cardinal directions. A spire rose above the brick square in thirteen levels—representing the thirteen levels of knowledge. We never did find a definition of a *chorten,* but we soon learned what they looked like. The *mani* walls were made of brick or shale; much of the shale was inscribed with religious symbols. These religious structures are important to the Nepali people; as a courtesy however, considerate visitors imitate the Nepalese custom and pass to the left of each. For good luck, a counterclockwise circle was recommended. We observed this custom even when a shorter and less steep route beckoned at the end of a hard day. And I, for one, made one counterclockwise rotation of one of these structures every day in Nepal.

Porters did not use a backpack. A large woven basket was secured to their body at their head by means of a tumpline. The basket was called a *doko*. Because of the terrific weight, they had to rest frequently. The loads were too heavy to set down or pick up without assistance. In order to rest, they wedged a T-shaped walking stick under the base of the basket to remove some of the load. Because the tumpline put tremendous strain on the head and neck, they used their hands to pull forward on the line as they walked. This made for some very muscular people—men and women. Near places to eat and sleep, rock walls had been constructed so that a shelf for the dokos would be at the right height for porters to leave their loads (see page 83). Some of those walls were built at particularly difficult portions of the trail. It was easy to pass groups of porters since they rested often. It was easy to feel physically inferior while you did so.

As I moved up the first pass, at 7,280 feet, I noted that porters did not talk much while at rest stops. They used a series of sounds, not as sharp sounding as a whistle, to signify a need to rest or a desire to start. Those sounds carried quite far and seemed to be a means of also alerting other porters above or below. The object seemed to be to travel in a group and have others to share the pace. I, too, would have wanted to be part of a group if I had been carrying loads such as those.

The map on page 91 illustrates the elevation gains and losses on the trek to Kala Pattar. I had not seen it before I started and had absolutely no idea what to expect. I had learned the name Namche Bazaar as part of the Nepalese inquiry as to where any given trail led. Namche Bazaar was the first major goal—possibly seven to nine days of trekking. On the first day, I crossed two passes and had started up a third when I finally reached Sete. I had just completed in one day what the guidebook stated was two or three days of trekking. It felt like it; the last hill had nearly done me in. I had trekked for eight hours of hill hiking—plus two long food stops. The sun was retreating behind the clouds when I found a lodge. I fell into bed as soon after dinner as I could.

Next page: Trails in the Himalayas travel over mountain ranges. During the trek to Kala Pattar, there are days when you have crossed two high passes but are lower than when you started. This graph shows our route. Page 93: Trying to carry part of a bridge isn't easy. This load weighed more than 200 pounds.

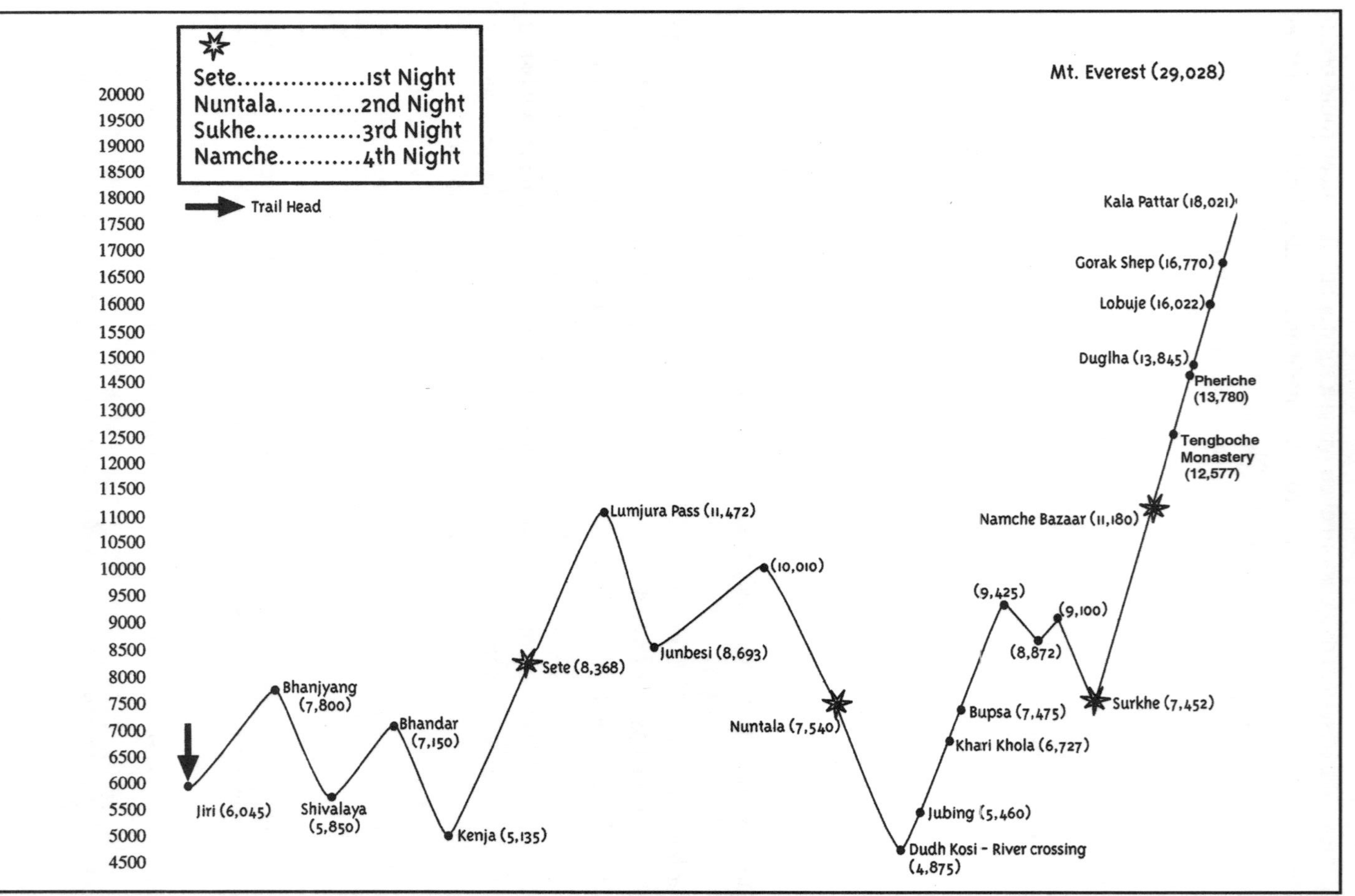

Sete.................1st Night
Nuntala...........2nd Night
Sukhe..............3rd Night
Namche...........4th Night
Trail Head
Mt. Everest (29,028)
Kala Pattar (18,021)
Gorak Shep (16,770)
Lobuje (16,022)
Duglha (13,845)
Pheriche (13,780)
Tengboche Monastery (12,577)
Namche Bazaar (11,180)
Lumjura Pass (11,472)
(10,010)
(9,425)
(9,100)
(8,872)
Junbesi (8,693)
Sete (8,368)
Bhanjyang (7,800)
Bupsa (7,475)
Nuntala (7,540)
Surkhe (7,452)
Bhandar (7,150)
Khari Khola (6,727)
Jiri (6,045)
Shivalaya (5,850)
Jubing (5,460)
Kenja (5,135)
Dudh Kosi – River crossing (4,875)
20000
19500
19000
18500
18000
17500
17000
16500
16000
15500
15000
14500
13000
12500
12000
11500
11000
10500
10000
9500
9000
8500
8000
7500
7000
6500
6000
5500
5000
4500

The next morning, as I was leaving, the hotel owner told me that most trekkers stopped in Junbesi on their third or fourth night. Therefore, if I intended to trek the same distance as I had the first day, I should try to get as far as Nuntala, another "guidebook" day past Junbesi. Not feeling sore or particularly tired, I thanked him for the information and started off. It was just before six o'clock. Based on yesterday, I decided to set up a schedule. I would start trekking early and eat breakfast after an hour or two—when the lodge and cooking fires were open for business. I would trek for three more hours and rest at lunchtime. Then, I would finish the day's work in time for dinner. There was so much to see and the pace was so slow that the time spent trekking didn't detract from the views. Breakfast and lunch offered me time to practice my Nepali and to gladly add more words to my vocabulary. At this rate of linguistic travel, I would be four years old by the time I reached the 18,000-foot level at Kala Pattar.

The second day began with the same problem the previous day had ended with: Lamjura Pass. It had almost killed me the night before, and in the morning it wasn't that much friendlier. It went steeply up. I passed lodge after lodge, beautiful view after beautiful view. There were changes in flora but no changes in angle. And, finally, I arrived at the top. Later, I would find out that this pass was higher in elevation than Namche Bazaar. That was not good news. The descent on the other side of this pass would plunge me to a lower level than Jiri. I was on the second day of what I hoped would be a four-day trek to Namche, but I would be sleeping lower tonight than when I started. I concluded that I was going to be climbing at least one other pass—in another form and by another name.

At the top of the pass there was a huge mass of loose rocks as well as prayer flags by the hundreds. I didn't understand the significance of much of the culture I passed through, but I sensed some celebration in what I saw there.

And, I was delighted to be going downhill. My heart sang. Within minutes, so did the forest. The sound of singing Nepalese porters came from above and below. Happier than I had been, they were ecstatic to be carrying their heavy burdens downhill instead of up, and they sang with great beauty and gusto. As I went by each group it was clear that passing over Lamjura was a common bond of great joy.

It remained so all the way to Junbesi and lunch. A beautiful town with a huge monastery, there was at least one roof that looked like solid gold from a distance. I had been told that there was a hotel in town that served terrific pizza and apple pie. Three sources had contributed to the rumor and all their directions had been the same. If it was a snipe hunt, then a lot of folks from different lands were in on it in a big way. I arrived prepared for the worst, but hungry enough for the best. I waited an hour for some of the tastiest food in a very long time. All the rumors were confirmed.

A number of other trekkers had come down the trail and were at the lodge for lunch. As with all major trekking routes, strangers typically asked where you were from (country), where you came from that morning, and where you were going that day. When two Australians struck up that conversation over our mutual pizzas, they seemed quite impressed with my progress. It seemed that I was doing about twenty-five miles per day and was on about the same pace as a South African who was a day ahead of me. He, too, hoped to make Namche in four days. I was amazed that anyone else would be pushing an eight-hour day, but was pleased that my goals were within the realm of possibility.

Nuntala was many hills away. It wasn't all uphill, but it was enough to wear me out for a second day. Fortunately, the last hour was downhill and the village itself was completely level. I stayed in the newest lodge and slept in complete oblivion in a never-before-used room. I made it through dinner and a language lesson before crawling upstairs. I fell into bed, reflecting on the biggest surprise of the day: As I had been lost in thought and trekking over a barren hilltop above a river; suddenly, a thousand crows rose up in front of me on a strong thermal from the canyon floor. It had been quiet, and then it had been very noisy as the birds wheeled and turned a hundred feet from me. My adrenaline had surged until I realized what was happening and could relax and enjoy the beauty of this strange scene. I fell asleep smiling at the memory.

My eyes were open at 5:45 and I was out the door by 6:00. It was downhill for a long way and then the trail crossed a metal bridge over the Dudh Kosi River. At the beginning of my third day, I was one thousand feet lower than the trailhead at Jiri. While not a kayaking enthusiast, I had heard in Thamel that this was one of the highest-grade kayaking rivers in the world. While crossing the bridge, it was nearly impossible to imagine one could survive an attempt to cross those roiling waters.

Descending to a river meant an ascent on the other side of the canyon. I started that almost immediately and crossed a huge area that had recently been swept by an avalanche of rock. Within an hour of starting my climb, I found the village of Jubing. A school there had been started through Sir Edmund Hillary's efforts. And there were flowers, flagstone courtyards, and gardens, and the air smelled like honey. A millstone capped a small stream that meandered between homes. No other village on my entire trip was so enchanting and I wanted to stay there on my way back to Jiri. It was beautiful.

There was another beautiful village farther up the trail. I topped another pass and I could see the village in the misty distance. It looked like Shangri La to me. Kari Khola might just be Nepalese for Shangri La (although they told me that *khola* meant "stream"). At that village I stopped and had breakfast at a very clean restaurant, complete with checkered tablecloths and hand painted signs in English. The food was tremendous and the people were quite at ease with Westerners and the English language. Had I known what the trail had in store, I might have wanted to stay much longer.

Just out of town, the trail seemed to be even steeper than it had been on Lamjura Pass. The Sherpas didn't seem to believe in switchbacks, and the labor never seemed to get easier. My thoughts about the picturesque village had been changed when I had looked at the thin outline of the trail leading up the next series of mountains. *"Bupsa"* was what the restaurant owner had said, smiling. Did that mean "up"?

After nearly three hours of nearly nonstop ascent, a series of almost level sections kept my hopes up that I was nearing the top. I wanted to reach Surkhe that evening, wherever it was.

Bupsa was the name of a village on the hill. The actual words for uphill and downhill were *ukaalo* and *oraalo*, respectively. You could be sure that I was one three-year-old who knew those well and asked them often.

On one of the more level sections a rather large group of laughing people sat at a table in front of a small lodge. Thinking that I could bask in some of whatever was causing the merriment, I sat down and ordered a snack. All but two of the people immediately stood up and started off down the trail. The direction of their hike explained their mood; I was too tired to wonder if I had anything to do with the abruptness of their departure. The two remaining men greeted me and I returned that courtesy. I should have remembered the dictum about the advisability of not talking to strangers.

They asked where I had come from and the younger of the two seemed oddly impressed with my forced march. In answer to more questions, he learned that this was my third day of trekking, which the guidebooks recommended as the sixth or seventh day. He introduced himself as David Blakeney and the gentleman with him as Malcolm, his father. They were from Norwich,

Opposite page: On top of Kala Pattar (18,100 ft.). In the background is Pumori.
Everest and Nuptse are to the right and across the moraine-filled valley.
It had taken ten days of trekking to reach this point.

in England. David explained to me that he was here as one of the group leaders for the Everest Marathon. Having learned that I had done twelve marathons and a few triathlons, he was eager for me to be a late entry in next month's race in Nepal.

Having only seen a few banners stretched across the main streets in Kathmandu, I had assumed that the race was there and given the Everest name to tie the event in with Nepal's most famous feature. David assured me that there was indeed a marathon up here, and that I was still a day and a half from the finish line and nearly a week from the starting line. A smarter man than I would have excused himself from the table and gone on to Surkhe with only a shake of his head to indicate his disbelief. There are a lot of men smarter than I am.

Both of the Blakeneys took a few minutes to tell me about the conversation they had just shared with the group that had just departed downhill. The descending group had met a South African yesterday. When they had stopped for lunch, they had met a very fit man and his wife. The couple expected to make Namche in just a few more hours. That was their fourth day of trekking from Jiri. The group had not believed it—they had taken nine exhausting days to get to Namche two weeks ago. Still, they had related it to the Blakeneys as a response to David's comments about the Everest Marathon and the fitness of the participants. Now David and Malcolm shared this story with me. I confirmed that this was the second time that a returning trekker had made mention of someone pushing the limit. Right now, this couple was in Namche Bazaar and undoubtedly resting and acclimatizing.

Malcolm left as he finished his meal. The Blakeneys, too, were headed for the same lodge in Surkhe. David and I chatted for a few minutes more, and then I was alone with my food and some thoughts. I had toyed with the idea of doing the London Marathon at the end of my trip. England was to be my final country of the tour and a marathon would certainly test my fitness level. I expected to train once I left Africa or the Middle East and would possibly be fit enough to finish. Now, I was suddenly faced with the idea of a marathon without having done any serious running beforehand. And this marathon was billed as the world's toughest. Well, if it was not the toughest, it was certainly the highest. The starting line was over 17,000 feet high. I did stay in Surkhe and the Blakeneys proved to be excellent conversationalists and interesting people. Perhaps this marathon thing was just a quirk. Sure that I would see them again, I left early the next morning for the last push to the Sherpa capital of Namche Bazaar.

Within ten minutes of the start of that day's trek, the trail divided. I took the most worn pathway since there was no one on the trail to ask. It seemed a safe decision. And it was. While it added some miles to my trek that day, it also took me to Lukla, where the airport was. The trail was again steeply uphill. I came out of a narrow canyon and onto the steep pastureland below Lukla only to find that several of the rock walls were not all rock. Two plane fuselages had been placed as part of the fencing for various livestock. As an advertisement for flying, it certainly had my attention. As I wandered into Lukla, I discovered that air travel for the wealthy had eliminated the need to do any of what I had just done. It reduced the trek by one twelve-hour bus ride and eighty miles of mountainous terrain; you could fly here directly from Kathmandu.

And, I discovered the polar fleece crowd. I wasn't aware that I harbored ill will toward other trekkers. But it was there. Strolling through the streets of this rapidly growing town were dozens of clean people with clean clothes. That was because they had just come from Kathmandu. I watched a particularly handsome couple walk toward me. He passed first and I could definitely detect some cologne on a freshly shaved face. She was wearing large earrings and makeup that included lipstick. As she walked by she mouthed the words "help me." And she smiled. She smelled terrific. I interpreted her gesture as a joke on where she found herself and the absence of the normal trappings of civilization. I smiled back. I had a pretty good idea of what awaited her above.

Before leaving town, I walked to the runway. That was it? I could see how you could land a plane on it; it was steeply uphill. And I could see how one could take off on it—in a helicopter. This was an exceedingly short piece of real estate and explained the fences I had seen earlier. The talk at a teahouse where I stopped for some bottled water concerned the weather. Flights in were postponed if the mountain weather was cloudy. With no flights coming in, there were no flights going out. Those with flights out of Nepal and tickets for the same became almost violent as they failed to get on the few flights that eventually came in and flew out. There was talk about bribes, threats, and upgrades to helicopters ($200 instead of $80). Because it could take as long as eight or nine days to hike and bus out, few people could afford that option.

I left Lukla with a big smile. Polar fleece! Having not looked at a guidebook or my trekking information sheet from Kathmandu, I was surprised to find myself at a lockable gate after a couple of hours of hill walking. And I was further surprised that the armed guard inside the office needed a Sagarmatha National Park entrance fee. I had the money, but this expense had not been fig-

The Everest Marathon trail. Some of the buildings of Namche Bazaar are visible in the upper right hand of the picture. This is also the major route for climbers going to Everest Base Camp in Nepal.

ured into the budget, and I was a bit concerned that it might cause a future fiscal emergency. I vowed to start taking better care of planning now that Bill wasn't there to cross every "T."

I reminded myself that this was a pilgrimage, and that the outflow of money might have mattered in another place. There were many pilgrimages for many people; this was mine. I wasn't sure if *karma* was the right term, but it was the right concept, and I didn't want to create anything negative. It was only money.

Chomolungma is the Chinese (Tibetan) name for Everest and *Sagarmatha* is the Nepalese equivalent. I had known those for years, and here I was. I arrived in Namche Bazaar at the end of a short day—less than five hours. I spent the last steep stretch in the company of a young British couple, Penny and Nick Wood. They had that "comfort in any circumstances" attitude, and I soon discovered that they were in the last stages of their own two-year world tour. We trekked the last few miles together and met again that evening at the Khumbu Lodge.

"Jimmy Carter Slept Here," the sign in the hallway said. Robert Redford had been here, too. But what was the most impressive to the initiated was the list of world-class climbers who had been here on their way to there. A great many of the successful expeditions to Everest had come this way. And Everest wasn't the only challenging peak in the area. Eight of the world's fourteen highest peaks are in Nepal's Himalayas. The walls were decorated with laminated copies of newspaper or magazine articles relating to Namche or this lodge and the land above us. Penny and Nick and I shared a dinner and listened to the talk of those coming down from the peaks and those going up. It was fascinating.

What wasn't fascinating was the lone smoker in the room who soon established considerable domination by virtue of having the loudest voice. He was dropping the names of people any climber would recognize and was doing so as though they were lifetime personal friends. Emboldened by the developing silence in the room, he launched into a series of stories extremely unflattering to climbers from other countries. The Russians were crazy and were risking everything with poor equipment and even less technique. A team of Bulgarian climbers had successfully climbed two major peaks by first-time routes, but he wasn't going to count those accomplishments until a team of humans made the same ascents. And there was far too much more in the same vein. Eventually, the room thinned.

A group of Australians asked a few last questions and sat through the answers. As they left, one asked him his name. I hung on the answer. His name was Joe Simpson. I had grown up as a friend of the Lowe family in Ogden, Utah, and knew Jeff Lowe well enough to make a mental note ask him about the chain-smoking Mr. Simpson. Jeff was a world-class climber and had recently done a solo winter ascent of the Eiger in Europe—by a previously unclimbed route. There were too many braggarts and wannabes in all physical activities and that was who I suspected Mr. Simpson was. I knew that Jeff had climbed both Ama Dablam and Pumori in this area and that he would know any climbers of note. We left Mr. Simpson sitting in the nearly empty dining room and writing in his journal. Hopefully, we would not be so blessed during the next day of acclimatization in Namche. As we walked out, I heard Nick mutter something under his breath.

"What did you say?" I asked.

He cast a glance back over his shoulder and repeated, "Nasty, British, and short." He was smiling to see if I had understood it.

"It was Thomas Hobbes," I smiled back, "wasn't it? And it was about life in nature being nasty, brutish, and short." We were both laughing now.

He looked back into the dining room one last time. "I rest my case," he said.

The next morning my luck ran out. Mr. Simpson was again in the dining room. Absolutely no one was talking to him, and I stayed only because it looked like that would continue. Two women from the night before finally asked him if he knew that he had been the only one smoking last evening. Instead of understanding the rebuke in the tone and content of her question, he told her that it relaxed him and he rarely smoked on major climbs. I remembered thinking that I wouldn't want my life to depend on someone whose fitness at high altitude might be in question. And then I found out who Joe Simpson was.

He left the upstairs dining room and was arranging his crutches, daypack, and a stereo headset on the wall outside the lodge. We could see him through the window. Someone near my table mentioned that he was the author of the best-selling book *Touching The Void*. It was the story of his near death and heroic struggle after a serious climbing accident. I was determined to find the book when I returned to Kathmandu to learn more. As I watched him work his way toward the downhill to Lukla airport, I wondered aloud that he was still this injured so long after the accident described in his book. A few inquiries

Nick and Penny Wood from Bedford, England. They did their own two-year tour, and dubbed themselves the "happy hamsters."

revealed that he had recently suffered a second near-fatal injury while climbing in the Himalayas, and it was this accident that confined him to crutches.

It took me a long afternoon a few months later to start and finish Simpson's book. Prepared to dislike it and all he had to say, I found myself enthralled by the style and pace of his writing. Had I not seen him in person, I would have wanted to meet the author of such a book. Even the preface to his book, written by famous British climber Chris Bonington, damned him with faint praise while lauding the telling of the tale. "Sitting beside him in a bar in Chamonix, it was difficult putting the stories and reputation to the person. He was dark, with a slightly punk hairstyle, and there was something abrasive in his manner. I found it difficult to take him in my mind from the streets of Sheffield into the mountains."

Meanwhile, Penny and Nick were proving to be delightful company. We were all learning Nepali together and comparing our accents in Hindi. They were also endeavoring to teach me English, proper English. It was a tough slog. Perhaps it would have been better if they had not been so playful with their new American friend. Nick took me through the game of cricket, which I had seen played all through England during previous travels and in every country on this one. Cricket had almost no terminology in common with any sport I knew. After getting the definition of a "sticky wicket" and "bowling a maiden over," I asked for and received a temporary reprieve. It was harder to learn than Nepali. Any country that called a bicycle a "penny farthing" was going to require some study.

Guidebooks and trekkers suggested a day in Namche to acclimatize and then a short hike to the monastery at Tengboche. Above the 12,000-foot level on this trek, all of the advice about altitude tended to relate to acute mountain sickness (AMS), which could be fatal. In the advanced stages it can kill in twelve hours or less, even though it is completely curable. At high altitude the body processes fluids differently, or barely processes them at all. When excess fluids accumulate, they can be found in the lungs (pulmonary edema) or in the head (cerebral edema). HACE and HAPE (for High Altitude Cerebral Edema and High Altitude Pulmonary Edema) kill a number of high-altitude trekkers every year. Expedition climbers experience it too, and a delightful book called *Clouds from Both Sides Now* by Julie Tullis is a posthumous work about these conditions. Her body is still near the summit of K2.

The day off for acclimatization was extremely informative. Namche was literally a bazaar. On Saturdays people from all over the region come to trade. It was not done for Western visitors; sales to them went on all of the time. On

Saturday, Nepali people come from all over the Khumbu Valley. Tibetans who had fled from the Chinese takeover in their country were there, too. There were over thirty languages in Nepal and a lot of them were spoken at the bazaar.

The Hindus we met in Kathmandu worshipped many gods and goddesses, but all were aspects of the one true God: Brahman, the "Self." Brahman is represented as "Om," the sound with no form. The Buddhists here appeared to have adopted many Hindu customs and beliefs, and the Hindus in Kathmandu seemed to have had some definite Buddhist influence. On our Saturday in Namche, we saw animals butchered for food. In a very smart move, the animals were herded to Namche and butchered only when actually sold. The buyers carried away the amount of merchandise they wanted.

There was a dental clinic in Namche Bazaar. The money from climbers and trekkers had helped the people of this area to improve their economy. Sir Edmund Hillary and others had helped establish schools, and the traveling Gurkha soldiers brought wealth and information back home. But the candy and sweets brought into the country had damaged the teeth of the adults and children. Bathing, brushing their teeth, washing their hands—those are all foreign customs. The candy given to the cute children in various villages along the trekking route had caused great pain and suffering. Decay created exposed nerves, infections, and pain. The dental clinic offered education and help for the local people.

I made it to Tengboche in a brisk three hours and had the rest of the day to visit with others and practice my Nepali. *Ma ali ali Nepali bolchuu* means, "I don't speak much Nepali." I should have started with that phrase. I discovered that Tengboche was the spiritual center for Tibetan Buddhists. I arrived just after breakfast and noticed that most of the trekkers at the teahouses were just getting out of bed. They stared openly at me. I learned that it was not of much value to strike off for the next destination at an early hour. Days were measured not in distance covered, but in altitude gained. The next day, I left late and sauntered to Dingboche—another three hours.

The small mountain towns of Dingboche and Pheriche were separated by a hill, Dingboche was in the Chukkung Valley and Pheriche was the site of a medical facility. This year it was manned by three American doctors who had volunteered their time. I hiked over the hill to hear their lecture on AMS, which was given regularly and was advertised everywhere. They had a Gammow bag, which allowed the pressure on a person placed inside it to be increased, simulating a descent—the best cure for the symptoms of AMS.

Right: During festivals the families break out their finest. This is a Nepali woman with her jewelry.
Below: A typical Nepali home with a mountain view.

They also discussed the drug Diamox, which helps the blood absorb more oxygen, but does not mask the symptoms of the disease. I learned that swelling of the face and fingers, headache, nausea, loss of appetite, and sleeplessness are some of the symptoms. In the more serious stages, these symptoms are much worse. Also, a victim might become ataxic, which is a loss of fine motor skills. At that point, the victim must descend to the last altitude where there were no symptoms, or lower. Failure to do so can result in death. It was a sobering lecture; so far there had been no deaths in the Khumbu this season. The doctors asked us to pass along some information to other trekkers. For instance, many people do not sleep well at high altitudes and take sleeping tablets to solve the problem. But those pills can be dangerous because they mask breathing problems and the symptoms of AMS.

I spent a day of acclimatization in Dingboche at the foot of Ama Dablam (22,282 feet). I went trekking with just a daypack and explored the glacial moraines, wandered near the ice fields and watched a group of climbers on an ascent of Island Peak. And I sat in the lea of a large rock and napped in the considerable warmth of the late October sun. Around me were views that most people only dream about. There had been nothing like it in my experience and I spent the afternoon feeling very close to Nirvana and all eight-fold paths. The Lhotse Shar, a huge, bright wall of ice to the right of Mt. Lhotse, constantly drew my focus. Even in the clear and bright light of day, it gave new meaning to the word ethereal. Had I awakened from a nap and found it gone, I would not have been surprised. It looked like something only possible in a dream.

The next morning was another steep but short hike to Lobuje, at 16,000 feet. There were only four places for shelter and food for those who did not have a tent. All sleeping areas were communal and the high altitude was playing havoc with any semblance of normal sleep patterns. Snoring was the least of the problems. A beauty of a malady called sleep apnea was common. Characterized by a failure to breathe and a sudden gasping when breathing did start, it was a great cure for sleep. Breathing could be interrupted for over thirty seconds. When others had it, they made enough noise to wake me. When I had it at those altitudes, it woke me. My dreams, short as they were, featured a lot of nonsensical scenarios and very vivid colors. I was glad I wasn't going to spend too much time up here.

At Lobuje the younger brother of our innkeeper's cook adopted me during a lounge in the sun. He was four and insisted that I listen to him count to ten in English. I was quite embarrassed that I couldn't count beyond three in Nepali.

We switched to vocabulary, and he was not very pleased with how few words I knew or how slowly I learned the ones he taught me. Clearly, there was a difference in what I thought I had achieved and what a real four-year-old knew. He signed my journal in English and Nepali and admonished me to study harder. I went for a walkabout.

There was one additional camp before either Kala Pattar or Everest Base Camp. Gorak Shep was at 17,500 feet and had even more primitive facilities than Lobuje. A few sheltering huts sat on the perimeter of a large flat area—about the size of three or four football fields. It was here that the trail divided. One trail continued on to Everest Base Camp through a labyrinth created by glacial moraines. The other led upward in three steep sections of trail and reached the top of Kala Pattar at 18,100 feet. Kala Pattar was Hindi for "black rock," and it was to this point that many trekkers aspired.

I planned to leave early from Lobuje, climb to the top of Kala Pattar, then descend all the way to Dingboche for the night in keeping with the adage: "Climb high and sleep low," the best way to avoid AMS. The lodge owner would watch my gear and I would pick it up on the way back. For the morning I needed only a light daypack with some extra clothing and a bit of food. David Blakeney had told me that a forty-seven-minute climb from Gorak Shep to Kala Pattar was the unofficial record among the 1989 marathoners. I wanted to keep that in mind in case I felt good without a real pack on my back. Just before sunrise, I started off up the trail.

At Gorak Shep, the least impressive mountain on the horizon was Mount Everest. When I faced Everest directly, the huge mass of Mt. Nuptse hung over the valley to the right. Just to my left and slightly behind was the even more massive Pumori. Everest won on height, the other mountains on pure spectacle. Gorak Shep was easy; the trek up to Kala Pattar provided insight. Every story I had ever read about 8,000-meter peaks and the expeditions that had challenged them had described the agonizingly slow progress toward the higher camps and the summits. I had hardly expected that the relatively low altitude here would be similar. After ten minutes of steady uphill walking, I revised my goal downward: I would be content if I could make the top without resting.

Even at my slow pace, I passed two groups that had left from Gorak Shep that morning. Over twenty-five miles a day of trekking below Namche was paying some conditioning dividends. And so was the absence of the pack I would retrieve from Lobuje on the descent. Still, I was one knackered American when I finally collapsed on the topmost rock at 18,100 feet. I had not stopped to rest, but some of those last switchbacks had been very slow and deliberate. On two sides of the summit, there were huge vertical drop-offs leading to picturesque tarns. Above me loomed Pumori. Below and to the left of the Khumbu icefall was the base camp. I could see three or four sets of different colored tents. Later, it would be confirmed that there were seven expeditions with permission to climb at that time. For the moment, I had my particular set of rocks to myself. And it was warm, perhaps fifty degrees. I spread the contents of the fanny pack on the topmost rock and thought of where I was now and where my friends might be back home. Was there anyone I had ever considered a friend who wouldn't be moved by the magic around me?

Penny and Nick arrived within an hour and we chatted and took pictures. I left as the wind came up and the temperature immediately dropped to below zero. I made a single attempt to do a handstand at 18,100 feet above sea level. Insufficient oxygen limited the number of attempts at anything. Fat game birds scattered at my noisy descent and advancing trekkers envied my direction. I reached Dingboche in just over three hours.

At the lodge where I stayed that night, I saw many of the people I had met along the trail from Jiri—and one that I hadn't. The South African was there. His name was Martin Cohen, and he was the epitome of absolute fitness. A veteran of over two hundred marathons, he had been all over the Chukkung Valley and had done many twenty-mile days of simply exploring. He confirmed that his wife had, in fact, made the trek to Namche with him in four days, but she had a sore knee and had remained there. When he was introduced to me and heard my accent, he immediately said, "You must be the American!" It seemed that as he had crossed the various trails above Namche, he had met many of the people I had met on the way in. The story of someone equaling his feat made him very glad that I had picked this particular lodge on this particular day. We spent a number of hours discussing our relative countries, our favorite challenges, and how much he loved running. Another instant friendship formed in one of the more remote areas of the earth.

He nearly joined me in a one-day effort to hike from Dingboche to Gokyo Ri. We had been told that it was possible to connect Duglha and Gokyo by means of Cho La (a high mountain pass with no food or shelter along its track). But we were also told that parts of that trail could be covered with ice and could require ropes, crampons, and an ice ax. Additionally, we heard that it was only an eight-hour hike. We were sure that it could be done in about half that time. What worried us was the questionable reliability of those who "seemed to know."

Neither of us relished the idea of hiking four or five hours, being turned back by an impassible trail and having to return to Dugla in another four or five hours. The other choice to get from Dingboche to Gokyo was to hike back toward Namche, take another trail that went around this section of the mountains, then climb up to Gokyo on a trail that paralleled the one I had taken to Kala Pattar—thirty miles of steep mountainous terrain. In the morning, Martin had decided not to attempt either route.

This paricular excursion was not for him, and it was probably just as well. I ruled out a solo attempt at the pass for obvious reasons. Martin was able to share something from the *Trekking in the Nepal Himalaya* guidebook. The planned one-day trek to Gokyo and one-day trek to Namche were both listed as five-day trips. He smiled as he said he just wanted me to be prepared in case I had deadlines to meet. His smile indicated he knew this information created extra pressure to complete each in a day. We shook hands as I strapped into my pack and we set off on different adventures.

It had been inspiring to meet someone whose fitness allowed him to see areas that most people hadn't the time or conditioning to see. I did make the one-day hike to Gokyo from Dingboche, but was relieved that I hadn't been pushed by Martin and his super fitness. It took nine hours and I saw no other Westerner until the trail I was on joined the main trail coming up from Namche. After Gokyo, I returned to Namche (another long push in one day), rested a day, and trekked to Jiri in three and a half days. I had never been more fit or happier in my life. I dreaded the return bus ride to Kathmandu more than any discomfort I had experienced on this trip of a lifetime.

Nepal had been one terrific adventure and I didn't want to leave. As it turned out, I didn't have to. Events were conspiring to keep me around and to send me back to Kala Pattar. My plans said India next; Dave Blakeney and a hundred other madmen and madwomen had other ideas.

Dieter Loraine before (l) and after the trek to Gorak Shep and the Everest Marathon.

Our group of fifteen stared silently at this magical scene. Then, the only word spoken was: "Camera!"

CHAPTER 9
THE EVEREST MARATHON

I am not a jogger!
– Dieter Loraine, Royal Marine

On my last full day in Kathmandu, I spent the morning at the bank and converted all my Nepali *rupiya* into Indian *rupees.* I packed my clothes, mailed packages and letters, and paid my lodging bill through the next morning. I had just enough loose change to pay for the day's meals. Tomorrow I would be on a bus back to Gorakpuhr in India. I wandered through the narrow streets of the vast marketplace and thought about how good the last month had been. I had trekked to Kala Pattar at over 18,000 feet, hiked through the beautiful Himalayan peaks, seen Base Camp and the Chukkung Valley—and had met some very fun and fit people. I wondered if any other adventure could possibly match this one.

Thirty seconds after having that thought I was almost run over by a mountain bike. The intent was friendly, but the brakes were poorly adjusted. It was David Blakeney, the British madman who had crossed and recrossed my path on the trek. He was overjoyed that his American friend was still in town. It meant that he still had a chance to talk me into being a late entry for the Everest Marathon. I told him that the chance was slim; I had not run seriously on my entire trip. One of the world's hardest marathons required training. David admitted that many of the entrants had been training for two years. I knew I was talking to one of the men who had marked the original 26.2-mile course with a calibrated wheel and who had run in both of the subsequent races. Neither of us convinced the other, but I agreed to meet him at Hem's Restaurant for dinner and a final decision. I had already made up my mind not to enter. I would return in two years and do it the right way.

Hem's wasn't crowded and I spotted David right away. He was in the company of a very attractive woman. Jennie Oliver, from New Zealand, had only been in Nepal a few hours; she was one of the doctors in the race support group. It appeared that she didn't know that marathon running was serious stuff, requiring a great deal of preparation and consideration. Less than twenty minutes of her smile and David's good-natured attack on American softness turned me around. A glimmer of thought said, yes, perhaps I could do it. The race organizer would arrive tomorrow, and the big question was whether a late entry would be accepted.

Diana Penny Sherpani listened a lot more to Dr. Oliver and David Blakeney than she did to me. The race organizer and director, she was leery until she talked with me. Then she said, "No." I was relieved, but my friends were persistent. Finally, she relented. There had been a couple of last-minute cancellations, and she allowed me to pay a late-entry fee. There were a few limitations. I could not be an official member of the party until the marathoners reached the Sherpa capital of Namche Bazaar. The plan was for official entrants to reach that point in eight days. Porters were already scheduled to transport the gear for existing entries. Not until Namche could my kit be worked into the mix. I would also have to carry some additional items for the small daypack that every racer was required to wear, making my pack about seven pounds heavier than it had been the last time I had trekked to Kala Pattar. But I was in. David and Jennie were ecstatic: I was "American."

We attended a meeting at the Blue Star Hotel in Kathmandu. All the marathoners except late entrants were billeted there. Shirts were given out—as well as parkas, daypacks, items required for race day, and advice. I listened carefully to the latter. The discussion ranged from AMS (we could die), to falling off the trail (we could die), to eating the wrong food or drinking contaminated water (we would want to die). Some of the natural playfulness of very fit people attenuated as Diana went through her list. That night three people came down with stomach problems. Even care and lectures weren't guarantees.

As a seasoned traveler, I knew what a lot of them didn't. Boiled water, for example, did no good if the water used for the ice cubes was not boiled. It was the same for water used to wash vegetables. And, it was the same for water used to brush teeth. Even water inadvertently swallowed during a shower was enough. And water was just one culprit. I knew there would be more sickness of this type and hoped it wouldn't include me.

During the discussion of race conditions, most of the first-timers missed the significance of the required daypack. Diana went over it. A runner would be disqualified if he or she crossed the finish line without the pack and the requisite items. We needed a waterproof top and bottom. That was in the event of a storm on race day or in case a runner had to be left on the trail overnight and a storm came up. A dry set of racing clothes also had to be carried. The need to be warm and dry if no longer moving did not need much of an explanation. The crowd was increasingly quiet. The whistle was in the event that a runner fell off the trail. Parts of the trail dropped hundreds of feet to the river below; no whistle needed. In the event that a fall was on a less dramatic slope, but out of the sight of others, the whistle would alert passersby. The pencil and notebook were for the benefit of those who attended an injured runner. It was cathedral quiet as Diana explained that someone might find an injured runner and have to go for help. In the event that the person in need of help lost consciousness, a note could be left to describe injuries, symptoms, and any treatment administered. "Any questions?"

I had just been there. She was not stretching the truth about the trail or the possibilities.

Because of my friendship with David Blakeney, I was allowed to read his copy of the first booklet published about the 1987 race. It was a good thing that Diana already had my entry fee money. The most severe critic of the idea of a marathon at that elevation was Dr. David Shlim, medical director for the Himalayan Rescue Association. In 1984, a race called the World's Highest Hash had resulted in one death and one patient in a coma. Both had fallen victim to HAPE (high altitude pulmonary edema). There had also been the death of an experienced mountaineer who had fallen off the trail at Pheriche. Dr. Shlim had been very concerned with the difficulty of effecting the rescue of casualties. In just one three-month trekking season, there had been over forty helicopter evacuations. A rash of such medical emergencies would overtax the small medical facility at Pheriche and those in Kathmandu as well.

Even the chief doctor for the first race was quoted as saying: "This event is an extension of man's desire to go to physical extremes. I would not want anyone to think I am overstating the case, but people die at altitude, whether they are running a marathon or not. It is a very risky business." I quit reading and returned the booklet to David.

There were seventy runners, ten doctors, and over one hundred porters. This was very different from my solo trek to the same area. At least it would be when I officially joined the party. During the eight days that everyone would take to reach Namche, I would have to carry my own gear, obtain my own lodging and food, and make my own way. In a way this was good. I could use that time to get as fit as possible. I wanted to equal my previous three and a half day pace

The moraines of Chukkung Valley. Everest is partically hidden by clouds near the center of the picture. The marathon's course runs through the area to the left of the picture.

to Namche with the slightly heavier pack. If the usual pain at the end of a marathon was going to be worse at altitude, I needed to take fitness to a new level. I had done twelve marathons and three triathlons, but I had trained hard for each of those. Some of the people seated next to me had trained very hard for this race for two years or more.

The size of the group was a logistical nightmare, which was partially solved by dividing it into two groups. Called "early birds" and "late birds," the groups would travel a day apart until Namche. I was a late bird in name only, for now.

I reached Jiri after being pleasantly surprised to find myself on top of a minibus instead of a public bus. It had been a month since I had last done this; now it was considerably colder in the daytime. This ride had actually started with all of us inside the bus. My seatmate was a very fit older runner named George Barris. As we had left Kathmandu, George had told me that he did a lot of "fell" running in the UK. He had also participated in the last Everest Marathon and had finished in nineteenth place. That was at age fifty-seven, and he was back to get serious about the race. I needed to find a new place to sit.

David Blakeney and I took to the roof as soon as we were beyond the legal limits of town. A few others sensed that we might be onto something and joined us. I hoped it wasn't a character flaw, but somehow I seemed to again be in the company of some very fit "irreverents." Dieter Loraine was a sergeant in the Royal Marines at Lympstone where he trained fitness instructors. He had competed in over 130 endurance events, including triathlons. Dr. Stephen Green was a dentist with a practice in Exmouth, England. A thriathlete, he also enjoyed cricket, squash, tennis, and golf. He had also been a Royal Marine. Roger Owen worked in the upper ranks of Gulf Oil and was a "42 Commando Royal Marine" in Plymouth. His company was partially sponsoring the Everest Marathon. Paddy Bettesworth was a chartered surveyor turned real estate magnate. None of his twenty marathons had taken over three hours and he had won several of them. He hadn't been a Royal Marine, but with running credentials like his, it didn't matter.

David smiled a lot. The lads couldn't tell if he was smiling because he knew a lot that they didn't, and I couldn't tell if he was smiling because we both knew what was coming. At any rate, Birds Eye doesn't do a better job of freezing than the last hour on top of the bus to Jiri with plenty of room inside. I still wasn't sitting in the right place.

During that ten-hour ride to Jiri, we all seemed to get along well. I was softer spoken than Americans they were used to and wasn't inclined to tell them what was wrong with the European world. Some of my soft-spoken demeanor was a result of hearing about the athletic feats of my new acquaintances. If they were at all typical of the whole group, I might have to deal with being last in a marathon, and by a considerable margin.

Porters were waiting in Jiri when we arrived. There was a camp for the late birds at the top of the first pass, about an hour's hike. Last night, the early birds had done what we were now doing. A day ahead, they were already into the Himalayas. It was very near sunset and the porters efficiently took the packs into their carrying baskets and started up the trail. I started off with my kit while the rest of the group carried only their light daypacks. On my first trek from this small town, I had been one of the most fit people on the trail. Now, I was one of the least fit. With my pack, I worked very hard just to fall slowly behind the men and women of the Everest Marathon. I hadn't considered the consequences of falling behind the group until a smiling Nepali porter at trailside sent everyone else onto a side trail toward the first night's camp.

Soon, I noticed how dark it was. I moved on as quickly as I could; I would need to find one of the trailside teahouses rather quickly. I could remember a very eroded and steep section of trail near here, but I couldn't remember whether the first lodge was above or below it. Then I heard footsteps behind me. As I kept moving, the footsteps kept following. I heard a man's voice say, *"Namaste."*

I turned around and found a porter with an empty basket. We exchanged pleasantries as night erased the last remnants of light. In English, he told me that the trail was unsafe ahead and that the nearest lodge was well beyond the base of the bad trail. My worst fears were realized. He then invited me to spend the night with him and his family. Sure enough, there was his home, not a hundred yards away. I accepted the kindness and followed him inside. His wife and two children were preparing dinner. Like most houses along the trail to Everest Base Camp, there were two levels. The kitchen, bedroom, and animal shelter were on the first floor. I was worried about the wisdom of accepting the offer. There were no dividing walls on that floor and the cow, pigs, and chickens looked to be a bad combination. I should have known better. My host ushered me to the top story where there was only a nicely finished wood floor and one large wooden bench. It was perfect.

I declined the invitation to join them for dinner. I knew that the amount of food they had prepared was just enough for the family. I would have a large breakfast the next day to make up for the missed meal. I slept very well and was awake at 5:30 the next morning. Leaving some money for my hosts, I tried to sneak past them so that I wouldn't disturb their sleep. That didn't work and it was just as well. We parted with my promise that I would return to Nepal and would stop to visit when I did.

Then I was out the door and on my way to as far as I could get. The early birds would be in Sete tonight and I hoped to catch them there. With my heavier pack, that would be challenging, but I knew the trail and that would help me conserve my strength for the effort. The morning was crystal clear with no clouds and beautiful rice fields all around. I was mentally prepared for a hard effort.

As I descended to the canyon below the pass, I was extremely happy to be trekking here again. This feeling amazed me because the last trip had left me on the verge of physical exhaustion. Now, it was as though the steep mountain ranges to be climbed were of only marginal importance. Those were the kinds of thoughts you had when the trail was descending. About two miles from the river, I had company. A Nepali student about sixteen years old with a small day-pack of books was moving to intersect the trail. Once there, he quickly moved ahead of me and cast a quick smile and a *namaste* back over his shoulder. I elected to try to stay with him and we were off.

As we crossed several small streams, he moved smoothly from rock to rock or rock to log. I didn't. He seemed to always emerge from these barriers with about a hundred-yard lead. I tried to make up that distance and would get to within thirty feet of him. We were on a slightly downhill grade and that made the weight of my pack less important to the speed we were going. Once at the river, there was still about three quarters of a mile of trail to the suspension bridge and a small village on the other side. At the river, the trail was level. Panting in earnest, I tried to keep up.

I really hoped that this village was where he attended school. It was. I wanted him to take his still smiling countenance into the building and collapse while telling a tale about the tough foreigner with the heavy pack. I knew that the reality wouldn't match my wish. For my part, I knew that I was going to be recovering from those miles for the rest of the day. It had been great fun, but it would cost me.

I reached Bhandar just after breakfast. This was where the early birds had been this morning and where the late birds would be tonight. I ate a snack and moved on. In another hour I reached a passport checkpoint. I went further and had a late lunch at the picturesque village of Kenja. Above me was Lamjura Pass. Somewhere on this mountain's flank would be Sete and the campsite for the early birds. For the last half hour, I had passed some of them as they slowly made their way. I envied them their light daypacks, their relatively short day, and their fitness. My heavy pack and long day were contributing to an increase in my fitness, but in several respects, I had a long way to go. Each day I would average a walking marathon with a full pack and a trail that constantly climbed or descended over huge passes. That, I reasoned, would give me a good base to build on once I reached the 13,000-foot level at Namche.

There were more marathoners on the ascent above Kenja, smiling folks who as yet did not know that I was part of the marathon. Some appeared very tired, and I realized just how much that first trip had helped me. There was a physical component to that fitness, but there was an even more important mental part that helped create the concept of success. Looking up the steep trail of Lamjura, devoid of switchbacks, was a character builder.

And then I was toast, as they say. I hit the wall, bonked...whatever. My pack suddenly weighed 150 pounds and my legs seemed to weigh twice that. The trail was vertical. My mind was no longer able to count to 150 steps before a rest. Had it not been for three women from the UK who walked by, I would have started life anew on the picturesque side of that hill. As I trudged up the rocky trail, all I could see was the boots of the person ahead of me. The women were talking of races they had done in Europe, and I used their conversation to help me forget that I was rapidly losing the will to move forward.

Finally, we were there. I cleaned up, ordered dinner, and crawled into my sleeping bag. The lodge owner cheerfully brought my dinner to where I was lying. I reasoned that I had better eat a lot before I fell asleep so that I wouldn't starve to death before I woke up. I had trekked for over eight hours and had taken another two hours to eat meals. It had been a long first day.

At six o'clock the next morning I was again moving up the trail toward Lamjura. This time I knew more about the pass. The summit was higher than Namche and the trail plunged to below Jiri's altitude on the other side. Knowing didn't make it less difficult, but I was going to try to get to Nuntala today and that would put me right on schedule. I felt great.

Each day's trek to Namche was approximately twenty-six miles long. Working my way toward Nuntala was no exception. Evidently, my memory wasn't nearly as sharp as I thought, since portions of the trail failed to register. Hills that I thought were not far away were two valleys from where I expected them. Long sections of trail evoked no memory whatsoever. I remembered the steep hills. Discomfort seemed burned into the neocortex. I reached the Nuntala city limits after almost exactly eight hours of trekking. Tomorrow would be the hardest day. I remembered that just outside Kari Khola the steep climb would take three hours or more. And there was a bit of a climb from the Dudh Kosi to Kari Khola. Sleep was sudden and deep, but I was out the door at six o'clock again the next morning.

I was still talking to strangers. At breakfast, I met an American who had almost died from AMS near Gokyo Ri at 18,000 feet. A porter was transporting his gear and he was doing very short days to conserve what little strength he had. He did not have enough money with him to fly from Lukla to Kathmandu and was planning on taking nine or ten days from Namche to Jiri. As we chatted, he told me of a shortcut to Kari Khola. His directions proved too accurate. I found the side trail just where he said it would be. And worse, I took it. The last trail leading up to the pass at Kari Khola is a monster and a shortcut seemed like such a good prospect. Not, as they say, in this lifetime…

An hour and a half hike became nearly three hours of slogging. The first few miles were fine, but once the trail crossed a very crude bridge, there was

Left: Dieter Loraine and the author on the trek to Kala Pattar. Everest is to the left and Nuptse is the imposing peak to the right.

Below: Kari Khola, "Shangri La," is a beautiful village nestled in a high mountain valley. The accomodations were inexpensive and excellent and the signs were in English. Rich Stephensen relaxes before lunch and leaves the packs along the wall where porters leave theirs.

nothing but ascent. Unlike certain portions of this trek, this was not a rapture of the steep. And the trail divided as often as someone's residence was nearby. No one spoke English and my *kuhn barto sibilai jansa?* (Which way does this trail lead?) was getting a workout. Instead of asking where each trail led, I found that looking hopeful and asking "*Namche?*" eliminated the problem of my accent and kept me on the right track. But I was in a foul mood when I staggered up that last hill to Kari Khola for a late lunch. Fortunately, the kind people at that restaurant with the checkered tablecloths and hand-carved signs in English soon turned my mood around. They brought me a magazine of scenic areas in the United States. I ate my fair share of complex carbohydrates and thought about the hill that awaited.

I did not spend the night in Surkhe as I had planned. The shortcut had cost me too much time and energy. Instead, I stayed at the lodge where I had first met David and Malcolm Blakeney. That fit with my sense of the appropriate. I knew that Namche would be reachable tomorrow and I was, as usual, nearly dead on my feet. There was another current being woven into the fabric of this part of the trip. Like Martin Cohen, the South African from my last visit, there was someone a day ahead of me who was doing the same kind of huge days.

Several people mentioned the Frenchman who had, supposedly, gone from Seti to Kari Khola in one day! If he was doing that kind of mileage with any kind of pack, he was one fit European. And, like Martin, he was purported to be traveling with a female companion. It is harder for a woman to carry her kit because of the weight of her body versus the weight of her pack, and the length of her stride. People were keying in on the accomplishments of the men, but I wasn't sure that the two women hadn't exceeded the efforts of their companions. Cohen and his two hundred marathons; now, who was this Frenchman?

Namche was a treat. The steep switchbacks above the Dudh Kosi River went by quickly. I was too tired to do much more than daydream about the Khumbu Lodge and some rest and a cinnamon roll. While I was delighted to be there, I could not imagine going for a run tomorrow. It would be painful, if not impossible. I paid my respects to the lodge owner and crawled off to bed at sunset. I smiled as I drifted off; the lodge owner had remembered me and had been surprised to see me again so soon.

Willpower got me out of bed and into my running clothes. And it pushed me out the door. That morning took all I had. No one who watched me hike up the steep hillside that was Namche would have guessed that I was fit, or a runner. A plodder perhaps, but not a runner. I was panting hard when I reached the level part of the trail at the top of town. That was a bad omen.

I started jogging and fully expected to have trouble. It was almost 9:00 A.M. and that was the best I could manage for early morning. After about twenty minutes of rolling hillside, I passed a trekker and his Nepali porter. We exchanged *namastes* and they moved aside to let me pass. I heard them conversing in rapid English as I started up a steep section of trail and then I heard footsteps behind me. I ran on and didn't look back. On the next level section the steps were still there. It was no use. I knew exactly what was happening. A Nepali porter who had never trained as a runner a day in his life was keeping up with me and my very light daypack, while he carried a twenty-pound pack of his own. He ran for the joy of experimenting with something that he had never had cause to do. He challenged my Nepali for a while, and then we both switched to English, and he ran with me for twenty more minutes. He finally walked on some of the short but steep uphill sections. I walked, too, and he thanked me for letting him continue. When he finally said farewell and turned back, I was very sorry to see him go. He had been right in his unspoken premise: It had been great fun.

During that section of trail I discovered the importance of the Everest Marathon in this part of the Himalayas. Porters, trekkers, and shop owners shouted encouragement or applauded. Everyone except yaks and their herders moved off trail to make way. It was heady stuff and just what I needed. If I felt this good and if people were going to add to my elation, I might just run all the way to the first river crossing.

On my way, I passed through a small village where leaves now covered the ground for four hundred yards of beautiful canyon trail. It reminded me of fall in upstate New York and I felt a twinge of homesickness for the United States. Unless I wasn't seeing well, I was passing maple, birch, and pine trees. In the Himalayas? As I continued on down toward the river below the monastery, every porter or Westerner seemed to know that anyone running had to be training as part of the marathon group. Their support continued. At the river, I felt fine. Perhaps I would try the ascent to the Tengboche Monastery. For a first training run at 13,000 feet, this was getting out of hand. I stopped at the small teahouse just beyond the river bridge. The sign above the door read, *"Phunki."* I smiled as I rested.

I only ran about half of the uphill grade to Tengboche. At the Monastery, I ordered some tea from some monks and then started back for Namche. Downhill was certainly easier and I was back to the river in twenty minutes. The uphill to the autumn village was a killer, so I walked and ran in what I hoped was a valiant effort. I could no longer tell. I had been gone over two hours and was beginning to tire. On a steep section of loose rock trail I heard a great deal of noise above me. I looked up quickly and saw someone running down the slope toward me. He wore a pair of shorts, a tank top, a headband, and some expensive running shoes. Two things clicked in my mind at the same moment: This man was one tough runner and he was the Frenchman. And the fact that he was running meant that he was almost certainly in the marathon. He nodded as he flew by. Going downhill, he went exceptionally fast, letting his feet move quickly from one tenuous spot to another. I did not know it then, but I had just seen the man who had won the Mont Blanc race twice and who was trying his first Everest Marathon. He was Swiss, not French, and he was running the same training run that I was trying to complete. My time was 3:20. His was 1:20. Oh, oh! That was my introduction to Pierre Andre Gobet.

The marathoners arrived over the next five days. I did not attempt to run as long as I did that first day. Usually, two and a half hours felt sufficient. I officially met Pierre Gobet and found him to be very unassuming and much tougher than I had thought. He and his girlfriend had indeed made the trek to Namche in three and a half days, but he had carried both packs on the last day and neither of them felt much fatigue from the hike. His timed descent from the monastery to the river was seven minutes. I had done it in twenty. My feet had actually touched the ground.

Mr. Gobet was not the only runner of note in the group. Gurkhas had competed in the two previous marathons. They had placed five runners in the top ten each time; their highest placing was second in both races. Kusang, who had been only a few minutes behind the winner in 1989, was back. Other members of his regiment were equally fit, and the group had already spent a month training near Annapurna and on this trail near Everest Base Camp.

And then there was Stefan Schlett from Germany. Less than a month before this marathon, he had done what he called a "five times triathlon." He explained that it was only an eight-mile swim and a 400-mile bike ride, but that it was a 100-mile run at the end. He had been in almost constant motion for nearly sixty-five hours. I began to think that there was no safe place to sit. Perhaps I wasn't even on the right planet. There were more stories about other runners. I did the only thing possible: I quit listening.

On the morning before our group picture an American died. He was not part of our group; he had come down with AMS a few days before; then other health complications had set in. He and his group had been waiting for

With Dieter Loraine (left) and Dr. Jennie Oliver
above Tengboche Monastery.

Top: The airport at Lukla is an exceedingly short piece of real estate. Fuselages from ill-fated take-offs are used as parts of walls for nearby farm fields.
Above: Tea houses range from free to $1.00 per night. Dr. Stephen Green and Paddy Bettesworth inspect their night's lodging.

a helicopter to take him back to the hospital in Kathmandu. They had waited too long. The helicopter had been available and had been scheduled to arrive the evening before, but an afternoon storm had made the conditions too risky and the pilot had not taken off. The American died as porters were transporting him to the helipad and the landing copter. Even at 13,000 feet there could be severe problems.

We moved up to the Tengboche Monastery as one group now and I was part of the move. A porter carried my pack and the daypack was feather light. Then we trekked up to Dingboche for two days of acclimatization and training. I took another glorious hike in the Chukkung Valley and attended another seminar with the doctors in Pheriche. And then we were on our way to Lobuje.

Dieter Loraine came down with a severe headache—a warning sign of AMS. With the start of the race only a few days away, we were worried that the British marine might not be able to compete. He had spent a lot of money to be here, taken time away from his family and work, and gotten through the hardships of the trail; now it could end with his being turned back before the start. He sat with his head in his hands near the cooking tent and waited for something good to happen. Fortunately, the day in Lobuje was another rest day. Most of the entrants hiked up to Kala Pattar and took pictures of Everest and the surrounding peaks. I remained behind with Dieter on the assumption that the Diamox he was taking and the rest day would allow him to make the hike tomorrow. I had already been there and he would not be able to safely go alone. The rest day felt very good.

The day before the race dawned cold and clear. The temperature was about twenty below zero. It was no problem to remain in bed until the sunlight hit the fabric of the tent. I had warm tea and was glad to have all my clothes on. We would trek to the last camp, Gorak Shep. Dieter was feeling much better, although weak, and we elected to continue past camp to the top of Kala Pattar. We did it slowly and with a lot of stops for pictures. There was a demanding race tomorrow and we didn't want to use all our energy on this ascent. Dieter's sense of humor returned and he started back to his recurrent theme of wanting the trekkers we met to know we were "runners and not joggers."

While we did our hike, Steve, Paddy, Roger, and David relaxed at a lodge and ate and drank. We had decided to abandon the tents because the area where they were pitched was at the confluence of wind from two directions. The lodge was sheltered by a few small hills and the rocks of the moraine. Many of the others came to the same conclusion and all of the lodges were full by bedtime.

The meal taxed the cooking pots of the lodge owner, but we were finally ready for another fitful night of high-altitude sleep. In one of those unfortunate moves of *karmic* consequence, we picked the same lodge where the "ambulance" slept. Dr. Amanda Isdale and David Blakeney were in the lodge with us. Amanda was to act as the chief medical officer at the start and could decide on the fitness of anyone with a problem. She and David would follow the last runners for the entire course and would have medical and emergency supplies in their fairly heavy packs. While it was terrific to have qualified people in charge, it was not a good idea to share sleeping quarters with them. Amanda and David were called on almost hourly to attend to someone who was ill. Several people had to have porters escort them down to Lobuje to see if their AMS symptoms would disappear. One of those was a Sherpa porter. No one, we reminded ourselves, was immune.

At each rap of the door, all of us would wake up. Several of the ill came to us personally. That wasn't good for us, as nausea was one of the symptoms of most high-altitude maladies. One such sufferer christened three sets of shoes placed on the floor near Amanda's sleeping bag. My shoes were also my running and hiking shoes and they were at the bottom of my sleeping bag so that they would not be frozen solid in the morning. At 5 A.M., I gave up on sleep and rehearsed my strategy for finishing this race. I was almost sure that the only hindrance I would encounter would be the desire to be competitive with others or with a specific time. Eliminating those was the theme of the rehearsal.

At 5:30 Amanda and David were up and out the door to check on various marathoners. The rest of us were free to eat or drink or stay in our sleeping bags until the last possible instant. It was easily twenty degrees below zero again, but there was no wind and the sky was cloudless. It was soon evident that the night had dealt harshly with two unofficial members of our group. Paddy and Steve had been ill all night. They left the lodge, only returning when the cold drove them back in. Both were having trouble standing and simply walking was going to be a problem. Running appeared to be out of the question. Most likely, the culprit was bad food or drink. It didn't seem to be AMS. Still, about the best they could hope for seemed to be a slow walk of twenty miles to Namche. Disappointment hovered over all of us.

At 6:50 most of the runners were at the starting line. We had practiced counting our assigned numbers in the relative warmth of yesterday afternoon. The race couldn't start until everyone had been accounted for. The practice session had not gone smoothly and David had repeated it until he was satisfied that he would have no problems in the deep freeze of morning. As I looked around, I thought I saw someone temporarily covering a pair of shorts. If he was going to run without long pants, he had to be certifiable. I opened my fanny pack and looked at the trinkets from home. I hadn't carried them everywhere to take them off during this race; they were a part of all that I did. I zipped it closed and looked toward David. All I could think of were several variations on "Get me down from here!" The marathon offered the fastest means of that. Below, there would be more air, warmer temperatures, better food, sounder sleep, pretty much all the finer things in life. The meaning of life seemed to be staring me in the face—if I could just get some food, air, and warmth…

David was the official starter and his speech was short and to the point: "You have trekked for sixteen days to reach this moment. I hope that you achieve all that you want and have a safe and enjoyable race. Ready, steady, go!"

And we went. Within the first two hundred yards of level ground, a lot of people walked. Twenty yards later we reached the moraines and the first uphill; the leaders were already out of sight and the struggle for oxygen was well under way. But it was a strange race. Before it had started, people who had already spent over two weeks traveling together sought out new friends and sincerely wished them well. On the course, people offered to move out of the way or would ask someone, by name, if they could move on ahead. Amiable didn't begin to cover it. If there were signs of competitiveness it was likely to be far ahead with the Gurkhas and Gobet.

Lobuje was the first station to provide aid for us. There, Dr. Oliver and the other volunteers collected excess clothes from us and encouraged our efforts. The first three miles had gone quickly and I actually felt quite fit. Below Lobuje was a long steep section of trail. Movement had been slow when we ascended that part of the trail and there had been little or no chance of falling or being injured. That wasn't so on the descent. The loose sand and rocks could give way at any moment. I was far enough in the back of the pack that those around me should have been conservative. They weren't. Above and behind me I heard what sounded like a rockslide of serious portent. Around me, no one was being conservative as we ran for our lives and tried to get to the next aid station at Duglha before the cascading stones. I didn't bother to look back. Someone would be able to tell me what the source of that slide had been.

Duglha came and went and the trail spilled out into the valley that funneled air and water toward Pheriche and the medical clinic. Through this section, the trail was mostly flat and was easy to negotiate. However, as I looked ahead, I could see no one running. I glanced quickly behind me and could see George Barris, the 59-year-old "fell" runner. He was just starting down the last of the switchbacks from Duglha. It was a two-man run.

We had great support at Pheriche and the doctors were out in force. There were many hardy trekkers lining the long main street of town. I drank as much as I could of whatever was available and started off just as George arrived. He was clearly gaining on me and I was sure he would catch me on the next series of rolling hills. At other times and in other races, I might have cared. Now, I just wanted to conserve energy and reach the twenty-mile mark with something left. I ran across the bridge out of town and up the first small hill. It wasn't bad. I was able to run all of the two hundred yards of ascent and I figured that the increased oxygen was paying a dividend or two.

We ran together to the base of the hill below Tengboche Monastery. Pheriche had been the seven and a half-mile mark; this was just over twelve. We had seen no one else and we had been able to have some nice conversations along the way. We were just two older gentlemen out for a little jog—through the Himalayas! Now, with the first severe uphill, we quit talking. Running downhill does some bad things to some of the large muscles of the legs. Running downhill on rocky and eroded trail is even worse. The uphill involved some different muscles and at first it didn't seem so bad. Breathing was much more difficult because we were near 14,000 feet. We came up the tree-lined trail and into the open field below the monastery to the applause of a large group of trekkers and support crew. We drank and ate and considered the long downhill run to the river at Phunki. We saw two runners who had been ahead of us the entire way. They had been taking a nice long rest. Another runner caught up with us while we rested and we welcomed the company.

Gobet's seven-minute training run to the river seemed unbelievable. Even my twenty minutes seemed quick at this point. I wondered how fast Pierre had done it today? And who was leading this thing? George moved ahead on the descent and I wished him well. I was not hurting too badly, but I wanted to be conservative and to see how the twenty-mile mark at Namche would be. I ran alone to the river.

I passed George on the uphill as he sat on a stone wall and ate some carbohydrates. The hill had not been kind to him, but he knew himself well enough to assure me that he would recover and catch me by Namche. He was almost right. I was only sixty seconds ahead of him when we reached the aid station above town. It was the twenty-mile mark and the race, as they say, was half over. Below me I could see the finish line, the tents, and our hotel. I wondered if anyone had finished yet. It was just over four hours. The winner would certainly be very close to the end. The course record was 3:59. Only 6.2 miles remained for us, but it was a hilly 10k that we faced. The best part was the support we would get since this was a loop. Those runners who were ahead of us would continue to the finish line with our encouragement ringing in their ears. And those behind us would do the same for us as we found a way to negotiate the 3.1-mile return loop. With that in mind, George and I skirted the upper reaches of Namche and started toward the small village of Thamo.

At the end of the second uphill, I told George to go ahead. My strategy had been paying off and there was no doubt that I could finish. But some of my leg muscles, the largest ones, were beginning to cramp, and I knew that I needed to run alone and pace myself just below the threshold of muscle tetany. We thanked each other for the good run and he moved ahead. Now I was running alone. Except for the increase in pain, this could have been any of my training runs: no one in sight and only the beauty of the Himalayan peaks and valleys to enjoy.

"Billy Bob!" It was Dieter Loraine and he was running toward me as I headed back from the turnaround at Thamo. I was probably a mile and a half ahead of him on the loop and he seemed positively jovial. His greeting was a take off on my Southern U.S. accent for "Say Hallelujah, Billy Bob." The Brits had found it funny. That he still had the presence of mind to remember anything and to try to make me smile meant that he was doing fine. We chatted about how we were feeling and he apologized for the small rockslide he had kicked off below Lobuje near the four-mile mark. Small? I told him I had heard it but had been too busy finding places for my feet to look back. He had tried to catch up with me by sliding on the seat of his pants. He had stopped himself when he realized that an avalanche didn't have to be snow. It was great to see him in such high spirits. He had not seen anything of Roger, Steve, or Paddy, although he expected Roger to be along shortly. We shook hands and I ran off to get the thing finished. I didn't have the heart to tell him that the pace we were now doing was definitely jogging.

Namche was below! From where the trail crested the ridge, I could see everything, and it wasn't hard to spot the finish line. I raced through the rock and cobbled streets and descended the small stairway into the open field that was the finish area. The official photographer took my picture just as I crossed the finish line. Four or five Nepali children who had run the last fifty yards with me turned aside just before that point. I would have encouraged them to finish with me; a smiling face was just what such a picture should have had. I received my medal and was told my time: six hours and twelve minutes. There had been two disqualifications ahead of me and I placed thirty-first. For the first time in my competitive life, I felt just fine about how I had done and the length of time it had taken—just fine.

One of the other racers brought me a coat and a drink of Kool-Aid. I was going to wait for some of the other finishers. Dieter was along in forty minutes. Then Roger. And then, Stephen! The good doctor was even running and smiling. He held hands with the young children who swirled around him and was obviously much recovered. His was a particularly impressive performance. And what about Paddy? We would later discover that he had not made the cutoff time to continue the loop. However, in the morning he ran to Thamo and back since he had made a commitment to those whose pledges he had accepted. This run was, after all, to raise money for the dental clinic and other projects that helped the Nepali people. Stephen and Paddy had completed a more impressive feat than I could have imagined.

Some of the day's toughest performances had also been back in the pack, very far back. The porters received my most heartfelt praise. Few people remained to cheer them on as they trudged the twenty miles to Namche. Each porter carried a double load—the complete camping gear for two runners. They did not arrive until after dark. I had tears in my eyes as I walked outside during our celebratory dinner and saw the last of these tough men bring in their heavy burdens. They, too, were smiling, as we had done after our finishes. I noted that many of the marathoners thanked them and complimented them on their effort. Some friendships had formed here, too. Diana had paid them double wages for the day and they had certainly earned that and more. And she gave each of them an Everest Marathon medal.

And what about the front of the race? I had seen Kusang during my run to Thamo. He had been walking and looked to be absolutely out of steam. Pierre had won the men's division by nineteen minutes—a huge lead in any marathon. He had not broken the course record, but that might have been because no one pushed him for the last part of the race. The Gurkhas had still not won, but they had again proven their toughness in difficult circumstances. Along with Gobet, they defined class act. Kareen Hogg, from Britain, had won the women's division in 5:58. She looked and acted like the race had been easy.

Crossing the finish line of the Everest Marathon.

My wish had been granted. The air was thicker, warmer, and the food was ambrosia. We hoped to spend tomorrow on the open-air balcony at Tawa Lodge eating our weight in cinnamon rolls.

In the meantime, I had to deal with a lot of pain. A veritable feast had been set out in the dining room of the hotel. I hobbled around as first one leg and then the other started to cramp. Worse than that was the dull aching of muscles strained to their limit. At times there seemed to be pain in muscles I didn't have, much like a phantom limb for amputees. My legs had always been thin. Now the pain seemed to belong to someone with much larger legs. I noticed that the course had not been any kinder to many other runners. However, Mr. Gobet, Ms. Hogg, and the Gurkhas seemed unfazed.

Then I gained a unique perspective on this world's highest marathon. I saw Dr. Oliver. Jennie was her usual smiling and untroubled self, wandering among the more seriously afflicted and giving encouragement. When she saw me, she couldn't wait to tell me how emotional the entire experience had been for her. She had been so inspired by the runners at that first aid station at Lobuje that she had run the rest of the race!

"Including the loop?" I asked.

"Including the loop," she replied. Twenty-three miles with no training and carrying her medical pack. As I looked at her smiling face, I thought that perhaps my legs did feel a bit better. Yes, they were definitely recovering.

If my "I haven't trained for this" excuse had to be eclipsed by anyone, this lovely doctor from New Zealand was the one to do it.

We flew to Kathmandu from Lukla and I caught a bus for the Indian border.

CHAPTER 10
<u>THE BEACH IN GOA</u>

For every traveler who has any taste of his own,
the only useful guide-book will be the one that he himself has written.
– Huxley

I again spent some time at the British Embassy in Delhi. On the heels of the Everest Marathon, I rested and relaxed in the comfort of British hospitality. Not much of the weight I'd lost had come back, but the nights of rest on mattresses went a long way toward healing the bruises on my hips, ribs, and shoulders. I discussed a possible import business with my new friends at the embassy, and I made a few purchases for friends back home. What I wanted to do was to go south to Goa and the warmth of the beaches. Penny and Nick had been there before they went to Nepal and highly recommended the area. So far, their advice and directions had been faultless.

My friends at the embassy had seen the contents of the fanny pack and heard the stories of the items I carried everywhere. They were curious about the small scrap of paper folded into my passport. I hadn't looked at it since Singapore, but I had been thinking about value rigidity more and more. The concept had changed from the monkey brains as a delicacy story to withholding judgement. My friends pointed out that the next step might be to try to see the world through the eyes of my various hosts. That, they reasoned, would certainly change the value rigidity I faced.

For the sake of the potential business and to see a different side of India, I decided to travel across the Thar (the Great Indian Desert). I would make my way to Bombay via trains and buses. From Bombay to Goa, I planned to take another train.

I tried to get to Churu from Delhi, but there were no trains. The alternative was a bus with metal seats and no padding—none. On that bus, I marveled that my fellow passengers showed absolutely none of the discomfort I felt. I continued to learn lessons like this and to understand that America had some entirely different standards for comfort and pain. I suffered in silence and amazement as I watched the sweep of the countryside and the calm faces of fellow travelers.

At the Churu train station no one spoke much English. They didn't get many Westerners here, and I was the subject of much staring. The train crew helped me out. There were handshakes all around, an immediate ticket and some heartfelt good-byes. While I was glad to be on the train, it was my first experience with a coal burner. It had only ten cars and I planted myself firmly in the doorway of the rail car.

I was coated with soot after about fifty miles and elected to return to my seat. A man and his two children were directly across from me. At the first stop, he bought me tea and interpreted the questions of others as we continued to travel. His English was impeccable. A college graduate, he was on his way to start a new job at the bureau of tourism, a job slated to last twenty years.

I noted an unusual feeling. Most of the time I wanted out of India. I missed Nepal and the lower intensity of the people. And then I met people on a train or a bus or in a city and I put up with the rest. What helped me to endure the over-crowding and manic cityscapes was the idea that I might never be here again. Hopefully, that wasn't true, but I felt I must act as though it was. There was so much to learn and experience.

I arrived in the Citadel City of Jaisalmer in the heart of the desert. It was the first of several cities where I could check out the possibility of an import-export business, which was really just a thin excuse to see a different side of India. This walled city was built on a high mound and was visible for miles. By coincidence, I found a guide to the city. One of the people who listened to my conversation on the train was an elderly gentleman. He politely introduced him-self just before we arrived at the station and asked if I would be his guest at one of the havelis in town. These were the mansions of the rich. I had certainly changed from the person I had been in Singapore, and I agreed to accompany him on the assumption that it would be safe. I seemed to have more faith in people; I didn't completely understand that.

In haste to allay any fears I might have, my new friend explained that his family would love to meet an American. His son, he said, taught English, but had never spoken with someone who knew English as a first tongue. I found that hard to imagine.

An *haveli* is a series of ornate and huge homes, each one set inside a larger one, and the largest one set inside a thick wall. Modern conveniences were present but were allocated to a particular section. My new family did not own this building;

they were caretakers for an absentee owner. "Mom" was very shy and listened to our conversations as she fixed dinner. Of the two sons, one spoke no English at all. The other was fluent but had definitely learned what he knew from others in the community who spoke English as a second language. We talked for the hour of dinner and for three hours after. His English was very good and his vocabulary quite extensive. I had been given a room of my own and felt very comfortable with their hospitality. I wanted to stay and learn more customs and language and history. The next day's tour was all the time I could spend.

I left Jaisalmer for Jodpuhr atop a crowded bus. Clutching some postcards and a book about the town I was leaving, I settled in among forty turbaned men, all of whom were staring at me. It didn't take much imagination to believe that the looks directed at me were malevolent and that I was in danger. Travel was either wearing me down or conditioning me because I knew that all I had to do to totally change the situation was to smile. Finally I did, and immediately a man threaded his way among the seated to see whether I was English, or at least spoke it. He noticed my postcards and asked to see them. Within seconds of my assent, the cards made the rounds of the rooftop. He asked me what I thought of India and this place in particular. I assured him that this was a place of great interest and beauty and that India was fascinating. Translated into Hindi, my remark brought warm smiles to all the faces.

He asked if I was British and I told him that I was not. "American," I said, and he looked puzzled. "I do not speak American," he said in a tone that seemed to add, "and, therefore, I am sorry not to be speaking further to your good self." I pointed out that we were speaking quite well in American and he looked around in astonishment at his fellow bus top riders. "I am speaking American," he repeated with a good deal of pride and amazement. In confused gratitude, he elected himself to be my guide to this area of the world. The confused gratitude should have been mine; another person who spoke four or more languages was helping me to understand the world.

He then informed me that the six different colored turbans being worn by those around me each represented a different culture. I had heard that in India the language and culture changes every fifty miles or so, but he assured me that it was more like twenty. While we chatted, we saw sheep, dogs, camels, deer, and many birds of prey. We were traveling on a one-lane road and sand often drifted across it to the extent that passage was very difficult. This was Rajisthan.

Once, this road had been part of a trade route to the rest of Asia. Caravans were offered protection from thieves and in return gave up a portion of their goods to each protectorate. Cities sprang up and great wealth was concentrated among traders as well as for those people who offered protection. The havelis, such as the one I stayed in, were the homes of the very wealthy from a bygone era. Ornate doors and windows and huge dwellings seemed to be everywhere in the fort-like cities throughout the region. Now, cities that once boasted 10,000 inhabitants were reduced to a tenth of that, and the level of poverty was often assuaged only by the tourist trade.

Out in the desert, I soon learned to spot encampments and villages by the four posts that rose above a well. Women in bright-colored saris carried heavy jars of water to their homes. Most of the water was drawn from the wells' depth by a long rope pulled by men or domestic animals. Along our route, families cut selected branches from trees as food for their animals. Camels were especially prized, and while they didn't drink much, they seemed to eat a great deal. It was a hard life in the best of times.

Still, I couldn't forget several businessmen in suits who carried briefcases and boarded or left the bus at various isolated areas. Those who departed just walked off along a path and into the desert toward the posts surrounding the village well.

When I finished looking around Jodhpur, I was able to take a train to Bombay. The second-class tickets were reasonably priced and allowed for a place to sleep. Although there were only supposed to be a certain number of people per seating area, I found that the rule was never respected. Where five people should have been, there were often eight or nine. Even with my significant weight loss, I was still six feet tall and needed a bit more room than the average traveler. The fact that I couldn't get the needed room without inconveniencing someone else led me to seek the doorway to the outdoors. And that was a very good change. I had terrific views of the countryside, fresh air, and relative privacy. Train travel was one of my favorite things.

The description of my arrival by train in Bombay was like nothing else on my trip. The poverty was overwhelming, with miles of the worst living conditions imaginable, or more likely, unimaginable. Freestanding water offered breeding grounds for mosquitoes. The ground was hard-packed dirt or mud, and the shelters kept out only part of the rain or sun. The bathroom was anywhere outside the house and the train traveled for miles among those relieving themselves. Shame or modesty was only for those who could afford it. Necessity would force you to do whatever it took to stay alive. It was hard to imagine life in such a place.

I arrived in Bombay on the nineteenth of December and wanted to travel to Goa as soon as possible. I had allowed myself one day to check for mail, advance some money via credit cards, and recover from five days of almost continuous travel. I did not feel up to braving the hordes of touts that were sure to descend on me at the train station. I thought about how short I was on money and how nice the beaches would be and used those thoughts to motivate me through the throng and to the first *tuk tuk* piloted by a Sikh. I had chosen that driver for two reasons: His beard and turban made him easy to identify as a Sikh and those of his religion answered requests about the price of a fare with: "What you wish." At this juncture, that was about all the tout-battle I could manage.

I needed to go to American Express, but my driver spoke only halting English. I spoke only halting Hindi. American Express somehow got translated as American Bank, and I arrived at five minutes to 5:00 P.M. at a place that, while still open, did me no good. American Express took another twenty-five minutes and was, of course, closed. My driver understood my predicament regarding money and food and actually stopped and bought me four bananas and a bottled drink. We both felt badly that I could not pay him for his services, and his kindness with the food added to my discomfort. He agreed to try to help me find lodging and we started off. I knew that I would be able to use my Visa and MasterCard tomorrow to get cash, and I knew that he would be paid and tipped generously. I could not imagine why he would think he would be paid and tipped generously. I tried to imagine how many of my countrymen would do what he had done. I could think of some friends who would have been as kind, but it was still a very impressive gesture. We tried several inexpensive hotels, but none would accept credit cards.

Finally, we succeeded. The hotel did not actually accept credit cards, but when I asked them if they needed payment in advance, they said, no, I could pay in the morning. Tired, hungry, and sleepy, I was over the moon with that bit of dialogue. The drama took a new turn as my driver came back up the stairs with my luggage over his shoulder and some credit cards in his hands. I had given him two expired cards as collateral, so that he would feel better about my scheduled meeting with him at ten o'clock tomorrow at American Express. He held them proudly in front of him, and, equally proudly, explained to the hotel manager that he was allowed to keep those until tomorrow because the American had no money.

Being thrown out of a hotel in India was done with such class and protestations of apology that it didn't hurt at all. What did hurt was the prospect of starting over again. I thought that my driver and I should part company before any more unintended harm was caused, and I again confirmed tomorrow's meeting. Then, shouldering a pack that felt increasingly heavy, I set off in search of something, or anything.

I finally stumbled upon the Grant Hotel. They were expensive by backpacker standards but they took plastic with no questions asked. And, better yet, they had room service that could also be charged. I took a shower, shaved, did laundry, and was asleep by nine. That adventure was over.

Not, as they say, by a long shot. The next morning at a bank, neither card yielded a dime. My mom was in charge of my accounts and my accumulated funds while I was out of the country, and she always kept the credit cards paid each month. What could have gone wrong? I tried another bank with the same result. I tried American Express. They never do a cash advance on their card overseas unless there is a checking account attached. I hadn't left home without it, but it wasn't doing me any good. I went back to the original bank, where the staff had been extremely kind and understanding. The manager had seemed to be a decent sort. I hoped that the payment had arrived and that the card would clear. The odds were heavily against that bet. Miraculously, one card yielded 2,500 *rupees.* I almost cried.

Another *tuk tuk* driver sped me to American Express where I paid two fares with generous tips all around. In keeping with the spirit of kindness that had been my experience in India, I loaned an American one thousand *rupees* at the bank. He was from South Carolina and was also out of money. He agreed to leave a repayment of the loan at American Express once his family wired him the money. I would have called home regarding my situation, but this was the first Christmas in a long time that my mom and her husband were out of town. Oh well, I was happy to be in a country where karma counted and hoped that by helping a compatriot I would pay off part of a larger debt.

The ride to Goa was sixteen hours of night bus. For someone who had been consistently warned about the dangers of night travel, I seemed to be incapable of heeding it. I didn't sleep. I never slept on a conveyance of any sort. I was more than ready for the touts when deposited in town. Fortune was smiling at me but was still unwilling to grin. I was down to my last 350 *rupees,* but I was near the beach, and I figured about two touts away from a shower and a bed.

Two lads from England sat next to me on the bus and we ended up with the same tout—which meant the same destination. That was a bit of good fortune since arriving and negotiating at the same time saved us all some money. We were just outside of the town of Mapusa, and it was there that I hoped to find an end to the money crisis.

"Mom" at our new digs granted me credit until such time as the bank cooperated. Then she fixed a breakfast of an omelet, six rolls, and three slices of dessert. Later, as I walked toward town, the oldest son caught up with me on his motor bike and offered to change money at bank rates. It was the first time in months that this type of offer had no connection to the black market. His offer was very generous, except that I had no money to exchange. Maybe what was changing was my luck. As I continued the three-mile walk to town, a taxi driver pulled up next to me and gave me a first price of five *rupees*. We both laughed at my expression and reaction. Most of the time a first price was three or more times what a driver would eventually settle for. This price couldn't be negotiated much lower. Here was a total stranger with a very welcome sense of humor. How nice. It turned out that he was going back to town anyway and thought that the joke would brighten two days. He was right. I was starting to like Goa very much.

The teller at the first bank in Goa solved the money puzzle for me. She pointed out that my cards were due to expire on December 31—a week away. I knew immediately what had happened. Mom had cancelled the cards and ordered new ones. A very organized lady, she would have already mailed the new cards to the American Express office in Bombay. Doubtless, she had realized the time that mail took and had done all that before the first of December. That was exactly what I would have wanted. I had let myself get a bit short of cash and now I was a very long way from the mail drop. While this was news, it was not good news.

I remembered hearing from other travelers that you could get anything done in India. I was about to find out. The American Express Card was all that I had that was valid. But it could not be used to advance money—a fact I had already established in Bombay. Few businesses in this area would accept anything but *rupees*. I would have to go underground. Or, in this case, I would have to go undergarment. The local cloth merchant was also a big time moneychanger, so the word on the street had led me to believe. Rumor had it that he had his own back room of highly sophisticated equipment and could check on your balance of account or acceptable charges as quickly as anyone could do stateside. There was a fair amount of overage for his service, but I walked out with 4,500 rupees and my problems were over. I had "purchased" quite a lot of cloth on my card. It was time to head for the beach.

I spent the Christmas season finding out that Goa had a very large Christian population. Huge churches were reminiscent of the cathedrals of Europe. Much of the architecture was Portuguese, and Spanish names were everywhere: towns, streets, businesses, and surnames. The world powers of bygone eras had left their mark. As I walked the streets on Christmas Eve, hundreds of Goans carried candles and walked to mass. Nativity scenes in the backs of large trucks were on the roads while children and adults walked behind. I joined the two British lads for dinner, and we selected the restaurant by sound. Everyone had music but we were looking for some that reminded us of home. Bing Crosby's *White Christmas* brought us to the Casablanca Bar and Restaurant, and we dined in luxury and listened to songs from Christmas past. My friends told me stories of Father Christmas and how this season was celebrated in Britain.

It was a very pleasant holiday. I moved from the somewhat expensive room near Mapusa to a less well known beach at Colva. It was another bus ride but only a few hours. There was only one tout as I stepped from the bus and he was ten. His parent's house had two extra rooms and one was available for forty rupees a day. That was about $1.50. There was the usual overhead fan, a chest of drawers, a bed, and one window with bars, a bare floor, and one light bulb. It was just right. I moved my kit into appropriate areas and changed into running shorts and a tank top and grabbed my towel. I wore no shoes. I was off to the beach.

My new lodging was several blocks from the beach. It was actually nearer to a large Catholic church. I walked through a forest of tall palm trees and noted that this was almost exactly what I had wanted when I stood at the starting line for the Everest Marathon a month earlier. I was warm, had gained a little weight, could breath large amounts of fresh air, and had no agenda. I missed Nepal very much, but this place took a lot of the edge off that feeling. Out of the trees I passed a barbershop where a shave and a haircut cost about forty-five cents—combined. Tomorrow would definitely be dedicated to that particular necessity. Right now, I wanted to rest on some warm sand, try to find some fresh fruit, and cereal, and relax.

Restaurants lined the beach for at least the first two hundred yards in either direction. Then, the number of places to eat dwindled to one every two or three hundred yards. The beach went on for about thirteen uninterrupted miles in either direction. Not wanting to be part of any particular crowd, I walked off down the beach for a half mile until I could see few Westerners. There were large boats resting well back from the water. Handmade, they looked like large dugout canoes with room for six or seven rowers. And they looked heavy and awkward. Each had huge nets resting near the front of the boat. As I walked along, one boat was returning from the sea. I was barely situated in a new area and already something exciting was happening.

I became an honorary Goan fisherman, because of my size more than anything else. It might have been my look of expectant involvement; I'm sure I looked like every kid who wanted to participate in a game but who knew none of the players. No, it was definitely my size. The fishermen motioned to me to come closer. And soon they had taught me how to drag the netting out of the water and move it along the beach. It was harder work than it looked, and I made it more difficult still by not relaxing and imitating the person in front of me. In fifteen minutes of continuous pulling, I had managed to get some very tired biceps and a considerable amount of net behind me. When I looked up, a few things were different. There were five Westerners with cameras who were taking pictures of us and the content of the net. Over thirty women and children created a semicircle around the outside of the net, and the fishermen were also moving toward some of the catch.

There was one shark and a number of large fish I had never seen before. There were crabs and there was one ray of some kind. These were dispatched and removed almost immediately. The women and children were sorting all of the smaller fish and a great deal of noise was made as they laughed and talked and worked. I hadn't been told what to do next, so I stood in oafish silence and stared. Nepal had made me a confirmed mouth breather and I resurrected that habit here.

One of the men who had originally motioned for me to help came up to me with his son, who spoke English. He asked me if I liked to eat shark. I assured him that was one of my favorite foods. The son pointed to a café farther down the beach and told me that they would have a large shark and vegetable meal for me at noon, if I wanted it. I thanked them both in Hindi, bowed a departing *namaste,* and returned to where I had left my few belongings. What a nice start to a day!

My plan was to rest and observe, and I did that for the entire time before lunch. What I discovered was that very few Westerners went much farther than a half mile from the road entrance to the beach. Indians did not go a third that far. Busload after busload of Indians would arrive and almost all of them would stay very close to the original spot of beach entry. The few who wandered down the beach were invariably men, and they were always looking for scantily clad Western women. It was definitely a cultural thing. The farther they went, the more chance there was for a topless Western female to be relaxing on the beach.

Of those who did not wander off, only the women removed no clothing. Fully dressed, they would wade into the water to a depth where they could begin screaming. The men removed all clothing except underwear and screamed at somewhat farther depths. At first I thought these were wealthy Indians who had not been to beaches and were coming to the coast for the first time. Another traveler explained that these were usually lower-middle-class people who had finally acquired the money to take such a trip. Far wealthier than the average person in India, they still regarded this trip as a major expense. I didn't question the explanation, as I often didn't. Obviously joy and terror were at work out there, and everyone would carry back sensational memories. I wanted no more than that from my own trip.

I had my free shark steak, and it was delicious. The restaurant was owned by the brother of one of the fishermen that I had helped, and the service was equal to the quality of the meal. After a leisurely repast, I walked back to the small town where I was staying, bought a book at a used bookstore and returned to my towel. By 4:30, I was doing what others were doing: I was resting in the shade of one of the many beached boats. I had had enough of the sun and heat. By 5:00, I had decided to go for a run down the beach. I wanted to run for about an hour. As it turned out, it was a particularly lucky choice of time.

I ran near the water's edge on the hard-packed sand. Tens of thousands of dime-sized pink and white crabs fled or ignored me as I jogged past. Not far off shore, dolphins rolled in the waves and fed. Wherever a dirt road intersected the beach, there were a few more people, but generally, there were only a few people per mile. It was not much of a stretch to imagine that I was in California before there were any crowds. Running in one direction for a half an hour, and then back for the same amount of time, I arrived at my towel just as the sun began to sink into the ocean. It was phenomenal.

The word "gold" does not begin to cover it. Within a few minutes, a huge yellow ball had started to disappear into the deep blue of the water. The sky was only a slightly lighter shade of blue and there were no clouds. The gold color reflected off the relative calm of the water and the sun seemed to grow larger and larger as it sank. At the last, only a small section rose above the waves, like a small pure gold island out on the horizon; then that, too, disappeared. Events had just selected the time for my evening run. Every day afterward, I wasn't

sure when I would start my exercise—that would depend on how I felt—but I knew that I wanted to finish just in time for the sun to repeat tonight's performance. The feeling was perfect as I walked up the beach to order dinner and watched the twilight fade to dark.

My existence fell into a nice rut. I arrived at the beach at sunrise and stretched and walked in solitude for a while. Depending on the tides, I would help launch or beach as many as three fishing boats. Within an hour, I ate breakfast at one of the restaurants and then I walked back to the barbershop for a shave and shoulder massage. As people started arriving, I took my books, journal, and stationery far down the beach and began to read or write. I managed at least a letter a day to someone at home and recopied many of my journal notes, which had been written in less-kind conditions. I memorized several pages of John Galt's speech in _Atlas Shrugged_ and practiced it as I walked up and down the white sand beach. After lunch, I did some reading—either one of my books or rereading letters from my friends. The latter were never sent home, but remained with me in an accumulating packet of precious treasure. Then, in the evening, I ran for an hour or more and watched the sun set. Before I noticed what had happened, three weeks had gone by. New Year's followed Christmas and it was mid-January. I could have lived there forever, but I was due in Africa in two weeks. Time to start planning for another continent. I would need to return to Bombay, but this time I would take the train. Ten pounds heavier and much more relaxed than when I had arrived, I packed up everything and took a local bus to the train station.

I took out my journal for a last entry at the airport in Bombay. The sign in front of the building said: "No parking for outsiders. If found guilty, tyres will be flattened with extreme prejudice."

I moved on to Africa.

Previous page: India constantly offers up architectural wonders. Dealing with Dehli's overcrowding was worth it to wander into marvels like this.

CHAPTER 11
<u>EAST AFRICA</u>:
Mount Kenya

Friends Always
– R. Stephenson

I was exceptionally tired when I arrived in Nairobi, Kenya. I was tired of Bombay and the travel from Goa. Funny how the trip toward Goa had been much more pleasant. The long flight across the ocean had not been restful either. I was still on my own and plunging back into ignorance. I didn't have a lot of what could pass for "knowledge" about Africa. However, in the back of my mind there was a growing feeling that something about this type of travel—the not knowing—added to it. On the plane, I listened to a very tall white man with a ponytail ask two Japanese girls if they knew who had won the Super Bowl. I slunk a bit farther down in my seat and pretended to be Australian. Sure enough, when the deplaning passengers queued for one of several midnight custom lines, I was right next to a fellow countryman. Maybe he was only gregarious around Asian women.

"Hi, I'm Brad." He stuck out a hand, and I shook it. "From California." I still hadn't said anything. I just stared. Other than Julie and Bill, he was one of the only Americans I had actually talked with. Or would be, if I ever said anything. "You Australian?" he asked. "You dress like an American." Brad gave me the impression that his worst nightmare might be a mute who couldn't even tell him his country of origin. I finally introduced myself, and then found that I was starting to like this easygoing traveler. He had a guidebook and we decided to try to find lodging and split the bill as inexpensively as possible. It was late and finding a place could be difficult. The changed time zones, the long flight, and late hour had taken their toll. Tomorrow we could figure things out. I was again amazed at the trust and camaraderie between virtual strangers.

The hotel was not exactly what the taxi driver had promised. It was more money, we were told, due to the late hour. It was nothing close to deluxe either, which I suppose could be a matter of opinion. The cab driver could look at the same shabby exterior we were seeing and still tell us it was "a fine hotel." For the four hours we would sleep in it, I hoped to see nothing but the inside of my eyelids. Brad was tired, too, but not so sleepy that he didn't remember to push a chest of drawers against the only door in the room while I checked the locks on the windows. We agreed that it wasn't Africa that elicited this behavior; it was the area of town and the fact that we were newly arrived. We had both done the same in many other countries we had visited. It was no different in some places in our own country.

Nairobi was a beautiful city and was far different than I could have imagined. There was an upper class, and beautiful high-rise buildings lined the wide streets and looked down on some very expensive automobiles. Pockets of extreme poverty existed, too, but it was an amazingly cosmopolitan town. With the plus side of wealth came the minus side of high prices, and I looked at Africa as though it was going to be a short visit. Safari touts were everywhere— and were especially thick at the Iqbal Hotel where my backpacker budget landed me. The Iqbal was definitely one of those pockets of extreme poverty. The cab driver from last night was starting to look like he knew what a deluxe hotel was.

I was still rooming with Brad, who was about as different from me as it was possible to be. Over six feet four inches tall, Brad stood out in any crowd. He was extremely gregarious and indulged in a fair amount of illegal substances. The saying "He never met a stranger" applied, and he soon knew several dozen residents of the hotel and most of the desk staff. Everyone seemed to like him. I had spent most of my trip and part of my life learning how to fit in and not be noticed. I didn't take drugs and was very shy among strangers. Our tenure as roommates should have been very short. Still, we seemed to get along well enough, possibly because of the previous traveling we had done or possibly because we both had an interest in an ascent of Mt. Kenya and a safari.

Before I could consider myself settled in, I needed to pick up some language skills. While wandering through a series of shops in downtown Nairobi, I got my chance. I found some shops that were not like those nearby. They were not constructed to last; they were mostly tin with wood bracing. In this merchant shantytown there were some values not to be found in the high-overhead stores. After an hour of hot midday shopping, I wandered out of the shops and was confronted with an ice cream store. In Africa I could have begun a lot of sentences with "I never would have imagined!"

Inside the air-conditioned restaurant I met Bwana Johnson. He was happy, friendly, and seemed pretty typical of the Kenyans I had met so far. I greeted him with the lone word of Swahili that I had learned: *jambo.*

His smile never disappeared but he said, *mwalimu,* and pointed at himself.

His nametag said "Johnson" so I assumed that his first name must have been Mwalimu. I pointed at him and repeated what I had just heard him say and then pointed to myself and said, "Mike."

I smiled. He grinned.

"No," he said. "*Mwalimu* means teacher. I will help you with our language." I should have known that he would speak barely accented English.

I was delighted to have met someone who was willing to help me at this early stage of my African trip. He talked to a coworker about taking a break, delivered an order to some people at another table, then sat down across from me for a quick lesson.

He told me that the language was Kiswahili. Here in Kenya and along the East African coast it was a first language, but 20 million people spoke it as a second language. Uganda, Tanzania, and Zaire used Kiswahili, too. I mentioned that I had been told that it was a language created by Arab traders, but he told me that it was a Bantu language. The story I had heard arose from the fact that the language borrowed heavily from Persian, Arabic, and other African dialects. Of the spoken language, nearly twenty percent was not of Bantu origin. He asked if I would like to know more. I nodded in affirmation.

"*Jambo,*" he said, smiling again, "means 'affair, matter, or thing.' It is not really a greeting. Usually it is said by those foreigners who do not wish to learn more than 'hello' in our language."

He did not say this in a mean-spirited way, and I could vouch that a lot of travelers learned only a greeting or a farewell in the countries they visited. I insisted that I was willing to relearn the one word of Kiswahili in my vocabulary.

"*Hujambo,*" he related, " means 'you have nothing the matter with you, do you?' The correct response is '*Sijambo,*' which means, 'I have nothing the matter with me.' It is another way of saying 'I am fine.' "

The Kiswahili language is much like Nepalese in that it is spoken most often by people who are not in a hurry or who would like to take a break from some very difficult work. As a result, it is considered quite rude to move directly to the purpose of any conversation. Sometimes there was no purpose. In the U.S., such dialogue can often be found among retired men sitting on a park bench in front of the post office. There is a ritual involved.

"*Habari gani* or *habari yako* mean 'What is your news?' " Bwana Johnson explained. "The response is always *mzuri*. That means your news is good." It was evidently inappropriate to answer greetings in other than a positive manner. Even if someone had been tragically killed, the answer was always *mzuri*.

Because I was going on a safari soon, I anticipated conducting all emergencies in English. Otherwise, I would still be somewhere between claiming that I had *hakuna matata* (no problems) and asking about the good news of the village when the rogue elephants stampeded over me. *Mzuri* might be a little lame at that point.

I returned to the shop three more times over the next two days and vocabulary was cheerfully added. I learned a pre-safari phrase: *leo tuleana,* which means "Today I saw…" I then began to plug in the missing words. *Punda malia* is zebra, *ngoya* is camel, *mamba* is crocodile, *unyoke* is snake, *fisi* is jackal, *tumbile* is monkey, and *twiga* is giraffe. *Tembo* is Kiswahili for elephant and *diki diki* is Kiswahili for dik dik (a small and harmless looking antelope about the size of a greyhound). I added the words *mingi* (many), *hapa* (here), and *sasa* (now) on the assumption that those were apt words to know when confronted by a large heard of *tembo,* or for that matter, some enraged *diki diki.*

Bwana Johnson taught me *asante* (thank you), *asante sana* (thank you very much), and *asante nimashiba* (no thank you, I'm full). Perhaps he had sensed that I was uncomfortable with the plans Brad and I had made, and he wanted me to be able to properly speak to my rescuers. Certainly, he knew that I spent a lot of time eating—ice cream. I filled up two notebooks with other meaningful words while adventures started to appear on the horizon.

I thought that Brad's idea of a safari was a good one. He had done some research and thought that trying to see animals and various tribes would be the most interesting. I agreed, and we signed up with Steve, our front desk tout. The trip did not leave for a week, which gave us enough time to consider a trek to the top of Mt. Kenya.

International backpacking travel was different from anything I had experienced before. With almost no expenditure of effort, we met Angelo from Australia, Charlie from New Zealand, and Debbie from Australia. All of them wanted to accompany us to Mt. Kenya and all of us fit easily into the casual friendship that marked such encounters. It wasn't my experience in the U.S. to find such trust and camaraderie among strangers. Here, it worked often and well, and we were soon intent on finding food, equipment, and information.

My very durable and warm sleeping bag and the accompanying warm kit had been mailed back to the United States. Succumbing to more preconceived notions, I had assumed that Africa would be hot like Thailand, Malaysia, and most of India. Kenya was, after all, very near the equator. I had heard of Kilimanjaro, but did not know where it was in Africa. No other peaks came to mind when I thought of Africa. Now, Mt. Kenya loomed as an adventure with a vertical rise to over 17,000 feet. There were many rental shops and we selected bags and cooking gear for both comfort and weight. Unlike in Nepal or at Hemkund Lake in India, food would have to be carried. This challenge would be more than I was used to, and I tried to pack accordingly. From the appearance of our final packing job, we had enough food to feed an emerging nation for a month.

Debbie was ill when we met her, but was trying to tough it out for the duration of her Africa stay. On the day before our scheduled departure, she was too ill and had to remain behind. Charlie, too, was unable to go. So, Brad, Angelo, and I further divided up the supplies and went without the others. On a mid-spring morning, we started off early to find either a *matatu* or a taxi to a town called Chagoria. After walking a few blocks to the taxi lot, we discovered that everyone wanted our money, but no one wanted both our sizeable luggage and us. With no place to store such large packs, space for other passengers would be taken up and profits would plummet. The answer was to double the already exorbitant fare for each of us. Since two other Westerners (*mazunga*) had joined us, the cost was much higher than we had planned. And, for one of the few times on my trip, the other taxi drivers were quite reluctant to wage a price war.

Finally, we decided to take an expensive taxi to Embu and a *matatu* the rest of the way to Chagoria. The *matatu* was a small truck-like vehicle with a long bench seat on each side of what in the U.S. would have been called a camper shell. This *matatu* was crowded beyond belief—our belief. At every stop, the few people who left were replaced by twice as many who were going. Somewhere in all that pressed flesh were five wide-eyed and staring foreigners. It was not the place for anyone with claustrophobia.

We reached Chagoria at just after noon on a very warm day. In the lobby of the hotel where we were deposited, we recognized at least six other people from the Iqbal Hotel. They all planned to start early in the morning. In Nairobi, we hadn't known that they were going to the park. We also didn't know that none of them would succeed in reaching more than the park entrance. What would stop them was a severe winter storm. Here in the jungle, such a storm seemed impossible.

Since it was a nineteen-mile hike to the Mt. Kenya Lodge at the base of the mountain, the other Iqbal residents wanted to start early to avoid most of the heat. Angelo, Brad, and I were reluctant to wait until morning and negotiated with a Jeep driver who offered to take us halfway to the lodge—today. Upon hearing his price for taking us all the way to the lodge, I started looking for the words Pan Am on the side of his jeep. I could have just looked at his smile; he had done this before, and with obvious financial success.

We took the halfway ride and were entertained by a driver who spoke excellent English and who regaled us with stories throughout the bumpy ride. We particularly enjoyed the tales of the snakes and leopards that inhabited this region. I had heard of the deadly mambas—one of the most poisonous snakes on the planet. Our guide did an imitation of a leopard's cough. That stirred some memories from other books and films. This was real and we were soon to be dumped in it. Because the speedometer didn't work, we concluded that nine and a half miles could just as easily have been three. We kept him telling stories as long as we could and hoped that we were near double digits when he finally applied the brakes. In a small clearing of hot and humid air, he repeated his price to drive us the rest of the way. We declined, but not without some hesitation.

Only one dirt road went to the lodge and we agreed to walk at whatever pace felt right for each of us. Angelo and Brad did not have the advantage of a month of beach running in Goa and moved at a more reasonable speed through the afternoon swelter. I pushed a pace that I felt I could hold for nine miles. By leading this trek, I was able to surprise large bands of black and white colobus monkeys and to occasionally hear something large race away through the stands of bamboo. *Tembo* sounded like a good word for elephant, and I stopped for a long moment to observe where one had very recently crossed the road from a small forest to the bamboo. Stories of rogue elephants had been circulating at the Iqbal before we left, and my proximity to their habitat was improving my imagination more rapidly than I could run. Run where?

After three miles of sweat, I heard a vehicle approaching behind me. A very nice family in a Land Rover stopped and asked if I wanted them to transport my pack to the lodge. In another move quite trusting, I threw my pack on the roof rack, next to Angelo's and Brad's. Then, with a heartfelt wave on my part, I watched the cloud of dust disappear around the next uphill bend.

I was now much lighter, having retained only some money, my "trinkets," and my passport in my fanny pack. I ran for a mile or two in celebration of the unexpected luxury of not carrying twenty kilos of gear. The vegetation changed

Lobelia and groundsels in the United States are often several feet high. On the flank of Mt. Kenya, they surround a mountain lake (tarn) and are gigantic.

and clouds moved in behind me. I stopped running and began to look around as the jungle gave way to a savanna-like plain. I walked another mile through the hills and ascended still further. The sun disappeared behind huge storm clouds. The perspiration generated by the run and brisk walk chilled me quickly, and I was forced to run again just to stay warm.

I crossed another mile of hills and saw still more changes in the surroundings. In the distance, I saw what seemed to be cattle. As they moved toward the road, I could see the unusual horns—short and tilted back. They had white rib stripes, black stockings, and large graceless looking bodies. At the time I could only guess that these were my first *eland*. They walked briskly as I ran and were much more agile in motion than they were at rest. When I crested a hill, I saw the Mt. Kenya Lodge (such shelters are called *bandas*). It was a welcome sight for a lot of reasons, not the least of which was the potential for food and shelter.

I negotiated a room for the three of us, retrieved our gear from the folks in the Land Rover, and started a fire in the fireplace. From a jungle beginning, we were now at 9,898 feet. That explained why it was so cold and why the last few miles had been so difficult. After I was warm and dry, I talked with

151

some of the other lodgers and learned something of what to expect on the trek. Brad and Angelo arrived in another eighty-five minutes, both feeling a bit unwell.

During my talk with some of the other lodgers, I discovered that the road we had been on was a forestry road. Logging had become a big industry at the lower elevations. In fact, I was told the dominant species of tree changed completely with every hundred meters of elevation gain. We had driven through Meru oak near Chagoria, then hiked through giant camphor (some over 130 feet high), then some yellowwood trees, and finally into bamboo. I didn't know that bamboo was a grass and had never imagined that it grew from thirty to fifty feet high. Usually not too interested in the flora of an area, I was fascinated to learn that this particular bamboo flowers only once every hundred years. Entire stands would flower simultaneously, reproducing vegetatively prior to that and dying just after. I was told that East Africa redwood and cedar bordered the lodge. Once they were pointed out to me, I saw them easily. Witch hazel was everywhere. Just as I saw Brad and Angelo working their way toward us, I was listening to a story about trout fishing in the nearby streams. The story was told with a straight face. It seemed too straight. The Kenyans with whom I was talking had learned that the best way to be mistaken for a liar was to tell the truth unconvincingly. Brown trout in Africa! Everyone laughed good-naturedly as I stood to go meet my friends and to direct them to our night's lodging.

The *banda* might have been primitive by most travel standards, but it was pure luxury for us. With three large beds, a completely furnished kitchen, and a fireplace, it was a more expensive place than we had anticipated. But the only other camping site was a communal dorm just across the way with beds only. That seemed a bit too spartan after the day we had just put behind us. We assumed, correctly, that "primitive" awaited us on the mountain.

Angelo proved to be an excellent cook and one prone to cooking with a lot of terrific spices. Brad proved to be a pyromaniac. If it hadn't been for his soccer skills learned at an earlier age, we would all still be in Kenya and working to pay off the cost of a lodge. All I could remember was trying to follow Angelo's instructions on the slicing and dicing of various vegetables. Brad put a canister of propane in the small portable stove we had rented. The canister had to be seated before you punctured it by tightening the small circular handle. If it wasn't properly seated, then neither was anyone else in the kitchen. And, we weren't in the kitchen for long. The fireball, which had once been an unpunctured canister, fell to the floor. My contribution consisted of yelling, "Get it outside!" Brad kicked it into the living room, Angelo ran to the front door and threw it open and Brad scored the first goal in an unopposed game as he drilled the can into the night. No more than a second of silence passed before the inevitable explosion. Once again, the rather flamboyant Brad had found a way to meet all of his neighbors—quickly. They all watched us from the protection of various vehicles or doorways. Angelo thought of asking if anyone wanted to join us for dinner, his way of suggesting an apology. I mentioned that such an invitation would invite aloneness—or whatever the opposite of togetherness is called. As soon as the fire was out, and the residents returned to the relative safety of their cabins, we finished our dinner.

The evening meal was terrific. It was amazing what Angelo could do to basic food with a few chili peppers and the correct means to cook it. It didn't hurt our assessment that we had spent a great deal of energy on the hike in. We talked for a while but readily agreed to an early night. Tomorrow promised to be a serious ascent. I didn't know about the others, but my dreams at high altitudes tended to be very bizarre and in vivid colors. When I awoke from the last one, I started to pack up.

The next day, Nick (the Land Rover driver) took our packs the several miles to the car park. His group was going to drive to one of the many lakes for a day picnic and would be returning to the lodge. If we started to walk well before they left, they would arrive at about the same time that we would. The car park was actually where the hike up Mt. Kenya began on the Chagoria side. We welcomed the assistance, and after breakfast and a few pictures, we were ready to start. Someone in Nick's party pointed out that by walking down a pathway parallel to the dirt road to the car park, we would avoid the official park entrance. That, of course, would avoid the official park entrance fee. We had not learned in our lives that saving money by avoiding the rules could be costly. We decided to be thrifty, inadvertently adding to the adventure.

After an hour hike to the car park, we were again united with our heavy burdens and could definitely feel the effects of our short exposure to these loads from yesterday. The trail was very steep and the travel was hot in the morning sun. There were beautiful views above and below us as we climbed. They weren't beautiful in all directions as we passed through some areas that had been blackened by fire. We passed through the sugar bush and heather lowlands and found that the lobelia and groundsel were burned over a really large area—especially leading to various slopes on the mountainside.

We were finally rewarded by a break in the ascent and a long ridge that offered green vistas untouched by fire. There were cool breezes cresting the ridge. We stopped for lunch and found a wind-sheltered spot in luxurious grasses that grew several feet high. Strenuous exercise was followed by lunch and rest. That seemed to be the right combination. We made the last one brief and started up again.

Brad and Angelo were still not feeling well, but the trail was clear, so they encouraged me to go on ahead if I wanted to. Where the ridge started back up, we saw that it worked its way along a cliff face far above a lush valley. That view was soon obscured as the late morning clouds rushed in and hid the cliffs and peaks above.

This was not fog on little cat feet; this was a malevolent cloud and it was cold in there. The trail wound among house-sized boulders and there were seldom enough breaks in the cloud cover to see several hundred feet in any direction. The direction of most interest was down, and there was plenty of that. For me, the danger was heightened by what I could not see, and I felt nervous in several places where the cloud cover was so dense that I couldn't see anything more than five feet away. It would have been easy to lose the trail and soon find that a steep cliff face had replaced it. I moved more slowly and all my senses were alert to the danger. Sound was deadened and even my own footfalls were subdued. The voices of Angelo and Brad drifted up to me as I entered the cloud zone. Then I heard nothing but my own harsh breathing.

With the exception of the ridge, we had been ascending for almost three hours. Finally, there was a downhill break for about fifteen minutes. When the clouds moved on up the peaks, the sun tried to shine for a few minutes. Then, there was a very steep ascent on a scree slope that was just a killer with a heavy pack. We had to be quite high to feel this knackered. It felt like about 15,000 feet (it was actually 14,000). There was a twenty-foot rock wall to negotiate and then a series of very small valleys to the hut. In the valleys were literally hundreds of hyrax, fat and furry boom-box-sized rock dwellers that are relatives of the elephant. If I hadn't known that there was a shelter nearby, the obesity of these locals would have given it away. A garbage dump had made them quite brazen around people, and they barely nodded in the direction of their shelters as I lumbered by. An immovable feast, indeed.

At the Minto's Hut, I met some others who had come up from another side of the mountain. There was another trail to this shelter: Sirimon. The third trail to the peaks was the Naro Moru and was opposite our starting point. We wouldn't

Top: The Temple is a famous part of the view of Mt. Kenya's twin peaks. A blizzard killed a porter the day after this picture was taken. Above: Timing is everything. About ten seconds before this photo was taken, this was a laughing and dancing group of happy children. Cameras often caused uneasiness.

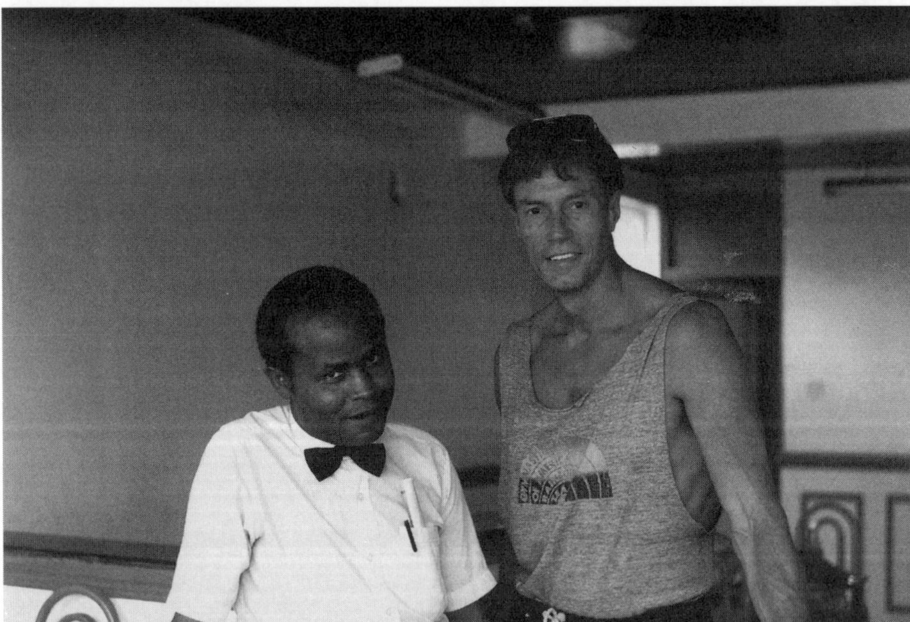

Top: Mintos Hut on Mt. Kenya housed as many as thirty trekkers uncomfortably. It saved us from a sudden mountain blizzard. Above: My mwalimu (teacher) in Nairobi was Bwana Johnson, who worked in a local ice cream shop and spoke excellent English.

see people who had come up the third trail until we were near the top of the mountain. I reserved three spaces in the very small tin shed, left my pack, and started back down to see if I could assist my friends. I found them at the base of the scree slope and quite done in by the day's push. Both needed some help, and I carried the two packs on the ascent. Brad wasn't ill enough to have lost his sense of humor and he kept us laughing at the expense of some particularly lazy hyrax. The hut, meanwhile, had become a zoo.

In an area where ten people might comfortably have "made bivouac," there were now twenty. We were told that more than thirty people had spent the night in there. From the outside, this "shed" looked about the size of those you saw in American backyards to store gardening equipment. Inside, there were two sleeping shelves; a large table for cooking took up the rest of the space. There were only a couple of small windows and I noticed a number of places where the walls, floor, and ceiling did not tightly join. We planned on a day of acclimatizing the next day, so we tried to cook, rest, and make ourselves heard amid the constant roar that was five or six languages and a lot of overcrowding. Still, it was a good-natured lot, and food and cooking gear were exchanged and used and cleaned in amazing cooperation.

By first light, most of the people who had acclimatized the previous day were off for their ascent to Austria Hut. The three of us soon had the place to ourselves. I left early, too, and hiked a short way to a nearby lake and found a rock ledge on which to write in my journal. It was very cold, but the sun was up and my fingers worked better with each passing minute. In an hour, I was lying on the soft grasses, enjoying the sun's heat, and nearly asleep in the clear mountain air. This was Africa? This was great!

In my absence, Brad and Angelo had started to clean the hut. All of us felt a little guilt over the attempt to save money at the park entrance. This wouldn't make it right, but this place was a wreck and so was the garbage dump out back. They had done most of it by the time I returned, and the three of us finished it off in another hour. Then, we split up and hiked around to various viewpoints. I found a place where a combination of grass and moss led right up to the edge of a small lake. There was no wind and the sun was so hot at 11 A.M. that I took off my shirt and was soon asleep. When I woke up, I decided to return to the hut for something to read and a snack. In the distance, I saw a bank of clouds rolling toward the mountain. I thought it would probably rain later.

When the clouds hit, the temperature fell very fast. And it wasn't rain but snow that began to fall soon after. Out of the storm came four white Kenyans and their porters. One of the porters was hypothermic from carrying a heavy load through rain and snow while wearing thin cotton clothing. Angelo, Brad, and I donated some warm and dry clothes and fixed him some hot tea. He was soon feeling much better, but his news was not good. A porter from a climbing expedition had come down with AMS and had been escorted down the mountain. He, too, wasn't wearing adequate clothing for these unexpected conditions. The word was that he was lost in the storm. There would be no more word today. No one moved on the mountain now. Our group was somber and cold as we prepared to spend the night in the Mintos shelter.

Our Kenyan friends were off at 3:30 in the morning. Their goal was Point Lenana (16,355 feet), just above Austria Hut. They planned to return by afternoon and were leaving early to avoid another afternoon storm. They exited the hut in frigid conditions and stepped into a world of pure white under a starlit sky. We remained huddled in our sleeping bags. Even had we wanted to leave that early, we lacked the headlamps that most high-altitude trekkers carried. Sleep wouldn't come, but at least we were warm.

I left at 6 A.M., agreeing to meet my companions at Austria Hut. Ice had formed in the night along and over most of the runoff streams coming down from above. It wasn't completely frozen as I proved by immersing each foot in several ankle-deep pools. With that as the motivation to hurry, I did, changing into a dry pair of knee socks and putting on my extra pair of running shoes. It was not the best alternative, but the snow was not deep above the valley and I had a good chance to avoid frostbite.

It turned out to be one of the most beautiful and silent hikes I had ever done. The twin peaks that made up Mt. Kenya loomed above me and I moved in muffled silence up rockfall after rockfall. When the sun came up, the reflection from the snow was dazzling. At the same time, it was possible to look far down the buttress of the mountain and see the jungle below. There, it would be hot and steamy already.

Austria Hut was nearly deserted when I arrived and I picked out three of the very best sleeping places imaginable. Then I talked with some of the porters who were there and some young German men who were hoping to climb one of the peaks: Batian. It was warm in the hut as the sun filtered through Plexiglas windows onto the boards of the various sleeping lofts. Outside, the wind swept up from the various valleys and swirled up onto the glaciers and rock. Huge boulders stood outside the hut and gave shelter to various people who soaked up some of the morning warmth. On the mountainside of the hut, a steep descent wound through tire-sized boulders to a lake. It was called "curling lake," the site of some very high altitude sporting games by early British explorers. Frozen year round and fed by the glacier above, the lake provided water only where holes had been made along the edge of the ice cover. Water could be boiled or "iodined" and I made several trips with the water bottle before I felt adequately hydrated from my rapid ascent.

One of the porters was a huge and well-muscled man named Stephan. He seemed quite the happiest of anyone at the lodge and received a great deal of deference from the other porters. As I talked with him, I discovered why. He was a climbing guide and regularly led climbers from all over the world up various routes on Nelion and Batian—the twin peaks of Mt. Kenya. Even better, he was the first Kenyan to have attempted the summit of Everest. While the expedition had not succeeded, he was preparing to go back with another group in the next several years. We were both glad to be able to share our tales of the Khumbu Valley. When he asked if I had seen any of the marathoners training near base camp, I was able to tell him a bit about Pierre Andre Gobet and the Gurkha runners. We spent a couple of hours talking while he sorted out his gear for tomorrow's climb.

Stephan told me an interesting story about a Meru tribesman named Efreme who had been found atop Nelion in 1979. He was barefoot and dressed in well-worn street clothes. Less than five feet tall and under one hundred pounds, he had ascended the peaks of Mt. Kenya on a number of occasions. Having felt the temperatures and seen the rock faces on both peaks, I could only wonder if this was a story designed for the gullibility of tourists. Later investigation showed that Stephan was, if anything, understating the case.

I asked Stephan about the brown trout and expected to be laughed at. Instead, he told me that he had often seen tourists fly fishing in streams in the valleys. The British had stocked streams worldwide during the days of colonization so that sport fishing would be available. This area had been stocked in the 1930s.

Angelo and Brad arrived at about 1 P.M. and were stronger than they had been in a while. Angelo, however, was showing some of the early signs of AMS—primarily the headache—and we were prepared to descend if he became worse. Their arrival had not been the only influx of bodies. Suddenly, the once empty hut seemed quite full. Porters with other climbing and trekking groups had arrived and taken every place I had reserved. I couldn't say much because their groups had permits, and I didn't want to reveal that we didn't. When the three of us finally found a place, I was in the kitchen on a small shelf about fifteen feet up the wall. Brad was on the floor near a doorway, and Angelo was on a dining room table.

I couldn't go to sleep until the last of the cooking and cleaning was done because the kerosene would asphyxiate me. My sleeping perch was warm, but the stay in it would be brief. Angelo had a version of the same problem in that he couldn't "get his head down" until all the campers were through eating. Because of the numbers and space available, the dorm ate in shifts. Brad could lie down any time he wanted, but he needed to be a heavy sleeper because frequent calls of nature would open and close the door all night. It was difficult to tell who had the best of it.

I finally fell into a headachey sleep around 11:00. There were some vivid dreams in color and then a dream where I smelled kerosene and heard the clanking of carabiners. The last dream was a 3:30 reality as Stephan and another porter began to fix breakfast and pack up their gear. There was no sense in trying to die in the rafters; it was too easy. I climbed down and talked quietly with the two Kenyans as they worked efficiently toward an early start. Stephan's lunch sandwich consisted of two slices of bread and a two-inch thick slab of cheese. Two of those were added to a few apples and the lunch bag was ready.

I stepped outside for a minute or two to escape the kerosene stench and to perhaps cure my headache. Cryogenics and Austria Hut offer the same solution. The wind, cold air, and lack of cloud cover combined to nearly freeze me solid. I spent some time looking at the differences in the equatorial night sky and sought some familiar constellations. Then I looked up at the peaks and out to the lights of the valley villages. Finally, I retreated inside, willing to trade the cold for the effects of the kerosene.

In the last fifty years of climbing on this mountain, thirty people have died. More than a dozen of the bodies remain there. All but six died on the descent— a strange statistic considering the relative safety of abseiling. As with most high-altitude climbing in glaciated areas, early mornings were usually ideal. Later in the day, warmer conditions could cause rockfalls and avalanches. That explained the early departure of our climbers.

Within an hour the group had left with their smiling guide and their head-lamps. Brad and Angelo were kind enough to come and get me and point out that where six bodies had been, there were now six spaces. And, there were six sleeping bags and pads. By throwing our own bags on top of those, we were in absolute padded luxury: warm, dry, and comfortable.

Angelo was worse and was now a bit nauseated. His Australian sense of humor was being tested and all three of us knew that we had to descend soon. Point Lenana was only a few hundred yards above us and the brief increase in height might make him worse. Whether he could summon the strength to make it was the issue. We decided to pack up our equipment and make a decision at that time. We could then all descend the Naro Moru trail, or have Angelo wait at the hut while we ascended, or try to all make the ascent. Angelo was to make the best decision.

When the time came, we all went slowly to the top, took pictures of some spectacular vistas, and came down very quickly. Then, we swung our packs to our backs and started the long trek toward Naro Moru. With luck, we expected to make it out of the park that day. Normally, the guidebooks said, the hike to the exit took two full days. Getting out of the park itself would be interesting because of our unregistered status. For now, we used the bent leg shuffle that heavily laden porters use on steep downhills and headed for the oxygenated warmth below.

We passed beautiful rock formations, lakes, and finally lobelia and some real vegetation. Angelo improved dramatically and within two hours of rapid descent, Brad and I had trouble keeping up with him. His quick wit returned; he was soon chattering away in Kiswahili, American English, and every Australian dialect he could remember. It was a happier group when we finally reached some flatlands and took stock of our situation. We found an informational booklet and map and consulted it for our best route. It was during that reading that we first saw the words "vertical bog." I wondered what it meant.

Just past a place called Mackinder's Hut, we found out. The trail became a mother's worst nightmare. Mud was everywhere. It wasn't just bad on the trail; off the trail was worse. At first, it was bog on the flatlands and we slogged along with packs that suddenly were real burdens. When we slipped, as we often did, the packs shifted unexpectedly and avoiding falls involved some quick contortions. When we sank, as we often did, the packs made extrication an energy-sapping exercise. After a very long time of this, we were all of the opinion that it didn't seem to be getting much worse. We had forgotten about the word vertical.

The landscape tilted and we tilted right along with it. Now a jump from rock tip to hummock to tussock had a real consequence for a miss. Falls were significantly aided by gravity. Landings were harder. Already weak from a few missed meals and a hard ascent, Angelo started to slow down. Brad went on ahead and his long legs soon had him out of sight. The bog seemed to never end, and a few more hours went by before we could see the relay tower that the map said marked the beginning of level ground. Hopefully, it would also be dry ground. When we reached Brad, we were all in agreement that the ascent of Mt. Kenya from this side would be exceptionally difficult. In fact, we would probably have done the ascent and descent from the Chagoria side except for the long walk out. Less than a hundred feet from the relay tower we struck a dry road.

The map and guidebook had been helpful and now offered some advice: "BEWARE. BIG GAME ANIMALS. STAY ON THE ROAD. YIELD RIGHT OF WAY. Several signs along the road were quite large and explicit. When we saw these signs, restating the danger we were now in, we all slung our packs over one shoulder and walked the next nine kilometers planning what we would climb in the event of a rogue anything. I made the remark that I didn't have to be fast enough to outrun the buffalo or elephant, I just had to be fast enough to outrun my two companions. That almost assured me that at the first sign of trouble I was going to have two additional heavy packs hanging around my neck. "Here," as they say, "carry this refrigerator with you."

Finally, we arrived at a point where we could see the park entrance about a mile down the road. If we were to sneak out in the same manner that we had entered, we needed to wait until late evening. Our food supply was almost gone. Dinner consisted of tuna fish covered slabs of onion. We called them breadless sandwiches and washed them down with some Kool-Aid flavored water. It was while slicing the onions with my Swiss Army knife that I noticed something on one of the blades. My name was engraved: "B. Michael Dennison." I hadn't seen that before. I turned the blade over. "Friends Always" was on the other side. It was the perfect time to discover a delayed example of friendship here in the jungles of Africa. Rick's gift was even better than I had thought. I felt better. With what was coming up, I needed to.

Bypassing the two opposing huts that we could see was one option. It meant leaving the road and following a river that was far below us. I was selected to scout the area—probably due to my comment on outrunning people and not animals. There seemed to be a trail near where we sat, so I started down toward the sound of the water. Within fifty yards I was in a tunnel of interlaced and overhead branches. It was much darker, hotter, and quieter than it had been in the open corridor of the roadway. The trail was obviously not man-made—a fact that I soon realized from the way the bamboo and small trees were bent or broken. The trail twisted a lot, too, and I couldn't see more than ten feet of trail at any one time. My steps were increasingly slow and my imagination was increasingly fast. The fear was real, too. I was descending a slippery and steep slope. Meeting a denizen of this particular jungle would mean racing up a trail toward the road. My screams, if I were lucky enough to generate them, would precede me to the road, but all I would find would be three packs on the ground and two friends in a tree. I turned around and retraced my slips and slides until I was back with Brad and Angelo. We continued to wait.

The second alternative was to stay on the road and to sneak by the guards in the dark. Finally, it was time. We started forward and discovered that the two guard posts had been abandoned some time ago—perhaps years. It was the park entrance all right, but not the new one. Between the old one and the new one was a village, and we were soon wandering down the streets of a nice settlement. We were jumpy; this time about what might happen if we were caught without permits. We had several stories ready and finally decided on one. There was no feeling like being ten years old again, and trying to make up an excuse that someone would believe. None of us felt very comfortable with the story that a fourth companion had become ill and had been taken to the hospital in Chagoria, and in our haste to arrange the evacuation, our official documents were also taken down. Since it was late at night, we reasoned that there would be no one at the park's other station high on the mountain. Therefore, no one would be able to verify that we had never paid or officially entered the park.

Like those who lie only often enough to be truly bad at it, we lacked confidence in our own story. We certainly wouldn't have believed it. However, instead of improving on it, we had started to speculate on what the penalty was for illegal park use. Our imaginations were working better for punishments than for viable excuses and we started to worry in earnest.

Two men exited a house and approached us. We tried our story out on them. One offered to drive us to Naro Moru in his car. The fee was reasonable and Naro Moru was still more than ten miles away. That would be an all-night walk and we had just done what most trekkers do in two days—just to get here. We agreed. Nothing was mentioned about a guard post or a gate or an entrance...nothing.

A mile later, we saw why. This was a magnificent entrance with a huge fence, large swinging gates, and an armed guard. It looked a lot like the enclosure in the film *King Kong*. This was not going well. The soldier was very professional and looked very serious. We took turns being a spokesman—probably so that we could try to improve on what we each thought was the weak delivery of the others. Finally, the guard asked us to wait in the car and he went inside to use the telephone. All the scenarios played out in silence as we tried not to talk in front of our driver. Had we been told that the guard was calling to have a new cell prepared or to get enough people together for some shooting practice, we would not have been surprised.

The minutes flew by like hours, but the guard finally returned. I wondered if he ever set that gun down. He asked us to write down our names, our passport numbers, and our country of origin; then he waved us through. I didn't know about the others, but I was in considerable shock. It was the one alternative that we had never considered: he had accepted our story.

The end of our problems left us drained but not totally stupid, and we were concerned when our driver stopped to make a phone call about five miles down the road. We waited and wondered what that would mean. Even paranoiacs have real enemies, and this was a total stranger with three foreigners at his mercy. When he returned to the car, he assured us that everything was fine. It was very dark now and on a deserted stretch of highway, we suddenly developed some not-so-fine engine trouble. I, for one, didn't like the idea that he had flashed his lights several times as he pulled over to the side of the road. And, I didn't like the idea of our driver being out of our sight in front of the raised hood of the car. This didn't look very good. There was no record of our having ever been in the park—except for one scrap of paper at the Naro Moru guard station. We had cameras, camping gear, expensive backpacks, and documents.

We had certainly suffered more mental anguish than we had saved in money, and we had also learned and relearned an important lesson. And here, on a narrow dirt road in East Africa, we learned something new about paranoia. After a few minutes of sweating the details of our imminent demise, both doors opened and in climbed the driver and a woman. Our driver had clearly been the patriarch of the household we had seen him exit on our walk through the village. This woman was not his wife. We realized that he had combined a lot of circumstances to allow him to see his lady friend and to be well paid for it. Having thought that your life was going to end in a hail of gunfire, this turn of events put us in stitches for the rest of the ride.

We were tired but feeling fine. The hotel where we were deposited was not one frequented by Westerners, and the patrons stared at us as we walked through the bar and restaurant on the way to our rooms. I drew the first shower and then took my clean self downstairs to see if I could get something to eat that we hadn't cooked. No one smiled much and I wasn't surprised. I had that effect on people. But I knew that Brad would be here soon and at that point no one would be safe.

Sure enough, Brad and Angelo were not too far behind and the jukebox was soon playing some songs that the three of us couldn't understand. Brad started to dance with our waitress and the girl serving drinks. Other patrons joined in. People danced alone or in pairs or in groups. I began to worry when the cook joined in. Everyone was smiling at the lanky American with the pony-tail and the obvious good time he was having. Africa was one adventure after another. And there was a safari coming up.

I remembered something I had read in a book in Nairobi: "*Ex-Africa semper aliquid novi*" (from Africa there is always something new). I couldn't wait.

A waterfall cascades into lush vegetation. Africa would use up all your film if you tried to capture every such beautiful scene.

CHAPTER 12
AFRICAN SAFARI

Nothing in Africa is adjacent to anywhere.
– Proverb

The African safari had changed and was continuing to do so. Once, it was reserved for a very few of the very rich, and there were many elements of danger involved. Now, it was often a luxurious stay in a rustic but nice hotel and was conducted from a minivan. Still, the animals were wild, and all the modern niceties couldn't cover up the need for signs prohibiting walking beyond the hotel's compound.

We, on the other hand, were traveling by way of a very old green Toyota bus and camping in tents near lakes or on riverbanks. Someone near the back of the bus made reference to the similarity of traveling inside a plant stem—noting that green was not his color of choice. It was scheduled to be an eight-day safari.

On the first day out of Nairobi, we traveled to Lake Baringo. I had seen flamingos in zoos and had had a brief look at this same habitat on PBS. Nothing had prepared me for mile after mile of pink and black. In a stark country almost devoid of trees, the lake and the birds offered a brilliant contrast. There was mile after mile of standing flamingos and mile after mile of flying flamingos. And the flying was what I had not seen before. The black feathers of their underwings were part of the graceful figures they cut as hundreds of them traveled up or down the lake. And it didn't take long to see that those birds flying with the wind were twenty or more feet in the air. Those flying against the wind were just above the caps of the waves and in a tight V-formation. Flamingos were drafting each other like race car drivers.

We had come to the lake to see the flamingos and to visit the hot springs, and we filmed and looked for an hour or more. Then, we climbed back in the bus and left for Lake Bogoria—a soda lake and our evening's encampment. Brad and Charlie (New Zealand) were along for this trip, and Brad did his best to disown us both. Not an early riser and certainly not a runner, he was suddenly traveling with two marathoners that seemed eager to talk of nothing else. Brad had asked me for a fitness program of push-ups and sit-ups and had been very conscientious about working with me daily. But running and early mornings were out. He was even less impressed when one of the girls on the bus went for a jog as soon as she arrived. It was our introduction to Ria, from Vancouver, Canada.

At our camping site our guide, "Banana," informed us that we were not to walk down to the lake after dark, not to go into the water under any circumstances, and to avoid hippos (*kiboko*). Funny how we listened to a figure of authority when he told us how to save our own lives. Those with guidebooks on Africa were busy informing the rest of us that a *kiboko* can outrun a man on land, has a nasty disposition, and accounts for more deaths than any other African animal. So much for what we learned at zoos. The yawn we typically see on a nature series is in fact an aggressive display.

Charlie, Brad, and I walked down to the lake just after we arrived and passed many campers with rented vehicles. This was a popular spot and wasn't unlike many roadside camping areas in the states. There were tents, VW vans with pop-up roofs, bicycles, and generators. At the water's edge it took a second look to realize that there was a motor boat in the water and that several water skis were positioned on a rack on the back. Unless I had misheard, these waters were not particularly safe, so the boat was a mystery. Several pairs of small flapping ears and large blinking eyes peered at us from twenty feet offshore. We knew that the water at that distance was likely to be at least one *kiboko* deep.

Down the beach a few hundred yards several large hippos grazed. This was the kind of reality that zoos hadn't prepared me for. These were wild and dangerous animals, and they were not far enough away to guarantee safety. The fact that no one else seemed particularly concerned helped quell my doubts, but as one hippo trotted rather quickly back toward the lake where we stood, the temptation was to trot rather quickly back to the bus. Brad, meanwhile, had noticed that I had been backing away from the hippo and toward the water's edge of a small inlet. He was concerned that if I continued to retreat, I was likely to step on several of the crocodiles (*mambas*) that were resting almost out of the water. In no time at all, I shared that concern.

The crocs were not large ones; some were as small as two feet in length. The largest that we saw as we walked along the beach was probably four feet. They seemed timid enough and retreated when our intent was definitely to approach them. I remembered that they grew to be really big and I remembered that they could also outrun a man. So far, running didn't seem to be a good method of self-defense. Brad was smiling at that thought.

After we set up the tents and had dinner, it was a thoughtful busload of campers that contemplated the one-block walk to the bathrooms in the middle of the night. Tents had been positioned away from large stands of vegetation to avoid the inadvertent step of a browsing herbivore in the dark. A smiling Banana wished us a good night's sleep as he climbed into his sleeping sack atop the bus. Value rigidity wasn't just about culture anymore; I was back to the monkey who couldn't see the big picture. Banana could help me find values and methods to stay alive; everyone else seemed quite clear on that point, too.

The next morning we were all up early—except Brad, who was decreasing his reputation for punctuality and drugfree living. We were going to travel 350 kilometers before our next encampment. Banana would again be our driver. There was no power steering and no automatic transmission; he was one tough person. There was a view window above the windshield in the raised portion of the bus. I could see out of it if I stood up. That sounded all right to me and I was hoping to ride there for the next eight hours. We had lunch in Maralal and then we were off in the direction of Lake Turkana. It was on this particular leg of the drive that the gearbox gave out. While we were assured that our driver and cooks could fix it, there was no guess as to the time involved. Charlie and I asked if it would be all right if we ran to the evening's campsite. Surprisingly, Banana gave that idea a thumbs up. Perhaps he shared Brad's suspicion of traveling in the company of runners. Only later did we realize that he had not told us exactly where the night's encampment was.

After a quick change of shoes, we were off into the African heat. The pace was about seven-minute miles and that was too fast for that kind of swelter. Fortunately, it was late afternoon and we were able to run in the shade of some hills for a few miles. And then we became famous. The Samburu people who live in the area had seen a lot of Westerners—as passengers on a bus or in a car. No one stopped here because there was no reason to. Now, suddenly, there were two half-naked white men running down the road, which turned out to be an occasion of great moment for all of us. Sharp-eyed Samburu men, women, and children spotted us from their positions near their herds. Many rushed on a course to intercept us. They were smiling or laughing and called out to us. Children of four or five raced from nearby huts and then stepped back in obvi-ous fear of having misjudged just how far they wanted to be from the *mazunga* (white foreigners). It didn't seem to matter if my Kiswahili was understood here as anything I said was met with smiles and waves. It was hard to tell who was having the most fun.

A small village appeared a few miles later and we had been running for almost two hours. At a Catholic mission we asked a priest in a Jeep for directions. He was almost as whelmed as the people of the countryside by our unexplained presence, but pointed to a continuation of our previous road and said, "Nine kilometers." That seemed a bit more than Banana had indicated and we talked about whether to wait there for the bus or not. Not.

After what seemed to be a long nine kilometers, there was another village. There were no Westerners here at all. Many Samburu men and some women immediately gathered around. The men were closest; the women seemed a bit frightened and stared from about twenty feet. My Kiswahili greeting and inquiry about the news of the village was directed to an old man who had squatted down in front of us and balanced by holding onto his spear. He did not speak English. From his quizzical expression as I spoke, we concluded that in his opinion I didn't speak Kiswahili. After a few painful minutes, he seemed to have decided that the words I was saying were almost Kiswahili-like enough for him to respond. Instead, he beckoned two young men to approach and stand on either side of us. Yes, they assured us, they spoke English. Their names were Phillip and Ben. One was Samburu; the other was Bantu. They quickly translated questions from both sides.

The old man was indeed their leader. He asked if Charlie was my son. I assured him that he was not. He wanted to know why we were running when nothing was chasing us; he smiled to show that it was a joke. Then he wanted to know why someone so old was running. That was the second time he had indicated that I was a bit too mature for what I was doing. We compared ages and he was assuredly two years younger than I was. He was 43! He seemed astonished at my age—as I often was. Perhaps it was in the translation that everyone seemed to be having such a good time. Ben and Phillip were smiling and laughing. When Charlie started to juggle three rocks and I did a few handstands, it was obvious that the circus had come to town.

What hadn't come to town was the bus. It was now dusk and there was no sign that it was coming. We had offers for free lodging at this village but knew that we would now have to retrace our steps. We hoped that didn't mean all of them. Either this was not the stopping point, or the bus had more serious problems than Banana thought. Before we left, Ben showed us a wound he had sustained on his calf and asked if we had any suggestions. It was a deep laceration into the muscle and must have been very painful. It was also in danger of being infected. Villages were havens for crippled people who had lost limbs to infections caused by wounds no worse than his. We mentioned keeping the wound clean and offered to try to get him some medication if this was the road we would be on when we were again united with our party. We waved to everyone and started back in the direction from which we came.

It was now completely dark and there were no villagers or country residents on the road. We remembered the fenced-in compounds we had passed all day in the bus. It was the kind of fencing to keep out animals rather than to keep them in. The buildings were called *manyattas* and the fenced in areas were called *kraals*—at least that was our interpretation of what had been said to us. Banana had told us that they were cow dung and wicker huts surrounded by thorn fences. It was no use speculating on the absence of any people and the possible meaning of the enclosure barricades. I told Charlie the story of the lowland portions of the Naro Moru descent and the Cape buffalo and rogue elephant stories. He was not impressed but guessed that he could outrun me because I was old enough to be his father. In my best Kiswahili, I told him not to push it.

We saw headlights at about that time and, sure enough, Banana had sent the bus out to find us. Camp, it turned out, was before the Catholic mission village and we would not have seen them even if we had waited there. We had overrun the goal by twenty-eight kilometers. The cooks had saved us a meal and there was plenty of lemonade to drink. We endured a lot of good-natured kidding—led primarily by Brad. Sleep came soon after the meal was finished and the dishes were done.

We arrived at our lake campsite the next day—on the southern shores of Lake Turkana. We were able to stop and see Ben and to give him quite a lot of valuable bandages and cleaning solutions. Fortunately, he understood the need for those modern medicines and wanted badly to save the leg. We instructed him to get to the Catholic Mission as soon as he could for further treatment or to travel to Nairobi.

The village was quite large and boasted a swimming pool of fresh water near our camping site. We would be here for several days before heading to an area where wild animals would be found. Here, we were among some tribes whose way of life had changed very little, and some whose way of life was almost totally different. Samburu huts were of wood and cattle dung, and the roof was thatched elephant grass with hides for waterproofing. We were camped close to several and our tents were on a grassy hillside with a view of the lake.

We did a brief excursion to see the El Moro tribe. There were fewer members of this tribe than of all the African tribes. Just outside their small village on the banks of the lake was a church with a cross and a Christian graveyard. The faces, shoulders, and hair of the people we saw were painted in red and orange. While everyone we saw seemed healthy enough, we were told that most of the tribes in the area suffered from tuberculosis. We saw fewer than a hundred El Moro in their single village.

The Turkanas, on the other hand, had 200,000 people, and most of them raised cattle. It was their source of wealth. They herd several kinds of animals, but cattle are their pride. I had heard that the Masai phlebotomized their cattle and drank the blood in ceremonies, but I was not sure about the Turkana. The tribe did not do well in times of famine caused by drought because plant death moved right up the food chain and wiped out their animals. While this seemed like an isolated spot to us, there was a story that we heard from the owner of a local hotel that was fascinating and sad:

Evidently the Norwegians had attempted to help the Turkana people. The Norwegians decided that the Turkana needed to have a drought-proof economy. The Turkana people had a lake 154 miles long by 35 miles wide in the midst of their territory. So why not cultivate fish? Why not frozen fish? Why not frozen fish shipped to Nairobi?

I don't know how many millions the two-story fish-freezing plant cost, but the road to it cost 20 million dollars. Diesel-powered generators had to be brought in and a large research ship, the *Iji,* was taken apart, shipped in, and put back together on the lake. To make the Turkana throw themselves into the plan whole-heartedly, the 20,000 Turkana involved had most of their herd animals destroyed. Nets and boats were provided and the Norwegians taught skills. Things went swimmingly.

Drought couldn't kill the fish in a lake that large (or the *mambas* and *kibokos* that resided there in large numbers). But it would dry up the bay from which eighty percent of the catch was coming. The *Iji* was suddenly at mud anchor and the catch was not doing much better. The amount of fresh water needed to run the plant exceeded the supply. Lake Turkana did not exactly qualify as suitable fresh water. But that didn't matter because the cost of cooling fish from over one hundred degrees to below freezing was more than they could be sold for—anywhere. After a few days of operation, the plant was shut down. The natives called it "the new mountain," and it sat empty and useless in the equatorial heat.

Anthropological studies tell us that in Turkana culture, fishing is for incompetents. A last resort. Fish were generally not eaten unless people were starving. Those who fished and did not have livestock were beneath contempt. It was a sad story.

We were fortunate enough to find several young Turkana warriors who were happy to explain about their life there. We noted that they dressed in skins, and they explained that there was no textile craft. Iron was for spears and tools and they were quite proud of their skill in fashioning both. The women we saw carrying water jugs on their heads often walked for over seven miles while carrying six gallons. After Nepal, I doubted nothing told to me by people who inhabited a region where privation was the rule.

Some of the men we saw decorated their hair with feathers. Others wore a skin cap made from a cow's udder and painted blue. These two young men had just completed the initiation rite for manhood. Where they once carried a spear-like piece of iron to ward off hyenas and other scavengers, now they had an authentic spear. Elders also presented them with shields that were made from the hides of hippo, rhino, elephant, or buffalo, four highly dangerous animals, and we tried to picture even a group of spear-carrying warriors facing any of those. Warrior became more than just a word.

For fighting among other tribes, men wore sharp-edged arm rings with a leather cover to render the weapons harmless. During battle, they were worn around the biceps; during less aggressive times, they were covered and worn around the wrist.

The women we saw around us wore a great deal of adornment. Our new friends told us that the way such ornamentation was arranged told a great deal: consecration to god, births or deaths in the family, marital status, son's initiation, even a husband's long absence could be told. The woman's hair was greased with butter or fat.

Both of these young men had tattoos on their chests and bellies. Neither had as many as one of the elder members standing off to one side. Many of his scars, we were told, were made by the witch doctor who was letting evil spirits out with the incisions. It was one thing to read of such things; it was quite another to see the living proof. We asked if it was permissible to know about marriage? *Hakuna matata* (no problem).

Marriage began with a kidnapping. While it was real, both parties agreed to it. Later, sometimes years, the marriage was ratified by a special ceremony and a bull was killed and the bride sprinkled with the dung of the animal.

Hyenas and vultures took care of the dead. Only the mother and father of a hut, or other important people, were buried. Unlike in Thailand, burial seemed to be an honor here. We thanked the young warriors for their information and returned to our tents.

Brad, meanwhile, had been to the only bar in town. It was run by some German ex-pats, and he had been informed about the Samburu tribe. We were interested in comparing the two cultures since they were geographically so close.

Samburu warriors wore an ivory ring in their earlobe. That confirmed that Charlie and I had, in fact, run to a Samburu village. They ate a diet of milk mixed with blood, meat, honey, and butter. The red ochre that we saw at the El Moro village indicated warrior status here. The males were circumcised as one of the many initiation rites. Showing fear of the ceremony brought great dishonor. There were other stages to manhood and other ceremonies. One that we found quite different involved swearing in front of his mother that he would not eat meat seen by a married woman.

Marriage was best done on an even day nearest the new moon. The bride-groom gave gifts. One example was a cow with calf and three other cows. The latter were for the father-in-law, the brother-in-law, and for the oldest relative of the bride. The bride had her own initiation rites and was circumcised on the day of the wedding. Then the groom and best man (and friends) would push a bull into the hut where it would be killed. That concluded the wedding contract.

Out of politeness, Brad had to explain our own initiation rites, marriage ceremonies, burial customs, and ornamentation. He would not tell us what he said but fixed us with an enigmatic smile. Perhaps he thought he could kill us with curiosity. It nearly worked.

During our stay, we noted that the lake seemed to change color. Sometimes it was blue. But, at other times, it could be gray or green. Banana told us that it was due to algae. The wind would often stir the surface enough to mix the algae and change the color. We asked him about the kind of fish in the lake, and he told us there were Nile perch that averaged about two hundred pounds. Some, he told us, weighed nearly four hundred pounds. He told us that there were from ten to twenty thousand Nile crocodiles in the lake, and he pointed to an island just off a peninsula as a good place to observe some of them.

We concluded our visit with an attempt to find some of the large crocs on the nearby island. In the heat of the day, five of us decided to walk instead of paying for a guide and a boat. A narrow land bridge was under a few feet of water and we used that to carefully negotiate our way to the island. Hippo's eyes and ears were visible just offshore and none of us wanted to be swimming, which could also be an invitation to crocs. After two hours of wandering in extreme heat and with no water, we saw some natives sitting in the shade of some rocks. After appropriate Kiswahili greetings were exchanged and all of the good news was confirmed, I asked, *"Mamba wapi?"* (Crocodiles where?). An amused and relaxed fisherman explained that crocs, El Moro fishermen, and hippos were only on the banks of the lake in the early morning and evenings. What he didn't explain spoke volumes. I had noticed the same thing about people running in Carefree, Arizona, in the middle of a 112-degree summer day. We returned to Banana, the bus, and the rest of our group.

Finally, we were on our way back toward some big game country. We were sure that this would prove to be exciting, too. I stationed myself at the front of the bus again. For mile after mile I saw the sentinel figures of lone herdsmen off in the distance. Sometimes I saw men or women walking along some of the trails. Because most of the people were barefoot, they used a series of trails through the countryside. Each footpath could be seen because it showed signs of a great deal of use, and every small pebble had been removed from its surface. That, of course, made perfect sense. These are the "roads" in this part of Africa, and every person in a tribe is a caretaker of that public trust.

It took a few minutes to register that I was not seeing another human being in the distance. Walking completely upright across the African countryside was a large male baboon. He appeared so human-like that no one else noticed for a few more minutes. Just after they did, he dropped back to a four-point gait and moved rapidly away from us. Then I saw an ostrich. I continued to bat almost zero in the knowing-about-the-country division. In less than fifteen minutes there were no herdsmen on any horizon and we saw reticulated giraffes (*twiga*) instead. Then we saw zebra (*punda milia*). It was clear that we were near the animals and our camp for the night. If it was dangerous at Lake Bogoria, what would it be like here?

What it would be like was soon perfectly obvious. Signs were posted everywhere. Some allowed you to use various footpaths, but only during full daylight. Others marked the boundary that you were not allowed to cross at any time. We drove past a nice-looking hotel and didn't even bother with the name; we wouldn't be staying there. We continued on to another of our nightly camping areas. Brad, Charlie, Ria, and I were out of the bus in a hurry and quite keen to do whatever exploring we could. As soon as the tents were set up, we struck out for the lodge we had passed.

People in the lodge were more than just a cut above the budget backpacker group. It was a safe bet that some of their vests cost more than our entire safaris. We knew they would dine in absolute luxury while they were there. Still, there was a side to Africa that their style of travel would never reveal to them. And it was just as well. We ate lunch in a very nice, raised, open-thatched dining room. Baboons and Marabou storks crossed and recrossed the dry riverbed that ran parallel to the hotel. There was a salt lick on the other side a few hundred yards away, and hotel guests could come here after dark to spotlight nocturnal visitors.

Others from our camp drifted over to join us for soft drinks. Brad and Charlie elected to walk back to camp along the riverbed; they assumed that it was safe during the day. Although it was not posted, several signs indicated the danger of straying from manmade paths. Ria and I took the trail and arrived at camp first. We sat in front of her tent to talk. That location put us at the edge of the riverbank and afforded a great view of our own baboon and Maribou stork population.

I had been teased a bit for my front-of-the-bus stance but as a result of my position had become the official camp spotter of things unique and worthwhile. My vision was quite acute at long distances and I had been charged with informing everyone about what would soon be visible to them. Ria didn't seem to have internalized that particular belief about my visual competence. She pointed across the wash and asked me whether I could tell if she was looking at a log? I looked the several hundred yards to approximately where she was pointing, and I assured her that logs didn't rest in the shade with their mouths open.

What everyone but Ria had missed was the presence of fifteen to twenty very large crocodiles scattered along both banks of the dry riverbed. A short inspection disclosed a few that were much nearer, and therefore appeared even larger. Brad and Charlie, who had arrived just prior to Ria's question, were much paler than they had been in a long time. The crocs must not have been very hungry. Or maybe they were content to rest and not outrun these human intruders. Where in all of the shows featuring crocodiles were they featured lounging in the shade of trees with no water in sight in any direction? That didn't make sense. Also, their open mouths and immobility were obviously a way to cool off in addition to the shade. This was fascinating. Brad indicated that he might be willing to add running to his training. Or sign reading, Ria added. Brad looked relieved.

Early the next morning we boarded the bus to see what animals Banana could find. The first thing we saw was that the great outdoors was constantly trying to come indoors. Banana thought his Toyota bus was a Jeep, and he took it through thickets that looked impassable. Anyone with an arm resting on the window frame would carry the scars of this trip for a long time. After that discovery, others learned that some of the bushes went after faces. In Arizona, we mountain bike riders had called most of the vegetation "wait-a-minute bushes." That was a mild epithet compared to what we called these. Since it was too hot to close the windows, the passengers nearest the windows were soon an experienced brush-dodging lot.

Impala were grazing just outside the campground, and just beyond them oryx fed near a stand of trees. We had seen squirrels, storks, and the ever-present baboons while we had our quick breakfast. Now every turn of the road seemed to present a different animal. There were even pheasants and grouse, which along with the squirrels, surprised me. We all hoped to see some carnivores and Banana wasn't long in presenting those. A few miles further down the riverbed we stopped a few hundred yards from five grazing zebras (I had learned to pronounce zebra to rhyme with Debra as per most "colonials"). The animals seemed unconcerned enough, but they were almost constantly looking our way and sniffing the breeze. It was Ria again who saw why. Off to our left were three motionless lions—all pointed toward the zebras. Their tails moved and their eyes blinked, but that was all the movement we saw. Someone behind me mentioned that these were female because they lacked manes; that same someone then wondered why they were hunting in a group. They crouched near a large boulder not twenty feet from our bus.

Nothing happened for ten minutes and one of the lions finally stood and started to wander off. Almost immediately, the other two followed. It was apparent that these were immature males, not females, and we all learned something about manes and lions. The lions learned about hunting techniques, zebras, and wind direction. Banana drove us to new ground.

We found lions again and this time they were feeding. The kill was a reticulated giraffe and the carcass had been fairly well cleaned. While there were no hyenas present, there were a number of scavenger birds attempting to outwit the two feeding lions. We drove up to a wash that intersected the riverbed. Along the top of this we were afforded a view of a leopard with a fresh kill. Moving

Resting along a jungle trail. It wasn't difficult to imagine the travails of early explorers, before there were any such passages.

A small herd of Tembo *wamdered by where we were silently watching two reticulated giraffe. We never got used to the lack of fences between us and the animals.*

like molten lava in and out of tree shadows, she could not be seen at times. Banana was proving to be capable of things we were not. We shared the same senses, but we certainly didn't apply them the same way. Between Ria and Banana, I was in danger of losing my title as camp spotter of things unique and worthwhile. The leopard appeared at the juncture of a rock and a tree and carried a small antelope into some branches above. Noise from another approaching minivan frightened her and she flowed down and out of our view and into the rocks below.

We did not discover the next predators. There were six minivans near some large trees and we arrived as quietly as Banana could manage. He needn't have worried. There were three cheetahs (*duma*) in the shade of a huge tree. Two were cubs. The mother had fed them and then herself. As she moved to the cub's sides, it was evident that we were not looking at a seventy-mile-per-hour killing machine. A full cheetah looked like the first animal that couldn't outrun a man— at least not without dragging a stomach over unfriendly terrain. I had heard of lions lying up after gorging themselves. A cheetah, with its small head and body built for speed, just looked a lot more ridiculous in the same condition.

During the next four hours, we saw elephants, monitor lizards, and more of the animals we had already seen. It was great excitement, but it brought up some thoughts about the original safaris. It must have been something to walk through these areas with no protection other than guns. Banana told us that it was now possible to go on a walking safari accompanied by a sharpshooter or two. Having watched the lions stalk some wary zebra, I would worry about such an excursion. For the rest of the day I imagined what it would be like for a Samburu boy during his rite of passage: trailing a lion with just a spear and no water or food. We had heard that such an initiation might go on for days and cover sixty or more miles.

On the last night of camp, Brad suggested that we do our push-up regimen in the ravine below camp. Banana and the cooks, Steve and Riki, wanted to join us. So did Ria. We started with fifteen repetitions. There was a fourteen-second rest, and then we did fourteen more. Then a thirteen-second rest, and we did thirteen. By the time we were at one, only Brad, Ria, and I were still doing strict repetitions. *Mingi* arms were shaking from the effort they were not used to. I told the men to stop when they felt that much fatigue, but I had forgotten that the presence of a woman would create a problem. Ria had been a gymnast and was still lean and fit. They would not stop while she continued. We did a few sets of slow pushups and stopped when it appeared that our friends would push too far. The next morning I expected not to be fed and perhaps not transported. Sure enough, Banana, Riki, and Steve were very sore. They fed all of us with great difficulty but seemed to be wary of Ria. They never lost track of where she was. In awe of a woman that fit, they forgot the source of their discomfort: me. It was a good thing, too.

The return to Nairobi was long and dusty, but we had accomplished a lot in eight days. Back at the Iqbal Hotel, we cleaned up and assembled everyone we could from the safari and Mt. Kenya trips and went out for a last night on the town. We had dinner at a restaurant called Carnivores. There were no apologies to vegetarians there. Some of my companions wondered how my normal bill of fare would stand up to a night of meat eating. They needn't have worried. We had eland, wildebeest, chicken, beef, and several others not identifiable from their Kiswahili name. Then we had salad, ice cream, strawberries, and cheesecake.

Brad led the after-dinner charge into a large area where a live band played. We were lucky enough to listen to a band play reggae, jazz, and most of Santana's best-known songs. It was a terrific change of pace from the wilds of Nelion and Batian or the shores of Lake Turkana. Our group was the last to leave after a very memorable night in Nairobi.

Everyone seemed to be going in different directions, and I was no exception.

Brad and Charlie were going on another safari—this time to the Masai Mara. I had heard that the Ruwenzori Mountains were not that far away, and that Uganda, where they were located, was no longer dangerous to tourists. I hoped to follow up on that lead and perhaps get to Zaire to see the mountain gorillas. If not, it would soon be time to leave Africa and make my way toward Turkey, Israel, and the Middle East.

I hadn't done much thinking about the meaning of life lately, which was strange because our lives had certainly been as much at risk here, as anywhere in Asia. I read back through some journal passages from the Iqbal Hotel era and looked for something profound. Banana and his skills seemed very important. He reminded me of Toy and our north Thailand trek. Both of them were looking at a world we couldn't see. Their knowledge and lore weren't anything we could grasp. I wasn't sure whether that meant we should try to learn what others knew or that we needed to learn that there are many ways to perceive the same things.

If there were answers in Africa, I needed first to be able to find the questions.

From the window of a train, we saw hundreds of smiling people. The smiles increased when they heard our attempts at Kiswahili.

CHAPTER 13
<u>RUWENZORI:</u>
Africa's Mountains of the Moon

The darkest thing about Africa has always been our ignorance of it.
– African Guidebook

I was in an alleyway in Nairobi and the sun had been gone for a half hour. As the dark had increased, people had moved toward me or sat on their haunches and looked streetward. A pile of luggage had grown as the number of people increased. Chickens cackled and struggled to be released. From where I stood, I could see what looked to be the handlebars of an elderly exercise bicycle. There would soon be a night bus and the destination would be the Ugandan border.

"They" said you should never take a night bus. They said it in Thailand and Malaysia. They said it in India and Nepal. And they said it here. Drivers worked huge hours and often took amphetamines to stay awake. Animals curled up for naps in the middle of the road. Larger animals, presumably, curled up for longer naps. This promised to be a night fraught with a lot more than just the unknown. Could Uganda match any of the adventures in the previous countries? Ria was asleep and I envied her that talent.

After Ria, Charlie, Brad, and I had finished our safari, we had tried to decide what to do next. I had asked some questions about Africa's Mountains of the Moon and had discovered that they weren't far away. Everyone thought that my description sounded like the most adventure we could have for the least amount of money, but Brad and Charlie wanted to go on one more safari with someone who appeared to be a little bit unscrupulous. We had all met him at one of the camping sites, and he was known to take people to places where the average tourist could not go. He operated by Jeep and was intent on telling us stories that made him sound very Hemingwayesque. But, they also made him sound likely to create problems for clients.

Ria and I elected to go on ahead and to meet them at one of the cities we would pass through. We arranged an elaborate message system based on guidebooks and then set out to organize our own transportation. My Canadian friend wasn't much over one hundred pounds and not much over five feet tall, but she had an absolutely fearless attitude and a great enjoyment of nearly everything that happened. That was what I thought during the safari; her actions would later show that I had underestimated her toughness and joy of life. For now, we had to survive another night bus and she was asleep.

I didn't fall asleep thinking about the danger. Sleep didn't come, but the Ugandan border finally did. It was a long walk just to get to the border guards. Many people walked along in brightly colored clothes and carried packages or animals for trade. In addition to the armed guards at the checkpoint, some heavy-duty fences stretched from horizon to horizon. It was amazing what an Uzi, albeit an old one, could do to the adrenal glands. Neither sleep nor its lack seemed at all important at that point. There were no other Westerners in sight, and it wasn't difficult to imagine that there never had been. Someone had told me that Uganda was safe, now. Well, that someone wasn't here and this didn't look much different than I had imagined when the trip had been planned.

You couldn't have read too many papers in the 1970s and early 1980s and missed the name of Idi Amin—"Mean" Idi Amin. I tried to remember everything I could, but it didn't seem to answer any of my questions. Amin had fled at some point. Some other African country had come to Uganda's aid and had helped overthrow his regime. There had been accusations of cannibalism and wholesale slaughter. The first new government hadn't done well for four or five years either. That was all I remembered. Who had replaced him? Was tourism a safe activity? What hadn't the smiling folks at the Ugandan Embassy in Nairobi told us? As we approached the series of guard huts, the wisdom of this trip seemed to be seriously in doubt. Everything seemed to be one huge question mark.

The unplanned nature of my trip had not kept me from reaching nearly all my African goals. I had been on a safari and had visited tribes and seen animals. And, I had climbed Mt. Kenya and seen snow on the equator. Now I was close to some mountains I had read about as a teenager: the Mountains of the Moon. Ptolemy had called them the Lunaes Montes thousands of years ago. Ruwenzori was roughly translated as "the place where clouds are boiled." I had first read about the Mountains of the Moon in the March 1962 issue of *National Geographic,* the home of red worms three feet long, chameleons with three horns, and butterflies the size of your head. I had never forgotten the article or the name. My source had told me that they were "very near Nairobi."

How close turned out to be almost three days of riding buses. First, we had to take the night bus to the border. From there we had to take a bus to the war-torn capital of Kampala. And after that, there would be a bus trip to a place called Kasese. We knew absolutely nothing about what it would take to trek in those mountains or what it would cost. But backpack travel often leads to this kind of situation, and after a while you expect the unexpected.

Brad and Charlie were probably two days or more behind us. We left them the first of several notes at an agreed-upon site. The guards posted the note on a board where tourists would see it. Other notes would be in other cities. We planned a leisurely trip through Uganda and hoped they would catch up with us.

We were tired and hungry after we walked across the border checkpoint. After the paperwork with the smiling government agents, we had breakfast. There was no need to wait until a bank opened; border towns take their neighbor's currency almost everywhere. If I couldn't sleep, at least I could eat. We ordered. In Nairobi, our food would have cost about 32 shillings apiece. Here it was 5,800 shillings. We hadn't been that hungry, had we? If we had just spent $175 U.S., then the Uganda trip was over. While the bill said 5,800 shillings, it was Ugandan and not Kenyan shillings that were being charged. The trick was to find out what was up in our new country. The war did more to Uganda than the killing and burning; the exchange rate was 1,200 shillingi to the U.S. dollar. That was about 24 to 1 versus Kenya. Breakfast had been a border town pricey $2.50 each. That covered a Spanish omelet, toast, *milo* (chocolate), and passion fruit juice. The monetary conversion took us days to get used to.

My trip to Uganda would have been a lot shorter had it not been for Ria. "Don't leave home without it" had a translation in Uganda; it meant: "Don't bring it here." I had learned not to carry large sums of money from one country to another because the exchange rate was costly. Uganda was the first country on my trip that did not advance money on a credit card, on any credit card. Ria's traveler's checks saved the day. She was such a good-natured person that she agreed to pay our respective ways until we returned to Nairobi.

I hadn't thought about what an exchange rate of 1,200 to 1 might mean in terms of paper currency. People would arrive at a bank with steamer trunks, fill them with notes and have strong helpers carry them out. The two hundred Canadian dollars became a backpack full of notes—the smallest of which was a denomination of one thousand. No cameras were allowed in the bank, for what I assumed were good and sufficient reasons. Money belts weren't totally useless, but they did give you the interesting contours of a large primate in the twenty-third month of pregnancy.

I stood on the bus for seven and a half hours on March 4 and had a terrific time on the third leg of our bus trip. We traveled from Kampala to Kasese. People were friendly, curious, and ready to join in the comedy that Westerners often present. Ria wedged herself into a space near the front door. There were no seats left after that and I had to stand. I wanted to be helpful and needed to do something active. Whenever the bus stopped to add or subtract riders, I would climb to the top. There, I helped load or unload luggage, and I ironed out the kinks from standing for so long. Of course, every time someone left, a seat became available—but I was scrambling around on the roof. The long-distance riders at first found this quite amusing and politely hid their chuckles when I returned to a full and seatless bus. After a few hours and a half dozen stops, even Ria had joined them to entreat me to take one of the seats that had become available. Finally, sensing that I wasn't the brightest Westerner in Uganda, they shamed a young man into standing next to a perfectly good and empty seat until I once again returned.

About halfway through the trip there was a roadblock. This was my first during the trip and the soldiers who boarded looked ominous. They each carried a short semi-automatic and went about the business of checking all documentation. A stout woman took the passport I offered her, opened it, and looked at my picture. Then she looked at me. Her face broke into a huge grin and she smiled at those around. "You were much younger then," she exclaimed. Everyone laughed; almost everyone laughed. Then, she noticed that today was my birthday. That news was greeted with much applause and even the bus driver joined in. Ria commented that, "If you look like your passport picture, you deserve the trip." As the armed troops left the bus, I looked at the bus driver and said, *"Twende"* (Kiswahili for "Let's go!"). We did.

There was a point during extended travel, especially comfortless travel, where impatience became almost more than I could stand. Often on the trips, this feeling occurred when we were close to our destination. As we neared Kasese, I was prepared for the worst. It had clearly been a trip of few comforts, but the countryside we traveled through was so park-like and beautiful that I was quite content to gaze out the window and listen as other travelers explained the area to Ria. We were passing through Queen Elizabeth II National Park. While we had seen large groups of impala for the last hour, we had seen no other animals of note; the Ugandans explained why. As Amin's troops had been driven out by Tanzanian soldiers, some had moved across this area. In the process, they had killed almost all of the game. Not just for food, we were told.

Some had been for sport and some for the collection of ivory, but most were killed just for the killing. Because there were almost no predators left, certain types of animals had grown far too numerous. As the highway meandered through rolling hills, we viewed all that we saw with a different understanding.

We arrived at the Saad Hotel in the late evening. It was clean, quiet and inexpensive—about five dollars per night. It had two double beds per room and an attached bathroom with a shower. It was quite a hotel and this had been quite a birthday. We agreed to unwind for a couple of days and to find out what we could about the mysterious Ruwenzori Mountains. Our plan would allow Brad and Charlie to catch up.

Kasese was a small town, but was a hub of activity, a juncture of much trade. In a place not geared to tourism, only two hotels advertised for Westerners. A walk through town produced greetings that ranged from *"mazunga"* (white person) to "Hello, John." The latter was a bit unnerving for Ria. Near a store that sold cassette tapes of mostly African music, a young boy greeted me with a thumbs up gesture and the comment "M.C. Hammer, YESSS!" It was a smaller world than we had suspected.

Men pushed bicycles laden with bunches of greenish-yellow bananas. The number of bunches so encompassed the bicycle that it couldn't be ridden. Still, it was a vehicle and a machine, and that combination allowed one man to transport much more merchandise than he could have without it. While going uphill was a problem for such traders, going downhill was even more dangerous. The brakes were not located on the handlebars; they were activated by pressing backward on the rearmost pedal. I marveled at the skill as a line of such bicycles negotiated a steep downhill. The owners would balance the heavy bike, hop on one leg, and apply the brake with the other. Ria took a picture of me holding at least fifty awkward pounds of bananas in each hand. And I remembered that one bike had six such bundles tied to it.

We waited a couple of days to buy our supplies. We explored and rested and I caught up on my journal entries. We were also waiting for Brad and Charlie. I needed a haircut and a shave. I remembered India's fifteen-cent shave and shoulder massage and could hardly wait. The local barbershop turned out to be a very polite and wizened man in the middle of the town quad. Dirt and rocks were his floor, and he did business in the shade of a very large tree. His English and my Kiswahili seemed good enough to get the job done. I wasn't worried about what the haircut would look like; I just wanted it shorter. He did that, albeit with scissors that seemed somewhat dull.

*Banana bunches are a staple of the local economy in Kabale, Uganda.
These weigh about 50 pounds each, and bicycles were used to acrobatically
transport seven or eight such loads.*

A shave and a haircut, Kasese style (with no cream)

Our communication had included the word "shave." Because of the fear of contaminated razors at home and abroad, I had always refused to have a shave with anything but a new razor. This habit resulted in a young boy being sent off to the local mercantile for one. A crowd had begun to form with the haircut ritual—one of the only things to do on a slow trade day. They had no idea how interesting this would become. My barber was more than happy to cut my hair; he welcomed the challenge of his first Western haircut. Now he seemed equally happy to shave my beard. A new razor, an appreciative crowd, a laughing Canadian. Nowhere had shaving cream been mentioned. When it was, by me, I was doomed. Ria snapped several pictures of me in severe pain as my beard disappeared s-l-o-w-l-y. Tears ran down my face and the crowd was delighted. Somewhere my African shaving story is lore. I thanked my barber and vowed to adopt a new and unkempt grooming code until the first modern city.

With the appropriate forms filled out and supplies purchased, we prepared to leave.

Our Ruwenzori trip cost 36,000 *shillingi.* Added to that was a 10,000-*shillingi* rescue fee. The area had been designated a National Park and there was a ten-dollar entrance fee. We spent twenty dollars each on food and miscellaneous clothing supplies. What we had not bought were rubber boots to protect us from the mud. Several local traders had them, but none in our sizes, so we decided not to wait for a new shipment. The entire week cost us about sixty dollars each. In a few days, we would have been glad to have spent that on the boots alone.

No one lived in the Ruwenzori Mountains. The *Bakanjo* (singular *Mukonjo*) lived at their base. Tribal names were biblical and the deity they worshiped was *Kitasamba*. When we emerged from the park office with the paperwork in hand, the wooden fence in front was lined like a parade route. But once they could see that we already had our required guide, they dispersed. With a few "Hello, Johns" and some smiles, most of the village strolled along with us for a while, singing and commenting on our group. There were now four of us with the addition of two Dutch backpackers: Enrico and Eric.

A guide was required, but Ria and I wanted to trek at our own pace. Eric and Enrico had hired a porter for some of their gear, and it was clear that they planned to go slowly. We agreed to share the cost of the guide, even though we did not intend to use his services. Our new Dutch friends agreed to this cost-cutting plan and we were ready to start. My pack weighed over twenty kilos and Ria's over ten. We were getting a late start and the farmlands and jungle were getting uncomfortably warm. According to the park service map, we would all stay in the same campground the first night. It looked like it would be up to Ria and me to make sure that our speedy progress ended at the correct destination. That was probably why there was a guide requirement.

For an hour and a half we hiked through cultivated areas where fields and stands of bamboo were the rule. The trail wound among banana and coffee gardens, passing *Konjo* homesteads. Some hollowed out logs puzzled us: We would learn that they were for brewing a local banana beer called *tonto*. We crossed a few streambeds, and I participated in the luxury of drinking from a stream for the first time in nearly eight months. The water was pure here, but it was with considerable effort that I drank the cool liquid. Most of the illness I had seen among friends and other travelers had been from contaminated food or water, and I realized what a strong habit I had adopted. It tasted great, but I hiked on with apprehension for the remainder of the day's ascent.

Three stream crossings and three drinks later, the trail began to start the steep gradient we had heard about. We had been hiking in a floral canyon of twelve-foot high elephant grass. There were fields of yams, beans, cassava, and coffee just beyond that barrier. We breathed the nearly stagnant air and noted that our progress was herding an increasing number of butterflies. Reluctant to fly above the tall grass, they were content to fly ahead of us. At first there were hundreds of multicolored wings rising up from spots of moisture on the ground. Then there were more and still more. By the time the trail opened up, tens of thousands of beating wings were like the spindrift of fine snow in the high mountains.

At about that time, we heard talking and soon a line of porters crossed the stream behind us. Unlike porters in Nepal, they did not carry huge loads. In fact, with no one living in the area above us, we were surprised to see anyone not connected with tourists. What they were carrying turned out to be tourist-related, and they balanced three or four twelve-foot-long, two-inch by four-inch boards on their heads. Each carried a backpack with supplies. These were not huge loads in terms of weight, but they were exceptionally awkward ones.

That they had caught up to us attested to their conditioning. They smiled and answered our Hujambo greeting although Kiswahili was not usually spoken here. One porter spoke to us in British English of such elegance that we utterly failed to hide our surpise, and we gave him our complete attention. What he said was wrapped in wonderfully accented English. He told us that the forest we were entering was almost entirely void of animals and insects. The notable exception was safari ants. They were either red or black, and they should be avoided. Their bite was quite painful and they numbered in the millions. We thanked him for the exquisitely delivered warning and moved on. The porters moved ahead of us.

As we began to climb, we soon discovered that the trail had been literally hacked out of the jungle. There were no niceties, and huge root systems from trees offered handholds where the trail moved among them. We climbed on steps chopped into the dirt walls of a hillside or on footholds where still more roots offered the only secure step. Surely, the porters could not have gone this way. We were using both hands and wishing for a prehensile tail. How could they have passed the boards up to others on some of the more difficult passages? The tracks on the forest floor indicated some adeptness we didn't have. The porter mystery was solved when we saw them across a riverbed. They moved up a sheer dirt wall with one hand turning the boards obliquely while they used the free hand to grab holds above. It was a marvel to watch. We were catching up to them, now. The trail was steeper and their loads were more of a burden.

The guidebook at the park entrance said four to six hours of hiking for the first day. We were going to camp at some huts at Niyabitaba and spend the night near the confluence of the Bujuku and Mubuku rivers. The names were so musical and reminded me in many ways of Native American names for things, but the "Indian" names were so familiar to me that I didn't always appreciate their equally magical sound. The hill finally slowed the porters and we passed them. After some more good-natured exchanges we moved ahead and arrived at the hut in two hours and forty-five minutes. The trees around us were spectacular, and we set our gear in front of a large shelter. *Symphonias* had no branches on trunks eighty to one hundred feet high. Above that they spread a canopy of dark green leaves and huge masses of scarlet flowers.

There had been no mud and no rain. Our clothes were soaked with sweat and we were glad to have a spare and dry set in the pack. We rinsed our laundry in the abundant water and placed our wet clothes on a huge tree stump to dry. We were on the side of a hill with the rivers below us. Water came from a pipe that disappeared uphill and toward another stream. Our view above was of peaks that rose steeply into some clouds. We started a fire and began to prepare a meal when the clouds parted enough for us to see impossibly high peaks rising above us. It did not take much imagination to conjure up images of dinosaurs just a day's march away. When our Dutch friends arrived, Eric greeted us with a rather agonized "Yeehaw"—an Americanism he had picked up from watching years of U.S. Westerns. He had survived his first day and was certainly trying to hike himself into shape. Or, as he said, an early grave. We were all asleep early.

At first light we noticed orchids growing in the trees near camp. We had still not had any rain in a place where two to five hundred centimeters fall annually. We unpacked our food from the various lines strung near our beds. We were more interested in keeping up our strength than in increasing the girth of various squirrel-like animals. We assumed that gnawing noises would seem louder near our heads, so we had hung our food very near to our faces as we slept. Bumping my head at night was better than losing what little food we had. It was a cold morning and we talked until just after seven before starting out. The map showed the next stop as John Matte Hut, seven hours away. It had both a bog and a "rough area."

It definitely had both. There was a lot of climbing up steep mountain trails. My Asics shoes, so good for running, were no match for the mud. At least they stayed on my feet. They did, but I didn't. In the bog, the branches and assorted stones meant to help us negotiate the shin-deep mud were unanchored or slippery—or both. I ended up end up many more times than I had thought possible.

While I was glad that I was twenty pounds lighter than when I left the U.S., I was not happy to be carrying that twenty plus twenty more. I thought about it every time I sank up to my knee and had to fight my way out. Still, we arrived in four hours. The "place where clouds are boiled" might also be called the "place where mud is deep."

It had only rained for fifteen minutes, and we had eaten breakfast beneath a leafy forest monarch during the downpour. Now we had arrived at a series of huts that were exceptionally well made. The porters with their milled boards were going to some camp above this. The main hut had a dorm and two large private rooms. Our Dutch friends and the guide and porters wouldn't arrive for another three hours, so we went looking for moss to cushion the sleeping bags. We rinsed and dried clothing and ourselves, and prepared some warm soup for lunch. Our friends arrived at about the estimated time and just behind them we had a rare treat.

There was another Westerner here. He arrived with four or five Lukonzo, and it was soon apparent that he was as much at home in the park as they were. He spoke to them in a language that was definitely not Kiswahili, but when I spoke to him in that tongue, he understood my words and my accent. His name was Guy Yeoman and he was a retired (1984) British doctor. In his early seventies, he had been coming to these mountains for many years. We learned that he was one of the people responsible for having this area set aside as a national park. His stories about the early explorations and his own adventures kept us spellbound for hours. In the middle of one of his tales, I looked at the upturned faces of my three seated companions and saw the same look that very young children have when hearing about the most magical of things. It made me realize that among the people I was hiking with, and with this new friend, I had heard no cynicism and nothing negative. We listened to as much as we could elicit.

One of the first things we learned was that the impossibly high peaks we had seen at Niyabitaba that first night were the southern Portal Peaks. While they were 6,000 feet above us, they were only the middle range. If we were lucky, we were told, the clouds might part during the three-day trek and we would see Mt. Stanley. During the course of his tales, he mentioned that the Mubuku River, below that first camp, was filled with brown trout.

He taught us some phonetics for the porters we would meet. The language was *Rukonjo*. A characteristic of Bantu languages (of which *Rukonjo* is one) is the custom of mediating word stems by the uses of prefixes and suffixes. Thus, one person is *mukonjo,* but plural (up to and including the whole tribe) is *bakonjo.* The language becomes *Rukonjo* and the country *Bukonjo. Wabukiri* and *wasubiri* mean "good morning" and "good evening," respectively. *Wahino?* is "How are you?" *Buchayi* is "good-bye." *Kuthi-kuthi* asks "May we could come in?" He told us that the Lukonzo could certainly understand as much Kiswahili as we could speak. He did not mean it as an insult, just as information.

Dr. Yeoman told us that Claudius Ptolemy first heard of these mountains from a book by Marinus of Tyre, *The Periplus of the Erythrean Sea.* A Greek traveler named Diogenes journeyed inland from the Indian Ocean coast. He thought that he had found the source of the Nile River when he discovered two large lakes (probably Lake Victoria and Lake Albert). Where did the water come from that fed these lakes? The answer seemed to be from the snowy mountain range that was only sometimes visible. Lunae Montes, he called them: the Mountains of the Moon. The physical discovery of the range is most often attributed to Henry Morton Stanley in 1888. This was the stuff that we had always hoped to hear—adventures from the past and firsthand experiences of more recent excitement. And we were hearing about them in the very place where they had happened.

The reason that even the discovery was at issue was that snow at the equator was thought to be impossible. Several early sightings were considered no more than visions. As Dr. Yeoman talked, it was easy to envision that brief parting of the clouds and the massive snow-covered range hanging above the African plane. The clouds, we were told, were due to the humid forests of Zaire and the monsoon climate of East Africa. These mountains were not volcanic and we were surprised to learn that Mt. Stanley was the third highest peak on the continent.

We really enjoyed that evening of interesting stories at John Matte Hut. We saw Guy Yeoman Camp on our map and noted that we would reach it during the return portion of our loop. But who was John Matte? Dr. Yeoman told us that *Mzee* (pronounced M-zay) John Matte was an agent of the Uganda Mountain Club. Or at least he had been. His title meant respected elder and he had spent most of his life organizing guides and porters for the exploration of this region. I immediately thought of Tenzing Norgay's role in Nepal. John Matte had not climbed Everest, but he was accorded a similar kind of respect among his people and foreign explorers.

We were off at nine the next morning. It was day three. There was an immediate stream crossing, so all that was dry was now wet again. Then there was bog. We had mud and water in great quantities, just like the day before. Still, no water fell on us and we appreciated that. After a half hour, we reached a large bog that looked deceptively like a meadow. Lobelia trees were everywhere and grew to a height of twenty feet or more. Today's goal was Bujuku Hut. We moved from 8,300 feet to over 10,900 feet, all of it on muddy trail.

In the middle of the climb to the hut there was suddenly a quarter of a mile of boardwalk. A lot of portages and effort went into this, and we assumed that the plan was to complete the entire trek from John Matte Hut to Bujuku Hut. But why not start at John Matte and work up? I didn't actually see Rod Serling, but I thought I heard: "Picture if you will...."

Spoiled by the boardwalk, we were soon back at the very fatiguing process of fighting the mud. I went knee-deep many times and even lost a shoe twice. The story of the Tar Baby came to mind as I stood knee-deep in one hole and reached my arm into another to see if a shoe was, indeed, at the bottom. The Tar Baby story was apt, but I remembered the tar pits at La Brea and found that not so amusing. This could have been a much shorter trip.

We arrived, and Ria started both fire and food. I went to the stream to wash shoes, socks, and myself. We had been hiking in shorts and tee shirts, but we were now forced to wear several layers of warm clothing. Amazingly, we were at 11,000 feet. Clouds flew by from the south, rushing over our valley and changing the colors of the lake near camp. Enrico and Eric arrived a few hours later and brought much better weather. We all marveled at the limestone formations, caves, waterfalls, and cascades from the peak nearest to camp. Dr. Yeoman had told us of Mt. Speke, and this was undoubtedly it. Above the largest waterfall, we could see part of a glacier. That meant a lake was just out of our line of sight.

It was March, and February and March were supposed to be the dry months. Dr. Yeoman had told us not to count on that too much. The new boards were intended for this area; a new hut was needed. The night was bitterly cold, and the great outdoors was constantly trying to come in. Someone had gone to a lot of work and had hauled a lot of corrugated tin to solve the problem of tourists getting too much sleep. The wind raged outside and the rains finally came. I consoled myself by thinking about what it would have been like if we had no shelter at all. There were other porters here and they built a huge fire inside an adjoining hut and talked and sang well into the night.

We ate a morning breakfast of Weetabix (a shredded wheat breakfast from the UK), UHT (milk), and jam. We used leaf and moss mattresses again. As in

Above: At the bottom of the photo, in the cloud shadows, is the Bujuku camp. Just over halfway up the cliff face, a small glacier lake accounts for a waterfall. The picture was taken below Elena Hut at nearly 15,000 feet.
Opposite page: The Ruwenzori Mountains with a handstand just below the summit and just before the storm that gave us a sleepless night.

Nepal, losing weight made our bones bruise just from the pressure during sleep. Rain and wind and cold had conspired to make last night quite memorable. And the rain—just buckets of it. The downpour was barely audible above the wind. Still, the morning was only cold; the weather during the days continued to hold.

That next morning, we left with our guide and our Dutch friends. We were assured that there was a shortcut to Kitandara, one of the encampments on the return part of the loop. We needed the guide to find it. Our path took us through frozen bog. I broke through the surface and into freezing mud many times. The shortcut was every rock climber's nightmare. As in Thailand, few climbers would trust any devices that they hadn't put into a cliff face themselves. We weren't being asked to climb the 300-foot rock wall, but we were asked to trust a 305-foot ladder that was attached to various places on the cliff. There were a lot of steps to that ladder and carrying a pack made it no easier at nearly 12,000 feet. I had purchased some leg warmers in Kasese as partial sleeping attire. Now, I put them on my hands and arms to protect me from the freezing metal.

We discussed the almost universal pratfall where someone atop a ladder falls (comically) to earth. Even into a muddy landing, this one wasn't funny at all.

At the top of the ladder there was a little confusion. Enrico and Eric wanted to head down to Kitandara. Ria and I wanted to go up to Elena Hut at 14,900 feet. This did not please our guide who was worried that he would have to explain this when we were never heard from again. Convinced that we were serious, he offered to lead us to the top while the other porters led our Dutch friends down the trail to a comfortable camp. While he was resting from the ladder climb, we started up the trail. We hoped to gain the top before an afternoon storm covered the peaks completely. Even at that moment, there were clouds scudding across the lower valley toward where we had camped on the very first night.

It was obvious from the trail itself that not too many people chose this path. We were through with mud and after a mile of circuitous climbing along an arête, we started to ascend for real. The rocky debris of the talus slope was difficult to negotiate with our heavy packs, but we pressed on without a rest. We looked up only to confirm the location of the trail ahead or looked down to check the incoming clouds. Our guide was probably twenty minutes behind us and we saw him moving out of the last of the lobelia at timberline. Just above us, two cliff faces seemed to join like the opposing pages of an open book. The trail appeared to lead in that direction. Surely, that wasn't right.

But that was exactly where the trail led, and when we arrived at the base we could see that a ledge traversed one face. Invisible from below, it was anywhere from three to five feet across. We started out onto the ledge as the first moist air from the clouds reached us. Within minutes we could not see our guide below. Then we could not see the base of the cliff. And then we couldn't see fifteen feet away. The abyss seemed more imposing when left to our imaginations, so we proceeded by ignoring what we knew was there. The clouds deadened the sound and cloaked us in dew-like drops of moisture. It was suddenly very cool.

Ria moved easily behind me and seemed quite content to continue. This wasn't a good time to discover a fear of heights, or a fear of the unknown. If the trail became narrower, or divided, or required actual rock climbing, then we would have to stop and consider how much danger we were in. Lack of visibility would be a major problem if it started to rain hard and the rocky trail became slippery. Then, even a descent would be an extreme move. On the other hand, to camp up here with no more gear than we had would invite hypothermia—or worse. I didn't share all this with Ria and I told myself that I was only considering unlikely possibilities.

In twenty minutes we had reached a wider place and the clouds broke apart to reveal a series of rock ridges that had been shaped by the retreat of a recent glacier. Rock cairns marked the trail. Three or more rocks were stacked up and placed in the line of sight. They were the only signs telling us which way to go. Less than a mile away we saw the corrugated metal roofs of the huts. There appeared to be three of them.

We chose the largest hut and stepped inside. Out of the wind and clouds it was still cold but much quieter. Our food supplies had fallen prey to our voracious appetites. The cold, altitude, and energy expenditure made us constantly hungry. We were not in possession of the proper clothing for this altitude and our sleeping bags were suspect as well. We arranged our gear and took enough time to get warm and drier. Our guide arrived, entered, and congratulated us on finding the hut. He was nothing but cordial and concerned. There wasn't a hint of disrespect for our lack of familiarity with the area or for our desire to be here instead of where the rest of our party was going. Still, he must have questioned our abilities at some time. He left for Kitandara and wished us a pleasant night. As the door closed, we saw what looked like sunshine on the rocks outside.

The sun was out and there were a few breaks in the clouds. Mt. Speke and the peaks above us would be more visible if we climbed to a ridge high above and to the right of the hut. As we did, I realized that some of what we were

*Left: Standing with Ria on some dry
ground in the Ruwenzori Mountains.
Above: Dr. Yeoman, Eric, Enrico, Ria,
and me.*

climbing would be a lot more difficult during the descent. With no ropes or
other climbing gear, this could be a chance we shouldn't be taking. Nepal had
four helicopters. Uganda probably had none that could fly this high—if it had
any at all. On the ridge, we saw Mt. Stanley (with peaks Mt. Margherita at
16,763 and Mt. Alexandra at 16,703) above us. Mt. Speke towered over last
night's camp. We could see the Savoia and Elena glaciers. There was even
another camp at Irene Lake (14,750 feet) on a ridge below us and at the head-
wall of the valley containing Bujuku Hut. We had been there last night and it
seemed a huge drop from where we were now.

The return was carefully and successfully done, and we were glad to fix
dinner and prepare for a cold night. We had noted two pitons placed in the rock
during our descent. That confirmed my impression that the climb we had done
had not been the best idea. A storm came in just after sunset, and as it got darker,
the wind picked up. There was a smaller sleeping hut, but we had evaluated it
and found that it allowed even more of the night air to come in. The third hut was
a cooking hut and offered little in the way of protection. It was all corrugated
metal and as we prepared for sleep we could hear the wind shaking it thoroughly.

I estimated the winds at from fifty to seventy-five miles per hour. When we
could make ourselves heard above the din, we discussed the idea that this was

probably the usual weather at this altitude. If that was our best guess, it needed a little work. Sometime about midnight, the wind took the cooking hut and moved it off the mountain. It did not go quietly nor quickly, but it went. We were a very sleepless couple of North Americans who spent the rest of the night tensed and waiting to spring for the door.

Before first light, we were already packed. We were out the door as soon as we could see the cairns. Tired, hungry, and cold, we were nonetheless glad to have experienced the top of the Ruwenzoris. Now, we hurried to join our friends who would be anxious to hear of our adventure. We saw nothing of the cooking hut during our descent.

Our rough calculations on our food supply were compared with our map of the route. We would have to stop at Kitandara for breakfast and continue on to Guy Yeoman Camp for the night. That was a "double day." There was no way to avoid it. It got worse. We would have to go from there to Niyabitaba the next day and continue on back to the park entrance. That would be two double days in a row. If the bog situation remained the same, we would be very tired. Enrico and Eric were in a similar situation for the last day and would travel with us out of the park.

There are a lot of combinations of falls in judo and gymnastics, and we did our share of them on the way to Guy Yeoman Camp. I led the categories of most falls and most spectacular falls. The latter gold medal was secured when I trusted my weight to an unanchored tree branch floating on mud. It moved. I moved more. I quickly started down a mud-filled ravine that in wetter times would have been a cascade. Ria saw legs and then arms and then pack and then legs again. What I saw was her face atop a hummock of native grass when she was finally able to reach where I had come to rest. She didn't smile until she saw that I was uninjured. She didn't laugh until she saw me smile. She would have to wait forever to hear me laugh about that one. If I said I was careful enough not to fall again, I'd have been lying.

When we finally arrived at Guy Yeoman Camp, we were bedraggled and not in the best of moods. Food and some rest would certainly take the edge off. Ria noted that we again had company. Guy Yeoman and his group of Lukonzo were there. Our moods improved rapidly—especially when he offered us some of his "extra" food. Either he knew something about our store of supplies or he actually had more than he could use. While we had refused the same offer at John Matte Hut a few days before, we now accepted both food and stories with equal enjoyment.

Dr. Yeoman had published a book on the Ruwenzoris and had helped establish the area as a national park. Now in his seventies, he had doubts about the wisdom of exposing such a fragile environment to the effects of tourism. By his best estimate, fewer than 7,000 foreigners had visited this wilderness since Stanley first arrived—over one hundred years ago. With the plentiful game on the plains surrounding the mountains, there was little reason for any tribes in the area to go exploring. Still, we could see his point. Perhaps when we love a place so much, our affection can bring about some undesired results. Certainly, we had heard nothing of these mountains from the Kenyans and even most Ugandans hadn't known where they were located.

The sun broke through that afternoon and we had clean and dry clothing by the time dinner was over. There was no use in saving any cookable food, so we ate a very hardy dinner. The next day would be our last trek and we would eat the cold leftovers from dinner and the packaged, pre-cooked, or raw food we had carried. The packs were light now with the reduced food supply. The guide and porter wanted our cooking gear, and we were more than happy to give it to them. They understood that we would have carried it to the village, but they seemed eager to avoid that circumstance. Perhaps they had seen other tourists arrive at the village only to give away valuable equipment to the first villagers they saw. We didn't know and we didn't ask. We were light, hungry, and in a hurry.

Our last morning in the Ruwenzoris was again dry. In our six days, we had endured only two short squalls during our treks and one night of torrential fury. We had been lucky. After breakfast, we again joined our Dutch friends and the porters and guide. The guide had mentioned that there was a very difficult waterfall to negotiate and that he would have to show us the way. We could not possibly do it on our own, he said. He assured us that we could race on ahead after we had crossed that most dangerous section. It took us an hour of bog to reach the waterfall.

Our phenomenal luck on avoiding rain had rendered the waterfall an almost completely dry expanse of rock. Compared to what we had climbed and descended at Elena Hut, this was very easy. Still, we watched as Eric had a bit of trouble on a few of the more technical areas and saw that if one did not like heights or exposure to them, this passage could be a problem. The guide had been very polite to us and willing to let us trek at our own speed. We thanked him for his concern and for all his assistance. He, in turn, congratulated us on our level of fitness—especially Ria—and smiled at his own attempt to compliment us on our unusual style of trekking. We were going to be one of the stories around some Lukonzo fires for a while.

We fairly ran on the drier portions of the trail. There were still areas of bog to negotiate, but we knew that would end at Niyabitaba where the trail divided for the loop we had done. Below that camp, we were familiar with the trail and it was dry. We were smiling and moving.

It took three and a half hours to reach Niyabitaba. We ate and sat in the sun to dry. Eric and Enrico were just behind us and feeling quite fit, too. They knew so much about American culture that I felt a bit frustrated to know so little of theirs. Perhaps if Dutch television reruns had been shown on American television for all of my formative years, I might have been their equal. Their English was nearly perfect. It was an oft-repeated theme on my trip. English was everywhere.

From Niyabitaba to the park entrance was a mere two hours of downhill run. We passed a total of fifteen incoming Westerners with their guides and porters. While we did talk of what we had seen, most of the conversation centered around which direction they should take on the loop, what areas to explore, and the condition of the trails. We added some warnings about terrain and weather and the condition of Bujuku Camp. We envied them their first-time enjoyment of what was to come.

Villagers were burning banana trees and bamboo as we passed by the outlying farms. There were still thousands of butterflies at each stream crossing, and their bright and varied colors were no less impressive this time. Ria chatted away and moved as though she had just started. Even into the Lukonzo Village, I marveled at her level of stamina. At the gatehouse, we took off our packs, and I found a place to change into some dry and less dirty clothes. It was worth the effort. A clean pair of socks and my extra shoes (worn indoors or at camps only) made me feel almost human. I returned to the front of the building to find Ria resting her head against her pack and seemingly dead to the world. She was fit, but she was tired.

The trip back to the Saad Hotel was dusty, bumpy, and long. All of us were hungry. More than that, we had hidden our hunger from ourselves and it wasn't until the prospect of food became a reality that we realized it. Ria slept in the truck—an amazing feat. But she was awake when we pulled up to the hotel and was one of the first to get to the dining room.

We ordered two meals each and showered and changed into really clean clothes while our orders were prepared. Then we sat down to the serious business of trying someone else's cooking for a change. We joked with other travelers and with some of the local residents and those of our tight little group. It had been a terrific adventure and we were sorry to leave this village and its friendly people. Ria talked about the gorillas in Zaire. It sounded like the next best adventure.

Enrico and Eric rested for an hour and ate again.

Above: At Elena hut in Ruwenzoris, before the storm.

CHAPTER 14
OSCAR:
A Silverback Gorilla

Nipe manemo launi mepesi kwa kukariri
yenye wema na amani na moyoni kufikiri
yenye wema na amani kwa watu yasikasiri
yawe tamu ulimini na moyoni kufikiri
yatie watu imani njema ya kutadhibiri

Give me colorful words, easy to hear
Give me colorful words, easy to repeat
Good and peaceful for people and not lacking anything.
Let them be sweet on the tongue and in the heart; to reflect upon
– A Swahili quatrain from the Marudi Mema

The trip to Zaire to see the gorillas was something I started under mild protest. I had very mixed feelings about intruding into the habitat of an animal that was extremely endangered. It was also expensive ($120 U.S. for as many hours as it took). I hadn't seen *Gorillas in the Mist* and had only read fleetingly about Diane Fossey's life. Jane Goodall's study of chimpanzees on PBS and Koko the gorilla's signing five hundred words had been the extent of what I had seen. Still, I had learned that almost anything on this trip wasn't what it seemed, and that the recommendations of other travelers were usually worth listening to. This trip around the world would probably be a one-time thing, so I decided it had to be done.

The money problem continued with Ria still floating a loan to the broke American. Stacks of money left the bank with us and we went out to spend it as frugally as possible. We were sad to leave Kasese because the Ruwenzoris and the quaint town had been so enjoyable. We were also sad because we faced more travel days.

To note in my journal that we arrived in Kabale in ten hours told nothing about the journey. Ten hours could be the luxury of a Greyhound or Trailways bus

Opposite page—Top: Uganda's recent wars have left the country with few resources. A vehicle rarely travels with fewer people than this. Everyone in this picture was eventually on board. Bottom: "Don't be taller than the silverback, and don't look directly into his eyes." I try and fail to remember either.
Above: "Do not touch the baby gorilla!" Our guide repeated that twice for our safety. No one told the baby not to touch us. Here, Ria shares some mutual interest.

on the open highway in the Western U.S., or it could be a minivan packed with thirty people or more. The relative nature of ten hours was easy to experience when we traveled via the latter. Wedged against bodies and metal, we couldn't move for hours; ten hours seemed more like ten days.

We arrived in Kabale and found the Sky Blue Hotel. There were more friendly Ugandan people, cheap rooms, and cheap food. It looked like we would be paying under four dollars per night. The staff immediately won us over just because they could win us over. We were not in the best of moods when we arrived and were only getting along with each other. Anyone else got short shrift. Within twenty minutes we were seated in the dining room and ordering our meal from a smiling hotel manager. Having showered and changed, we sat down to a delicious meal in relative isolation. It was a definite case of *ninapenda sana Kabale* (I like Kabale very much). The waiters all wore crisp white shirts, blue bow ties, and dark-colored slacks. The emphasis was on service and Western customs were observed. We both noticed the smile and genuine enjoyment of the staff. Thailand's "*sanuk*" was here under some other name. Africa!

The next morning I went for a forty-nine-minute run through town. Kabale is Uganda's highest town (over 6,300 feet). Being a foreigner was a great icebreaker anyway. Being an early morning, Western, running foreigner got me a crowd. Bright-eyed smiling children ran with me for a block or two near their school until it was clear to them that I really intended to run up the steep hill leading to the hospital. Their physical enthusiasm slowed, but their vocal enthusiasm continued as long as they thought they were heard. People descending on the roadway smiled and said, "*Hujambo,*" as we passed each other. I smiled and waved but was well into oxygen debt and didn't trust my voice. I returned for a shower and breakfast.

We recognized travelers from the Iqbal Hotel in Nairobi, and they were quick to interrupt our breakfast with news of the riots in Nairobi. Over fifty people had been killed in the violence and much of it was near the area where we had been staying. While we listened to the little that was actually known, I thought about how much this trip had already changed my viewpoint. A year ago, I would have thought that a report such as this meant that Nairobi was unsafe to visit. Now, I wasn't so sure.

Letters I had received from friends back home had generally expressed concern for the violence I might encounter in various countries. It had become clear that such violence existed in each of the countries I had visited. But I saw articles in the papers in these foreign countries that reported on my own country. And I noted that one disgruntled employee was often responsible for as much carnage as an entire mob in a Third World town. All of the dead were Kenyans, no foreigners had been involved. The papers reported this as a tribal problem. From reading papers in Nairobi I knew I didn't understand the fierce hatred many tribes held for outsiders. Some of the same ingredients for violence were the same here as for back home: a poverty-stricken section of the populace, high unemployment, and drug and alcohol use. We were glad to have been somewhere else, but such senseless killing saddened us. Ultimately, violence spilled over into the lives of the innocent and being away from it was the best solution—for those who could.

There were some practical considerations awaiting us too. The prices for having our laundry done were hard to resist. The list near each room read: "Shirt 150, T-Shirt 150, Trousers 200, Trouser-Jean 250, Ladies Dress 150, Skirt 150, Socks (pair) 100." One of everything on the list came to 1,150 shillingi—just under one dollar! Nearby, a sign for "Bicycle Hire" listed 2,000 shillingi for the whole day and 1,000 for a half day. The town was somewhere that would be a fun and affordable place to stay for a few days.

We walked around town while waiting to arrange final transportation through five checkpoints to the Zaire border. We noted that while the country was certainly in the throes of some serious poverty, the people seemed extremely outgoing and friendly. American tee shirts had found their way throughout Asia, and we noted that Africa had its fair share, too. Two of them gave us pause: "I Tanned For Jerry's Kids" was seen several times, as was "Our Baby Is Here" (with an accompanying down arrow)—worn by a young man. Humor or ignorance was at work here, and we were sure it didn't matter.

While we walked down the streets, we saw many families gathered under large trees. They were cooking meals or playing games, and we noted that there was great enjoyment of family life. There was a mental click in my mind as I realized that these people didn't have much in some ways, but they had every-thing in some other ways. We stopped to chat with a few of the women and children. Because of their curiosity about Ria, other families moved toward her wherever we stopped. She acquitted herself well and was wonderful with the children. The mothers didn't miss that attribute, and I was allowed to stand back and watch as mutual friendships were born. It was not hard to fall in love with Africa.

The next morning we were at the "bus stop" near our hotel. There was no bus, but there was a small, white Toyota truck with a few sacks of grain and a

Ria and the silverback. At just over 100 pounds, she sits calmly next to an animal four times her size.

few people in the back. We were assured that we could also be some of the people in the back, so we purchased tickets.

While we waited, Ria snapped some pictures of a large number of people trying to get a ride on a small truck. It was a swarm and redefined the term crowded—in a way that not even *matatus, tuk tuks,* and buses could. Leaf springs and tire pressure seemed certain to fail the system, and we saw people literally hanging onto each other as the truck pulled away. From behind, only the back wheels of the truck could be seen.

Steve and Kristi were the only other Westerners going to the Zaire border with us on this particular "bus." The four of us joined six or seven smiling Ugandans, and we sat in the truck and awaited our imminent departure. Sixty-five minutes and sixteen people later, we were not the happy campers we might have been. Kristi was a complete stranger. Now she sat very close to me on one knee while Ria sat equally close on the other. The downside of that arrangement was that others in turn leaned or sat on them, and the tears in my eyes were not always going to be tears of joy. Steve was buried under luggage and more bodies. When Kristi and Ria finally obtained a moving count (actually underway), there were thirty-four people, seven of which sat in the cab of the truck. There were no children; we were all adults.

The pavement ran out in answer to the question "What could be worse?" Now a thin cloud of fine dust settled on the just and the unjust alike as we slowly drove through what I was assured was beautiful mountain country. Through the dust and tears, I was doing well to make out Kristi and Ria. People shifted about and that was often a bit painful for those of us at the base of this particular pyramid. One energetic fellow, who had been causing me a bit more pain than the others finally shifted enough to cause several riders to seek higher ground. And that opened up space enough for me to both breathe and to see some of the sights. I endured more hours of no movement atop a moving transport. Stopping meant an end to the pain in my knees, but didn't guarantee I could walk well enough to carry my pack.

The four checkpoints before the border came and went without incident— although we kept our cameras out of sight as a precaution. Uniformed and armed Ugandan guards checked passports and kept us nervous about what could happen. The border checkpoint was a different story. We had to do all of the paperwork and tout work that was typical of a border crossing. We were in for another financial shock: The rate of exchange in Zaire was ten times worse than that of Uganda. Here, a U.S. dollar was worth 100,000 Nouveau Zaire. A short inquiry of the checkpoint administrator gave us the monetary picture. Until 1967, the currency was the franc (100 centimes). Then, in 1967 it became the Zaire (100 makuta). The Nouveau Zaire was worth 3 million Zaires. With no more facts than these, a person knows a lot about the conditions of a country.

We were required to leave most of our Ugandan money with the man in charge of the station, and we were a little concerned about that. He left us with our U.S. dollars to pay for the gorilla trip. After two or three such border crossings, we were immune to the time spent and taken and it was just another ordeal. We tried our best to ensure that our money was safe, but in a place where our lives might not be safe, the condition of mere money seemed less important.

Having been told by the touts that "our driver will wait you," we discovered that our new hosts spoke fluent French. They also spoke tribal dialects, Kiswahili, and English. The whole trip had been linguistically humbling and adding French to the mix was just more of the same. It was a short ride to the trailhead.

Once we arrived at the starting point for the trek to the night's lodging, we discovered that our guide was a young boy—very young. He couldn't have been more than twelve, and that was giving him the benefit of considerable doubt. He was a charming lad and talked a great deal. He seemed to be babysitting a younger brother who walked with him. Both made excellent time since they were fit and unencumbered by packs. They offered to fix the latter in each hamlet that we passed through. Young porters or porters-to-be were out in great numbers. Several Westerners from other campsites were in our group and we now numbered about fifteen. Most of us were reluctant to ask small but wiry children to carry a pack of nearly their own weight.

We arrived at the lodge after a steep climb up some farmed and forested areas and our guide extracted his payment: one dollar each. We paid. His "assistant" also asked for a dollar, evidently on the assumption: nothing asked, nothing gained. We turned him down *en masse*. Other boys who had tagged along took this as a sign that their assistance was not highly valued either and they smiled, waved, and started off down the hill. We headed for the lodge.

There had been a bit of a mix-up and everything was backed up by one large group of British tourists. The only sleeping area was on the floor and we took that. Dinner was one dollar. It was a bit expensive, but this was a captive audience. There was no menu. Potatoes, beans, and cabbage were ladled in huge portions. A drink of soda was one dollar. Only beer cost more: $1.50. There would be a one-day delay, but we had been warned that the wait might be three or four days. We were content to read or write or wander about the countryside.

The next morning, two groups started out in search of two different groups of gorillas. They left in the company of two guards for each group. Each of the guards wore an official uniform and carried an official rifle. At first, we were told that the weapons were meant for poachers. Presumably, that meant to shoot at poachers. Someone in the group left behind wondered whether there was any danger from poachers. Then, the rest of us wondered, too. A kind of game developed from that conversation, and in a very short time a good-natured debate swirled around the idea that the guns were, in fact, to protect the tourists from the gorillas. Realists such as Ria and I believed that the most we could hope for in a gorilla–tourist confrontation would be a mercy shot from the armed guard. Shooting a gorilla, we reasoned, would clearly result in a severe loss of product—not to mention employment. Others believed that no one could watch someone being torn to pieces by a savage beast and not do something. I hadn't been gone from the mean streets of parts of America long enough to give that argument any credence. In some major cities, it was considered a cultural contribution. Nothing came from our good-natured musings except that we were all anxious to ask our guide some questions tomorrow.

To find the gorillas, the guides had to travel to the previous day's nest and then track from there. Gorillas were nomadic and hungry, and they traveled surprising distances in a short amount of time. The day before, the gorillas we were going to see had been quite far away. The two groups of tourists left our lodge in torrential rain for what promised to be a long day. Ria and I talked with some of the others, wrote in our journals, discussed gymnastics (her competition and my coaching), and ate our simple fare. By late evening, the people from our hut returned. They were ecstatic.

It took them almost four hours to find the gorillas and three to return to camp. Still, the hour they spent at the feeding site seemed to have impressed everyone. The cost had been $120 each. That was a very dear price, but two of the people immediately tried to see if they could work their way into either of the next excursions. It must have been impressive and the rest of us looked forward to the next day with real anticipation. Of those who had gone, some had taken over a hundred pictures per camera. Ria's concern that she might have over-purchased film faded quickly.

The next morning we were out the door early and followed our guides. Abdullah was the leader of our group. In the distance we could hear the distant thunder-like sounds of the war in Zaire. The instability of this country was a concern, and these morning sounds didn't help to dispel any of my doubts. At that moment, the best news was that the sounds were distant. I concentrated on talking with our guide, who seemed glad to take his own mind off the war.

Information flowed back along the line of fourteen people. Abdullah said that the guns were for several purposes. It was open season on poachers and the guide said that he could kill on sight. It was also true, he said, that poachers were often armed and that the guns could lead to a pitched battle. And, yes, the guns could also be used to protect the visitors in the event of a serious gorilla attack. I hung a lot of my next thoughts on the hope that his definition of serious and mine were roughly the same. It turned out that they were not.

Last night, someone from the rain-soaked group had told us about what had happened when they first found the gorillas. The silverback, Oscar, was the dominant male and normally was quite easygoing with about an hour of tourist visitation. He was not tame, our informant told us; he was just habituated. Perhaps it was the rain, but Oscar had rushed toward the guide and had pushed him down. Then, he dragged the guide across the clearing by one leg and finally stopped and stared fixedly down at him. The guide was purported to have said, "Keep…taking…pictures." I assumed he said it in the tone that golf announcers used to describe a winning put on the eighteenth hole. I thought it was a pretty good thing to have said and was less concerned with whether it had actually happened and more concerned with writing it in my journal. For me, leg dragging definitely constituted a serious attack.

Abdullah told us that he made twenty dollars per month at his job and that he had worked every day for the first year. Now, he had one week of vacation per year. He confided that he made from five to ten dollars per day in tips and would retire in a couple of years with a great deal of money. He also explained why he never put the rifle down. He was charged with it, and if it was lost, he claimed that the government would "cut his head." Further inquiry indicated that he meant decapitation. In a war-torn country with few weapons in the general populace, a gun was a powerful commodity. Sold or used, it conferred wealth and power to the person who possessed it. We saw that these guards considered the threat from the government to be very real.

We passed through several miles of tilled fields until we reached a field that looked quite different. The guide stopped, pointed off trail, and said, "*tembo*." Someone's hushed tones reminded us that Abdullah was indicating one or more elephants. He then said, "*mingi*," which confirmed that there were many. It was clear that he was right and that this field would bring in no crops this season. The guides were obviously nervous and that was transmitted to the rest of us. When he pointed to a pile of still steaming dung nearly two feet high, we all understood that the *tembo,* the *mingi tembo,* were still in the area. In Nairobi, Bwana Johnson had taught me the word "*sasa*" for "here." I hoped that Abdullah wouldn't be saying that next. I asked Ria if "*rogue*" was a French word. Suddenly, the narrow trail through waist-high grass took on a new and more foreboding aspect. The guide moved off and there were no stragglers and no casual conversations. We might not have known where the danger was, but we knew where it wasn't.

Another mile went by and we passed through a village where people were going about their daily tasks in what appeared to be a normal way. At least they did not seem to be worried about being trampled by a herd of *mingi rogue tembo.* The children danced and sang around us and our mood lightened considerably. We seemed to be a parade of sorts and everyone stopped to watch us pass by. A hundred yards outside the village, we passed through a large field of potatoes on our way toward the jungle beyond. Suddenly, our guide held up his hand and crouched down. "Gorilla," he said.

Abdullah had joked with us before and we were all sure that gorillas did not live at the edge of potato fields. As he cautiously walked the last forty feet to the wall of trees ahead, we all waited to see what was really happening. Not only did we not see any gorillas; we did not hear any gorillas—as if we knew what wild gorillas sounded like.

The guide reviewed our instructions: Do not touch the gorillas, especially the baby. Do not dominate any of the male gorillas by being taller than they are or by staring directly into their eyes. Do not make sudden noises or movements. Do not touch the gorillas—especially the baby. We assumed that his repeating of this last rule meant that it was quite important. We knew that gorillas could catch human illnesses, like colds, so touching them was not in their best interest. Why it was not in our best interest for them to touch us went without saying. The guide pointed out that the males and females could misinterpret holding the baby. That was good enough for me. Sudden moves, Abdullah said, could startle a gorilla. Good, fainting wasn't likely to be interpreted as sudden. And from a horizontal position, I'd be unlikely to be taller or be able to look directly into the silverback's eyes.

"*Pole-pole*" means "go slowly." As with many words in the language, saying it just once means something different. "*Pole*" is a word for commiseration. Ria was quite quick to point out that if you only heard it said once, the speaker was sorry that there was no reason to continue to remind you to go slowly. Around wild gorillas, one "*pole*" was perhaps all the sound you were going to get. Canadian humor was starting to make sense.

"They like people," the other guide said. "As what," I thought, "Frisbees, boomerangs, pets, or lunch?" You could argue that gorillas are vegetarian, but I had seen the look in their eyes on PBS from the safety of a couch.

We all stood next to the line of trees and listened as the guides made some strange noises and began to hack at the vegetation with machetes. With nothing to see in front of me, I looked up and over my right shoulder. And, less than twenty feet above me and off to the right, the silverback was eating a tree. At about that time, Ria caught an armful of baby gorilla. It was not her fault that she had been chosen as babysitter, but I glanced back and forth to see if dad could see her from where he was dismantling the forest. Evidently he couldn't. Ria and her charge received a lot of attention and were soon part of an intense photo shoot. The guard's instructions to the baby gorilla seemed to have gone unheeded. He clung tightly to Ria as she tried to appear a victimized hugger—or huggee.

In pictures of Ria and the silverback, she appeared quite at ease with an animal four times her size. The picture was made possible by the adaptation we all made to the idea of no barriers. A person at a zoo who discovered the animals all roaming free from their cages would feel the same shock we did. In a moment we realized that death or serious injury could be only seconds away, and our confrontation with the silverback truly brought that feeling home. If there was going to be significant aggression and physical harm, it seemed likely that this huge beast would be its source. The guide's *sotto voce* comment to move slowly toward the gorilla seemed almost suicidal. He didn't have to tell me: This was yet another animal that could outrun a man. Still, it couldn't outrun all of us and I was determined that if the need arose, I would not move slowly away from the gorilla.

Ria was a lot more relaxed about the entire situation; it showed in almost all of the hundred pictures we took that morning. When I took my turn next to the 450-pound lead ape, he was sitting on the ground and munching on some leafy branches. He would eat up to thirty pounds of trees, bushes, and vines daily. I stepped over some felled limbs in order to sit next to him. For a few moments, I looked directly down and into his face. Alarm bells about dominance and leg dragging were going off as I slowly sank to my haunches and hoped for natural shortness. The silverback looked away. Unfortunately, my branch clearing steps placed me much closer to him than I had ever intended and our shoulders actually touched as he turned to look toward the retreating guide. Retreating guide? Then, he started to scratch his side with a hand that was bigger than my head. His wrist collided with my ribs on each of a succession of scratches, and I did my best not to move suddenly or to acknowledge that it was more than a little bit painful. When he stopped, I moved—*pole-pole.* The adrenal cortex worked just fine and shaky legs carried me to the outer fringe of the group—surely the safest place from which to move quickly to the safety of the potato field.

As Ria handed me the camera, the baby decided that she was free to play. I looked quickly dadward and saw that he was, indeed, watching. I looked for Abdullah. He had his back to me and was chatting with a girl from Australia. There was nothing in sight we could climb that we couldn't be shaken out of, and there was nowhere we could run that wouldn't prove that man was slower than the great apes. Perhaps it was time to develop plan "B."

An hour seemed to be about the limit of tolerance for the gorillas and we were encouraged to leave by our guide. As we started back on the trail, Abdullah pointed out that we had company. A young teen-aged male gorilla was paralleling our course across the potato field. His goal, however, was some goats tethered to the side of a hill at the other side of the farm. It seemed curious. The gorilla was primarily a vegetarian and would presumably have no interest in killing a goat. The guide solved the mystery just before we saw the answer ourselves. The gorilla was just playing. He would frighten the goats until they pulled loose from their tethers and ran off into the underbrush. He seemed less than concerned when a five-year-old village boy charged down the hill throwing stones and yelling at the top of his lungs. A few of the missiles actually landed, however, and the young gorilla ambled back to the jungle a bit faster.

An interesting day had been spent among a vanishing breed of animal. Poachers could make so much money from the various parts of a dead gorilla, that the temptation, even for farmers, was to trap them or to kill them. Visits by Westerners kept a form of protection on a daily basis and let villagers see that tourism was a continuous benefit to the countryside. No gorillas, no tourist dollars. It was a close battle that was certainly not being won. However, I saw that my visit was of more value than harm, and I was very glad to have made the effort.

It was time to return to Nairobi.

Sometimes, the desire to communicate in someone else's language brings unusual dividends. Here, the house, grotto, and pool in Mombassa.

CHAPTER 15
MOMBASSA:
The Landed Gentry

There is one phrase that indelibly haunts all East African conversation,
that epitomizes everything in the East African soul—
The Kiswahili words: 'Bado Kidogo.'
They mean, "not just yet." It is more futile than mañana,
slightly more optimistic than maybe.
All will come, but 'not just yet.'
– African Guidebook

I repaid Ria's loan for the Uganda and Zaire portions of the adventure; her largess had allowed me to experience two of the most memorable adventures of my entire trip. We couldn't find Brad or Charlie anywhere, and it was nearly time to leave Africa. I wouldn't have enough money to visit the Middle East, and the volatile situation there made that into an even better decision. Perhaps another trip at a better time would be possible.

Ria and I decided to leave Nairobi and spend our last African week in Mombassa—on the East Coast of Africa. Returning travelers had told us of beaches that were supposed to be very nice and a place called Lamu that had also been given a high rating. I was a confirmed train addict by this part of the trip, and Ria liked the idea of any form of travel that wasn't a bus. We took the slow train instead of the express and hoped that we would see more that way. It was a bit expensive by our standards, but we had been very frugal the last several months. We splurged and bought second-class tickets.

Trains in Africa were very luxurious compared with those in India. While there were still different prices for various classes of travel, there was none of the "cattle car" overcrowding that characterized many of India's trains. These were old-fashioned cars, paneled, and cooled with ceiling fans. A uniformed attendant walked the length of the cars and announced dinner by playing a xylophone-like instrument. Because of the luxury and style, something had been lost. It was not possible to stand in the doorways and see the country roll past. Ria and I stood at a partially open window outside the compartment and watched animals and villages go by. I loved this kind of travel, but I missed India's lack of regulation.

At least two trains a day ran on these tracks. Still, in a country that had not yet seen an explosion in the use of the personal motor car, there wasn't much that happened in each village that hadn't happened the day before. The train worked its magic on the children and then on their mothers. There was no music but the smiling and waving groups gyrated to some sound that Westerners couldn't hear. We heard the friendly cry of "*mazunga, mazunga*" and remembered back to Kabale where the two dancing preschool brothers had wanted to hold our hands and sing. We waved back and I noticed that over the next three or four hours of waving, standing, and talking, Ria's enthusiasm for each village remained as strong. She waved, smiled, and laughed as though each time was the first. Perhaps that was what the African children were doing. Perhaps each train was magic because it held the promise that something unusual might happen. We reflected on what early pioneer life must have been like in the U.S. and Canada a hundred years ago. Kids still ran toward the iron horse as it carried people across the land.

Mombassa itself seemed like a place well worth getting out of. We were sure that it had its own fascinating history and informational gems, but crowding was not what we wanted. We took a taxi across town to a bus park and noted that traffic was a bit more aggressive than in Nairobi. For one thing, the traffic lights didn't often work. As a result, when they did work, they were often ignored. An intersection became an opportunity to exhibit extreme bravery or stupidity. Ria noted that both extremes accurately described the same driver in the same situation. If a driver failed while making a daring move, he was stupid; if he succeeded, he was brave. Our driver was of the old and not-bold school, and we were pleased with that.

While we waited for the bus we noticed some Westerners giving some coins to some very small and cute children. Ria made a negative remark about it. It struck a chord with me, too. As we talked about it, we agreed. For my part, I had seen begging in every country in Asia and Africa. People begged for food or money from those who had both. In Kathmandu, Nepal, and in Goa, India, I noticed perfectly clean children rolling in the ashes of doused fires and dirt near various roads. They received instructions from older children and then put on the saddest faces they could manage and went "to work." A six-year-old with an outstretched hand may be cute; a sixteen-year-old is not. It was easier to beg from tourists than to do menial work day after day. But that was not the saddest part. When a boy or girl reached a certain age, sexual exploitation often replaced the begging. Thailand was infamous for that result.

Ria agreed that the example I gave was bad, but there was one that was worse: In some countries, mothers would cripple their own children so that they could use the child's infirmity to gain money from tourists. I had to agree; that was worse than the prostitution. All of it was bad. What we had seen during our wait seemed innocuous enough: foreigners being kind to little children. They did not understand the damage that they were doing. We reminded ourselves that it wasn't just Mombassa; it was the depressing side of much of the Third World. Our bus arrived.

We had obtained some third-hand information on an area to visit. The hotels were supposed to be inexpensive and the beaches very nice. Our source and the guidebooks said that the public access roads were not always safe and robbers plied their length looking for unsuspecting tourists. Oh good. I wondered out loud if they also preyed on suspecting tourists. Our bus dropped us off at the entrance road, and we learned from a taxi driver that it was three miles to the beach, the roads were most unsafe, and it was very expensive to go by taxi. We smiled at that last information but were unwilling to hear why. Our driver smiled in return. He was not disappointed to omit that particular story.

At the first cottages, we released our driver from our pocketbooks and elected to walk to as many potential lodges as was necessary. Guidebooks in the Third World were our worst enemy, and we discovered that Mombassa would be no different. Once a place of lodging was in a book, the rates rose dramatically. Neighboring lodges generally raised their prices a little and relied on the disgruntled for their clientele. Suddenly, our bargain hunting did not seem like such a good idea. Usually, when someone told us that other hotels were even higher in price, it was only a ploy to close the best deal on the "last" room. Here, we were faced with an outbreak of veracity. Everyone's rates were high.

And it was hot. Every possession we had was strapped to our perspiring backs. The beach and ocean remained hundreds of tantalizing yards away. In terms of actually sitting on a lounge chair and sipping something cool, we were nowhere close. I asked Ria to watch the packs for a few minutes while I set off through a mile-long stand of palm trees toward what I hoped would be one hotel too isolated to have much bargaining power. The breeze was cool and my sweat-soaked shirt and pants made it even cooler. In a few minutes I had started on the road back to optimism.

A very large caretaker greeted me in a big booming voice from fifty yards away. I returned his greeting and altered my path toward the spot where he was working. We chatted in Kiswahili for the obligatory three minutes and then switched to English. His discourse on Mombassa and the history of this particular section of the coast was fascinating, and I almost forgot that I was on a mission. When he asked where I was staying, the memory was quite clear. I explained the problem.

His look was one of deep concern—even more so when he learned that a young lady was also stranded. In my life before my trip, I might have been suspicious of the look on this total stranger's face, but I was beginning to understand that there are many truly good people throughout the world. He asked me to wait for him and he disappeared in the direction of the house whose grounds he was maintaining. In fifteen minutes he was back.

He had hoped that he could arrange a room here for us but had been told that the company that owned the property could not allow that. I was ready to thank him for the attempt when he mentioned that he had spoken with another caretaker for an adjacent property. It was unfortunate that we might be charged for the favor of allowing us to stay there, but at least it was a possibility. I asked how much the charge might be and was told six hundred *shillings* per night. That was about one third of the cost of the cheapest room in any of the hotels in the area, so I said yes, sight unseen.

I almost ran back to where Ria was still patiently waiting. Our only trepidation was the state of disrepair of our new lodging. We had stayed in some pretty bad accommodations, the Iqbal in Nairobi and Bujuku Hut in the Ruwenzoris among others, and we were working our thoughts around to the acceptance of nearly anything. The mansion that greeted us seemed like a case of misdirection. Bwana Harrison was smiling at our reaction and was quite happy to take us on a tour of the main house. There was a huge living and family room on one end of the house and a kitchen and several bedrooms on the other. All the rooms were huge and spacious with the airy look that only vaulted ceilings provide. The kitchen had refrigeration and the beds had mosquito netting attached to the ceiling. Wow.

There was more. There was a beautiful grotto just outside the front door. One part of the grotto had a cement floor and furniture was placed for the maximum enjoyment of cool breezes that flowed through. The other part of the grotto opened onto a large swimming pool. Running water came from a slide via a

Ria at poolside. The grotto provided a breeze, and the pool was heated by the equatorial sun. For backpackers, it was a luxury we never expected.

small pool above the grotto. The deck was wide and lined with trees. It was possible to see the ocean and the beach while lying at pool's edge. More wow.

We put our packs in the living room, took showers, and changed into our bathing suits. Within a half hour we were landed gentry. After a few hours of cooling off and relaxing, we realized that we were getting hungry. The caretaker had made it clear that we should provide our own food and that meant a trip into town. We decided to brave the thieves together and prepared for the three-mile walk each way.

I wouldn't want to make light of any warnings given to tourists. And I wouldn't want to suggest that we were blithely ignorant of the potential danger. We did carry one of the large *kukri* knives from Nepal with us, and we picked our roadway course so that we could remove ourselves from sight at the first sound of an approaching vehicle. As to thieves without vehicles, we tried to stay within eyesight of the many huts dotting the countryside. After fifteen minutes of waving villagers and smiling children, we were almost convinced that the guidebooks' findings must have changed with the newfound influx of tourists. There was nothing worse for business than a reputation for thievery. And there was no one better to police the thieves than local businessmen with their liveli-

Here I am with the day's catch. The actual fisherman shyly remained in the background, refusing to be photographed holding the family meal.

hoods at stake. We remained cautious until we reached the main highway.

There were no markets in sight. This was a rural Mombassa area, not a tourist hotbed—at least not here on the highway. Our good luck held, however, and a young boy on a bicycle directed us to his uncle's "store." The directions led us to a seven-foot by nine-foot shed with a door that sagged on the one remaining hinge. It was, it turned out, a drop-off site for farmers who were paid when their foodstuffs were picked up by a truck headed into town. At the store, we were able to buy six bottles of Coca-Cola, some vegetables and fruits, and even some eggs. It was a heavy load, but it would last us until tomorrow afternoon. Perhaps we would get some exercise and run to the "market" in the cool of the early morning. We discussed that possibility on a thiefless walk back to the house.

For three days we ate, basked in the sun, ran on the back roads, and forgot that we were tourists. After dinner, we celebrated sundown and our good fortune and relaxed in the cool pool waters. Sodas were cold, the food was healthful and plentiful, and we were able to put off the thought that we would soon return to Nairobi and then continue our respective journeys. We had a very comfortable friendship, and Africa had been made better because of the people we had met and the places we had traveled.

We made it to the beach only once. Offshore, the water was actually quite warm because a line of coral paralleled the beach and allowed the partially captive, shallow water to heat up. As we walked along the coral, we looked for treasures. We found many shells, some with animals still using them. Then, a flash of bright orange caught my eye. Breaking waves made it hard to know for sure, but it seemed that there was a shell in a small, fist-sized hole in the coral. We had trouble getting it out and discovered when we did that it was both beautiful and occupied. There was a fair amount of soul searching about whether to leave it or take it with us. Taking it with us meant the death of the occupant for a trinket. We still hadn't decided as we neared shore and prepared to work our way back to the house.

A man with a snorkel mask and a trident spear suddenly stood up in front of us. He was hunting octopus and had several on a line staked to the rocks. He showed us some different types and told us how much the hotels paid for these delicacies. It was a meager living, but it was the only work he had been able to find. When he saw our shell, he asked if we were going to keep it. We didn't understand his intent and thought that he wanted it because it might bring him money at one of the hotels. That wasn't so. He wanted to help us remove the denizen from its home. Before we could protest, he raised the shell over his head and slammed it down on the hard wet sand of the water's edge. He repeated this many times, throwing the open part of the shell against the sand. Obviously, this was not his first experience with such shells. There was a lot of animal inside and there was no medical hope when our fisherman ended his ministrations. He assured us that he had been happy to help and showed us where we could find some many-colored starfish for pictures. We waved goodbye and walked away with another story and another souvenir.

On the return train trip we used the money we had saved for lodging and treated ourselves to first-class accommodations. There were a lot of things to talk about: people we had met, places we had gone, and what we had learned about ourselves from our respective trips. Ria was thinking of settling down to raise some fat and happy babies in a house with a large fireplace. She wanted to travel, too, and there were conflicts between those two desires. Knowing her, I felt she would find a way to do both. And if the babies tried to keep up with mom while they were growing up, they would never be fat.

I had no dilemma. When I ran out of money, I would go home. There, I would work at something and would save for my next trip—perhaps to South America. I wanted to see the Andes and Tierra del Fuego. And I wanted to see Patagonia. I would return home, practice my Spanish, and try to create enough wealth to do this again. We talked long into the night about how good all of this had been. Within a year of my return, Ria and her boyfriend, Yves, were in South America, writing me funny and inspiring letters.

Things happened fast in Nairobi. We purchased tickets and exchanged addresses. Ria was going to Kathmandu for purchases for a small business she had started in Vancouver. I would be flying to London. I wasn't out of money, but the turmoil in the Middle East and depleted funds made Europe the next stop. Kathmandu for my Canadian friend; London for me. Of the shock awaiting our respective landings, mine would be the most severe. What I had always thought of as civilization rushed to greet me. I no longer knew what I would think of it now.

As I sat in the waiting room, I thought back over the past year. What had been the best? How could I compare any two of the adventures I'd had? Kala Pattar? The first or the second time? With the marathon or without? Everest or Mt. Nuptse or Ama Dablam? In October's warmth or November's icy chill? Or Goa? Huge pink burnished clouds at sunset with the sun a giant orange ball sinking slowly into the sea? Hours of barefoot running on a beach of fine sand while porpoises rolled and fed in a calm sea? Or Africa? Climbing the second highest mountain on the continent and finding snow and cold on the equator? Viewing Kenya from over 16,000 feet of breathtaking glacially carved arête? Or the Ruwenzoris? Or the gorillas? Or the safari?

Finally, I realized that it was the wrong question. A decision never had to be reached. Nothing needed to be thought of as second best. There wasn't an also-ran. I could keep it all—from Singapore to Salt Lake City. I had learned a lot of things, and I'd be realizing what they were for years to come. At this moment, I realized that I had been working full-time making memories and had taken advantage of every chance to maximize enjoyment. Somehow, I was getting closer to the meaning of life. Just the new friends alone…

CHAPTER 16
ENGLAND

For my part, I travel not to go anywhere, but to go. I travel for travel's sake. The great affair is to move; to feel the needs and hitches of our life more nearly; to come down off this feather-bed of civilisation, and find the globe granite underfoot and strewn with cutting flints.
– Robert Louis Stevenson

Culture shock is a relative thing. It had started for me as Ria and I parted company at the Nairobi Airport. Her flight would take her to Kathmandu; my flight would take me to London. As I walked from her gate toward mine, the human landscape began to change. Caucasians were everywhere. British Caucasians were everywhere. I saw freckles and red hair, blue eyes, and Western-style clothing. I was no longer the one easily identified tourist out of every one hundred people. My trip was about to take another very large turn.

I had written to Penny and Nick, my friends from Nepal, and had mentioned my flight number and date of arrival. Mail, however, had not always been timely between countries and I had no idea if I'd be met at Heathrow's terminal or not. Had I been able to stay in Africa longer, I would have gladly done so. Asia and Africa had been my home for over a year and it had been a very action-packed time. During my flight to see my friends in England, I read back over some of my early journal entries and thought back to what huge differences some of the experiences had wrought. Then I thought about the reason my trip was being shortened.

Four people in America owed me money before I left. One source of remaining-on-the-road money was a former employer in Arizona. Another was a loan made to a friend almost a year before I left for Singapore. Two others were from the sale of personal items just before the start of my trip. The total was almost $2,500—enough to remain in Asia or Africa for almost four more months. Repeated letters had not worked, I had never received an answer. I went back to reading the journal. Thoughts about what might have been always led me to thoughts about what should have been. And that led to resentment toward friends. Or, as such negative thoughts seemed to suggest, former friends.

Air travel was such a treat to a backpacker that even the long trips were quite pleasant. There was time for reflection and journal reading. Then, we were over England and in a very short time we rolled across the tarmac to the gate. It was early morning. Would my friends be there?

Nick was both waiting and smiling as I walked out of the customs area. We exchanged *namastes* and the *wai* of greeting. It had been an early morning for him and he had driven from Bedford, nearly forty miles away. Still, he was his usual animated self and wanted to know everything that had transpired since I had left Nepal. He had read my letters detailing some of my African accounts, and it pleased me a great deal that he remembered most of the information I had sent. He also asked for my comments on the culture shock I was obviously experiencing.

My immediate observation was that I was no longer special. All through Asia and Africa, my Western origins had been obvious. It was a fact that couldn't be escaped. It led to hordes of touts, but it also led to language lessons with families, offers for lodging in homes, and many chances to meet people from each country—special. Now, in England, no one stared or walked up to me to ask what country I was from or what my good name was. No one placed his or her hands together in a *wai* of greeting. My looks were no longer affecting my travel.

Now, in a largely Caucasian society, I was only special when I spoke. My accent was now the key to my difference. Nick, too, had experienced something like that after his two years of travel. However, he had returned directly to England and had slipped quietly back into the society in which he was born. My return had this intermediate stop called Europe. Certainly, there were linguistic adventures to be had in Spain and France. The trip was not over. In the meantime, our discussions of the adaptation to familiar cultures helped me over the slight depression of feeling quite ordinary. I wasn't home yet, but it felt closer.

Penny was teaching school when I arrived. At day's end, she was her animated self and the three of us spent a pleasant evening discussing some of the highlights of our respective trips. It was not lost on any of us that such conversations could only occur with fellow travelers. They had discovered that untraveled friends had varying degrees of disinterest in most of where they had been. I hoped I wouldn't face that when I returned. We savored this time for all that it meant and would mean.

"Bedford-my-Bedford," was how Nick referred to his hometown. I didn't actually have my nose pressed against the side window of his car but the forty miles from London to his residence certainly had my undivided attention. There were lots of cars, but the pollution seemed minimal. Buses had people in them, but none rode on the roof or spilled out of windows and doorways. School children wore shoes, and there were generally several adults near any group of them. Policemen didn't carry guns; they especially didn't carry semi-automatic weapons. And the homes…

You could think about the differences for days. Running through the countryside with Penny and Nick was thought-provoking. I was thankful that they had shared some of their experiences and that they had spent two years of their lives as backpackers. While I didn't exactly slip back into Western society, I found that Penny and Nick offered a sort of halfway house of adjustment. I stayed for a week.

I had been to England on two previous occasions and had spent most of my time in the north. Now I had been asked to visit some of the marathon runners in Devon. Everyone who learned of my impending excursion told me how wonderful that part of their country was.

I traveled from London to Devon with marathoner Dieter Loraine. The Royal Marine and non-jogger was in town to pick up his son at the airport. It was good luck. It was even better luck that the day we met at Heathrow was the date many of the entrants in the London Marathon arrived. Dieter and I had both chosen to wear our white and blue Everest Marathon sweatshirts for this particular reunion. We received much more attention than we could have anticipated. More than half of the marathon participants in Nepal had been British, and we had many questions from those in town for a tamer version of distance running. Those runners who had never heard of such a thing were as incredulous as I had been when David Blakeney had told me about it. A 17,500-foot start line, 4,500 feet of ascent, "fell" running, twenty degrees below zero… Now that I was in the clear light of day, it sounded pretty difficult to me, too. Dieter seemed quite happy that he was finally answering questions from a group that would not refer to what he had done as "jogging."

Dieter and his wife and two sons lived in the very quaint village of Budleigh Salterton. Like most places on my trip, it wasn't what it seemed. While there were a lot of older residents and many retired people in the area, the Royal Marine base of operations was not far away. It was not uncommon to see a large number of exceptionally fit young men training in and around the confines of Budleigh. Dieter's job was to train the trainers. It sounded a lot like the position I had been in before my trip. I had been getting paid for something I liked to do and something I was good at. Dieter and I agreed that it was a good life.

After I had settled into the top floor of the Loraine home, Dieter and I went for a run. I discovered that my lack of running in the last few months caused a real physical beating. On days when I should have been resting, I ran the same course with Dr. Green. For a change of pace, we would drive to Dartmoor and run with Paddy Bettesworth on the moors. To be precise, I've never actually run with Paddy. He was ill on the day of the marathon, and he was well on all the days we ran on the moors. I could see him in the distance, though, and I took some solace that at least he wasn't more than a mile ahead of me.

I was accorded the kind of hospitality that might be expected of family. It was a tremendous feeling to be the recipient of that much kindness and I reflected on just how lucky a traveler could be. An hour or two of running was always interesting, and I never turned down an opportunity to join my friends.

One afternoon, I was recovering from a one-hour run with Dr. Green and his two golden retrievers when Dieter called from the military base. He wanted to know if I wanted to have some fun. Having learned that unquestioning acceptance can be painful, I asked, "What kind of fun?" It seemed that Dieter had told his students—the future PTs—that an American friend of his was in town. This American friend had done the Everest Marathon and was a personal fitness trainer in the U.S. The natural progression had been to extend an opportunity to join them in a workout. I agreed only to save face. Everyone knew that I had nothing else to do.

To get to the base required a forty-five-minute bike ride. I assumed that the lactic acid I had acquired on this morning's run would disappear if I biked. The guards checked my ID, confirmed my visit through Dieter, and waved me through. It was tight security.

Inside the gymnasium I had doubts that this was going to be "fun"—at least for me. There were twelve men in their mid-twenties listening to Dieter. He was explaining what we would be doing. Around me stood young men who looked like they were waiting for the body building contest to begin. There wasn't an ounce of fat on any of them and I thought I knew the reason. I told Dieter that he could have been more honest and just asked me if I wanted to have some "pain." He smiled.

I could do all the exercises he outlined. What I couldn't do were the warm-up exercises and that was clear to everyone in a hurry. Dieter's job was to teach these young men how to instruct. One of them led the exercises and his task was to have everyone perform with military precision. I set them back a long way. There were some very unregimented smiles. Dieter was not so restrained and made fun of me unmercifully. Then we were on to the fun.

The exercise program consisted of rope climbing, push-ups, chin-ups, sprints from one end of the gym to the other, and a number of other familiar movements. The key was to pick the order according to my own strengths and weaknesses. While there were one hundred push-ups to be done, we didn't have to do them all at once. Each time I finished a set of twenty, for example, I would run up to a chalkboard and record it under "Yank" in the appropriate column. Then it was on to another exercise to let my arms rest. This was a mental and physical challenge. Those who did their chin-ups first, and did all of them, might find that they lacked the biceps strength to climb the rope.

It was a madhouse. There was no military precision here. But there was a sense of teamwork. Between exercises, encouragement was shouted to anyone who struggled. I had my fair share of verbal assistance. I did finish. It was thirty minutes of strenuous movement. Dieter said there were at least four hours a day of physical exercise for these Royal Marines. It was no wonder their instructor thought nothing of all the bicycle and running races. It was just business as usual.

It didn't take long to decide that Devon was a great place to stay. Dr. Green let me stay at his home for a lot longer than guests normally do. He couldn't have been more amiable, and I enjoyed listening to his stories as we ran with his two beautiful dogs. However, I was still on the schedule that had been set before the trip started and I was supposed to travel with David Blakeney to France and Spain. The group leader for the Everest Marathon worked for Acorn Ventures and I had volunteered to go along and to help at the various recreation camps that he would visit. And then I was supposed to meet my friend Rick in Germany. I looked forward to seeing someone I knew from America.

It was time to see the rest of Europe.

Land's End.

CHAPTER 17
<u>EUROPE</u>

I stood at the motorway entrance ramp in the south of France and tried not to build up a severe case of anxiety. It had been so comfortable in England among the friends I had met in Nepal. And it had been equally comfortable to travel with David Blakeney from Devon to Cherbourg and to the various Acorn Venture camps in France. Because he was fluent in both Spanish and French, there was never any question about where we were going or how we would get organized. Now, I faced travel to Munich, Germany, and I was going to hitch-hike. Money was really becoming a problem.

It was easy to imagine more trouble than could possibly occur so I confined my worries to situations that seemed quite probable. One was the legality of hitchhiking. Was it legal in the countries I would cross? If not on the freeways, would taking back roads be either legal or safe? Would the people giving me a ride speak English? I felt more comfortable with the last question because almost everyone on this entire trip around the world had spoken English. The first ride was with a couple going to Lyon. They spoke less English than I spoke French.

"*Morgen,*" said the driver, a gentleman in his mid-fifties.

"*Morgen,*" I replied. He must have thought that I was German because of my sign: "Munich." Well, it was a language I was a lot more comfortable with than French.

"*Wie geht's?*" he said, smiling.

"*Zer gut, danke, unt enan?*" I saw a puzzled look on his face. He had understood what I said, but he seemed to have picked up a non-German accent on my part. Was this couple German or French?

After he told me that he was fine, in German, I plunged very uncomfortably into the very limited French that David had taught me.

"S'il vous plait, monsieur, y a-t-il quelqu 'un ici qui parle anglais?" I might have just asked him if anyone spoke English. David had taught it to me for environs more crowded than an automobile. I also thought that it established that I not only was not French, but I also didn't speak it.

He smiled courteously at my discomfort. *"Un pue,"* he said. Naturally, I didn't memorize any of the answers to questions. He had told me that he spoke a lot of English, some English, or no English. Well, maybe not a lot of English or we'd have been communicating in it then. We needed to get some dialogue established soon. The speedometer read eighty.

"Je veux me rendre a Munchen." That was me, again. Bless both their hearts, they spoke to me slowly and clearly, but I still had no idea of how close they were going to Munich. I could only hope that they knew where to let me out of their car.

After discovering that conversing was nearly more work than it was worth, the three of us settled into silence. I had heard stories about the rudeness of the French and had not seen it at all in the last week. And I didn't see it here, either. It was a half hour before they spoke to each other, and they apologized to me before conversing. Just beyond the first sign I saw for Munchen, they slowed. We could only smile at each other and gave Gallic shrugs for our linguistic problems. Then, they were gone.

I was deposited at the road near Avignon. David had given me a map but had cautioned me that French maps often showed, out of national pride, roads that did not exist. I was careful to stay on the main roads and hoped that the gendarmes were going to be lenient in enforcing whatever ban on hitchhiking might exist. One ride down and who knew how many to go…

The next ride was also with someone who spoke no English. He also spoke no French. He was from Bosnia and was delivering some goods from one friend to another. It had turned out to be a linguistically sorry state of affairs, and this time I was not sure if he understood my destination or how I would go about getting there. The old joke about the good news of making good time and the bad news about being lost was not so funny. I carried all my worldly possessions and relied on the good will of others. My new chauffeur talked a blue streak, apparently on the assumption that eventually I would recognize one or more words, and we would communicate. At least he wasn't trying to teach me his language by speaking slowly and loudly. What finally happened was that I saw a major intersection with a sign that said, "Munchen." It hadn't taken me very long to note that Munchen and Munich were one and the same. For the duration of this part of my trip, Munchen was the answer. He slowed to let me disembark. We shook hands and wished each other luck. That is, I wished him luck.

I was about to cross the border into Switzerland. But for a while, it was not to be. Almost all male hitchhikers have experienced that long stretch of time and road where no one looks at you, no one slows down, and your spirit sinks by the minute. An hour went by and I felt increasingly like Casper the friendly but invisible ghost. Another hour went by. Along a crowded highway, this did not look good. I wanted some attention, any attention. I had forgotten the cardinal rule of wishing: "Be careful about what you wish for, you just might get it." A horn honk from a decidedly official-looking black car on the other side of the freeway was accompanied by an extended arm motioning me off the entry ramp. Things had gone from bad to worse. I didn't want to be arrested, to continue standing here, or to find another route less traveled. If there was a connection or a solution, I didn't see it.

Slowly, to comply with part of the law's letter, I started to walk back toward the frontage road. My thumb was still extended, but not as obviously. I still had my Munchen sign, but now I hung it around my neck instead of holding it up. If there was going to be justice, this would be the time to find some.

And, sure enough, a large brown van honked as it went by and the driver pulled over into the emergency lane of the road. As I ran toward the partially opened passenger door, I hoped for someone who spoke English. The driver appeared to be James Bond. You can't get any more English than that. (Franz Kafka was still choreographing parts of this trip, and the man behind the wheel was about to prove that he belonged.)

He wasn't actually James Bond, but he was decidedly British. He started off by telling me that he was with international drug interdiction. I looked over the exceptionally elderly van and its strewn interior and marveled at the expert disguise. Behind the two captain's chairs in front was a large open area filled with shelves of electronic equipment, a clothesline, and remnants of fast-food dining. He informed me that he had a full passport, an empty passport, and a Turkish passport. The latter, he informed me, couldn't be taken out of the country. I thought I understood full passport and empty passport, but I felt confident that a passport you couldn't take out of the country of issue should probably belong to Yossarian. If *Catch-22* had a real human embodiment, he was driving that van.

There was more. The minutes flew by like hours as he enlightened me as to the value of the equipment he had on board. He estimated that it was over 1.5

At St. Peter's in Europe.

million U.S. dollars. He had personally driven 2 million kilometers in this vehicle in the last two years. In front of me was a damaged television set, a water depth gauge, and a number of disconnected speakers resting on the dashboard. Everything was dusty. I committed his comments to memory as quickly as possible because I sensed a great story to tell my friends. I did it quickly because there seemed to be an increasing chance that I might have to shorten the story and jump out before I had the opportunity to find out what the water depth gauge was for.

He didn't speak French or Spanish or German or French and had a lot of trouble deciding where he was and where he was going. I reflected on the idea that the very expensive "eavesdropping equipment" stored behind me would only be of use to him if he quit racking up miles and stopped to use it, and only if drug dealers all decided to work their schemes in English or Turkish.

I told him I was going to try to get to Geneve (Geneva), Switzerland, by evening and meet some friends. I gave him road directions from the map, and he seemed genuinely surprised when we reached the Swiss border crossing. It seemed that he thought Geneva was in northern France. He had just decided to show the border guard his international drug enforcement badge as I was preparing to make the truth sound believable. Fortunately for all concerned, the

With Rick at Neuschwunstein

EEC and the border crossing agreements allowed us to pass through without slowing down. Nonplussed to be in a country he hadn't intended to visit, he asked me if I knew what the Swiss *shilling* was worth?

We stopped for a moment to consult my map so that he could get to his secret drug busting rendezvous. Even confronted with the map, he was sure that Germany and Austria should be interchanged. When he told me his van was named George. I decided it was time to bail out. It was not to be.

No sooner had we reached the outskirts of the Swiss border town than we entered some steeply descending canyons. He was chain smoking cigars and telling tales that were even more unbelievable than his descriptions of his immediate surroundings. Then he decided to instruct me on driving techniques. If it had been instructions for vans and not Ferraris, I might have emerged with fewer gray hairs. His premise was that one did not need to use the brakes on a descent but could, instead, use the engine compression and special steering techniques. I stopped listening when he mentioned not using the brakes. When I was much younger, an adult had tried to impress and scare me at the same time with other absurd driving techniques. I had said then that I would admit to fear if he would quit trying to escalate my reaction to his near-death driving. Mr.

Bond was worse. Driving *"dangereaux"* became tailgating, and curves were used for passing. He rolled his window down twice and tried to adjust the "special antennae." We nearly hit the railing on each of those failed attempts. The antennae must not have been working because it was deathly quiet inside while the tires made up for that outside.

We reached Geneva and we continued on to Lusanne. It was there that I assured him that I was going to meet my friends. If he noticed that my friends had mysteriously changed meeting places, he never said. (It probably fit in with the world as he knew it.) For my part, if I had to ride in that van again, I would consider taking up residence right there and would learn to speak Swiss.

I arrived in Munchen by train. Hitchhiking problems and stress had made the cost from Urdorf increasingly reasonable (eighty Swiss francs). Aside from the James Bond adventure, there had only been one other incident of note. A brand-new Mercedes had stopped on an entrance ramp in Switzerland in the rain. The driver was a beautiful, mini-skirted Asian girl who spoke German, French, and English. Unfortunately, she had been unable to see my sign and was going to the exit toward the city where I had come from. There was a universe between her and James Bond, but by that time I was just looking for a train depot.

My friend Rick was flying in the next day from California. I had part of a day to explore downtown Munchen and then would go to the airport to meet his plane. In Germany and Switzerland, planes and trains run on time. You can set your watch by their schedules. I arrived several hours early and was amazed at the number of people at the airport, most of which seemed to be a human squall line. I couldn't even find a bench or a chair to sit on and opted for the floor. After a while, I sensed that all was not well. There were more people coming in and none seemed to be going out. I went to the one airline counter that was deserted amid the crowd.

German transportation workers had gone on strike. That was perfect. This trip had forced an increasing amount of Zen on me. The plane, I was told, would be landing in Frankfurt and the passengers would travel by bus or train to Munich. That was because the planes could not land in Germany. I pointed out that Frankfurt was in Germany, a fact not lost on the German airline representative. If they could land there, they could land here, couldn't they? Evidently they couldn't. He told me that he would have an answer or an update in two hours as to which bus or train might be used. It depended on when the plane landed. I waited, read, and wrote in my journal.

Two hours passed and the clerk had been unable to find out anything except that they "should" be traveling by train. He said that I needed to be at the train station that evening, but I departed the airport with no idea of which train to meet. At the train station it was even more confusing. For the first time in twenty years, trains were late, delayed, or canceled. The information counter staff were very polite, but all they could suggest was to stand on the second floor observation area and watch the fifteen arrival tracks for trains from southern Germany. And that's what I did.

I did it from 4:30 in the afternoon until 1:00 A.M. I saw more people than I had taken careful note of in a lifetime. I saw people twice or three times if they stayed around the station. I recognized the vendors when they walked to and from their kiosks, and I felt like part of the station employee's extended family. It seemed like I saw every country represented and every social stratum. What I didn't see was an American friend, and I thought that this situation did not bode well for our meeting. I called my mother in the U.S. and asked her to call Rick's wife, Anita. That was in case Rick called home. I gave Mom the number of the hotel that would have a vacancy tomorrow so that we could find each other that way. I had already discussed the call with the hotel staff. At 1:30 A.M. it was cold; I was tired and there were only two or three more trains scheduled. Or, more likely, not scheduled. Evidently, they didn't arrest foreigners for loitering. If they did, I would have qualified several times over.

It was too late to get a room in this part of town. The strike had made accommodations scarce. I tried to curl up on a bench, but a cruel wind blew through the hangar-like station, and I could only shake. An Australian girl had been standing near another track for a few hours and we struck up a conversation about the bad luck of trying to meet friends under these circumstances. After a few questions, she felt better about her situation because mine was worse. I could see that she wanted to invite me to stay at the residence where her friends had given her lodging. The fact that I was a stranger and unknown and an unacceptable risk decided the matter. She left to get her car and sleep warm. I resigned myself to being a street person.

There was an opportunity for rest in the upstairs waiting room. It was for passengers with tickets only, and I was a great believer in signs. Clearly, however, this room and the signs were being misused tonight. A few families and at least twenty street people were already in the room. About a half-dozen tired and dazed foreigners like me were near one of the two exits—in case the message on the sign was to be enforced. At 2:30 in the morning, enforcement arrived. The police rousted us all and I spent the rest of the night walking back and forth in the deserted station. There was a lesson here, or maybe more than one, but I just wasn't ready for anything more meaningful than sleep, warmth, and privacy.

I was back at my observation post at 7:00 A.M. I took a quick break at a Burger King about fifty feet away. Food was important but so was appearance. When you are out on the street, you can go to seed very quickly. Or, at least I did. I washed and combed my hair, brushed my teeth and changed into a fresh shirt. Perhaps Rick would recognize me. On the assumption that we weren't going to be touring Europe on separate tours, I trudged back to my post.

With the idea that maybe I was missing something, I decided to walk out one of the very large doors where German commuters were pouring in. The habit of scanning every face was still active and it took a second for me to recognize a familiar countenance. Looking rested and refreshed, Rick and another grounded traveler were walking through the terminal on their way to breakfast. The story, as it unraveled, was that a group of disgruntled passengers rented a car and drove to Munchen. They had arrived last night and stayed in a hotel.

A new adventure was ready to begin, but not until I had some rest

CHAPTER 18
<u>THE TYROLS</u>

The adventurer is an outlaw.
Adventure must start with running away from home.
– William Bolitho

When I joined up with Rick, I was curious about several things. One of my questions was answered right away when he made a very smooth transition to German while negotiating for a hotel room and a meal. Somewhere in the past few months he must have been very busy with tapes, books and…who knows? Somewhere outside of Munich, I'd get to find out if he had trained for running on his vacation. One feature of most of my friendships was that the months before a vacation included intense sessions in the gym or on roadways. Running was always part of the plan. We bicycled when possible and hiked, too. For this trip, Rick had done that along with taking care of the linguistic side of things.

We arrived at a hotel in Garmisch just after sunset. With no sleep and a busy day of sightseeing in Munchen, I was out as soon as my head hit the pillow. Tomorrow morning we would go running.

It was a memorable run. There were some kayaks on the river near the trail and we both noticed that there was no litter anywhere. The river water looked glacially fed and I remembered back to the Dudh Kosi in Nepal. We clocked a 54:13 run with the last twenty minutes on steep hills. We were both fatigued and had some difficult moments pushing ourselves to the limit on the hills. But this was Germany and I was with the first person from my life before my trip and I felt too good to worry about temporary discomfort.

Our friendship went back through almost a quarter of a century. In 1976, we had done our first marathons. He had taught me to snow ski and had helped me learn to do somersaults from jumps. I had introduced him to weight training and the trampoline. Now, he had three wonderful children, a second marriage, and a very good job in southern California. In the last few years before this trip, we had done some long bike rides in Mexico and California. I had even convinced him to do the 200-mile Seattle to Portland bike ride.

Now, for some reason, there was a bit of tension on my part. I tried to figure out what was wrong. Several days of sightseeing went by, and then I was able to see what had changed. For Rick, this European trip was a short adventure and was only a little bit stressful in terms of the unknown. He had studied the areas he wanted to visit and was comfortable with understanding more German than he could speak. He had a reasonable amount of luggage for such a trip and enough money to enjoy above average accommodations. That was fairly typical for a vacationer from my country.

On the other hand, I was newly released from the Third World, where I had spent over twelve months. I had not studied or prepared for any of the areas I had traveled to and had spoken none of the native languages when I arrived. My possessions had been only what I carried on my back, and I had purchased only a few items of clothing to replace those hardest hit by rigorous use. I was nearly out of money and knew that there wouldn't be any waiting when I got home. I had become exceptionally budget-conscious as a result, which is fairly typical for a backpacker traveling around the world.

Rick offered me a few of his shirts and a pair of pants. I was a good enough friend to weigh the gesture instead of just rejecting it out of politeness. His gifts would be the nicest clothes I had worn in twelve months. This small gesture illuminated the tension I had been feeling, and we discussed it. Neither of us had expected that this trip would offer a sort of halfway house for my return to the civilization I had grown up in. But of the five or six people I considered my closest friends, I was quite sure that Rick was the ideal person to gradually ease me back into the world of my past.

We traveled to Grainau to a lake for another run. For the miles of car travel before the destination we looked at various rugged mountains and discussed routes for possible ascents. We could have been in our early twenties for the excitement in our voices and the plans we discussed. Rick's enjoyment of adventure often exceeded my own; the more mature sides of our older selves must have been hoping that we were on a tight sightseeing schedule. We were approaching the Zugspitz. Our itinerary would take us to Lake Constance (Bodensee) tomorrow, and there would be no time for mountain climbing. Rick didn't have the time, but I thought I might return here and climb to the summit by one of the easier routes.

The road from Garmisch to Bodensee took us through the Austrian Tyrol.

It was exceptional and very different from the mountains in the western United States. There were stacks of wood everywhere. Some were huge. Many seemed to be rotting because they were so old. Everyone had a considerable storehouse of winter heat, and some homes appeared to have an inexhaustible supply. In each valley, there were wooden sheds with nothing in them. It was a mystery and we chose to let it remain one. We toured by observing and didn't try to find explanations for everything. We were very interested in the bicyclists we saw plying the steep roadways over pass after pass in the high mountains. There were some very fit people here.

I told Rick about the first time I had driven a car on the trip. David Blakeney had let me drive through France and it had been an incredible experience. I had taken driving for granted before the trip. After a year of deprivation, I understood the power that came with being able to select your own destination and to go there directly. I could stop when and where I wanted, change my mind, take care of my own safety. The personal motor car was personal power. Those who have walked or taken buses for years understand exactly what I mean. I couldn't wait to retrieve my Dodge van and drive somewhere when I returned to the U.S.

We drove from near Meersburg to Innsbruck and were stopped by the sheer beauty of this place. We knew that the Winter Olympics had once been held here, but that told us nothing about the area away from the ski resorts. As we drove through the long valley leading to town, we saw gliders being towed aloft by planes. There were also hang gliders and parasails in the sky. Brightly colored kayaks were negotiating the river and in-line skaters, runners, and bicyclists were everywhere on a trail near the river's edge. Winter sports were not the only attraction in Innsbruck. The chamber of commerce could not have created a better advertisement for us than this fitness paradise set in the beautiful Austrian Tyrol.

Innsbruck had other aspects that brought smiles to our faces. The police cars were made by BMW and the taxis were Mercedes. The size of the beer steins was amusing, but we knew that there had to be some problems with alcoholism lurking somewhere. These people loved to drink.

We continued on back to Munchen and prepared for Rick's departure. His vacation had seemed far too short. I no longer thought in terms of time. I would be home soon, and we agreed to get together and continue my rehabilitation, if that was possible....

Rick boarded a plane and I returned to the hotel in the car. In the morning,

I would leave, too, but I wouldn't be going by air. I felt myself reverting to the backpacker mentality even as I dropped the hotel key at the desk. The only ripples on the pond of my Zen outlook had been the drive from the airport to the hotel. It was a powerful feeling to have that much control. Now, putting that in the past, I walked to the nearest bus station. My destination was somewhere in Spain. My new outlook solved a lot of the potential problems that might have concerned me a year ago. I'd had many nebulous destinations with no idea how to get there. And all of them had been terrific adventures. I was sure that this would be too.

I took bus 91 and S6 to Hauptendorf, the location of the train terminal. After I parted with 247 Deutschmarks ($160), I was on my way. According to the schedule the arrival time would be the next morning at 9:00 A.M. in Barcelona. Finally, I was moving toward a language I could speak and understand—I hoped. In the meantime, I settled in for a long ride and was content to observe my fellow travelers and to see the beautiful countryside. And it was beautiful. Most of what I had seen in the countryside of Germany, Austria, Bavaria, and Switzerland had looked like a park, and what I saw now was no exception.

In the morning, we entered Spain. There was a change. I was back in the Third World. At one time that statement would have seemed a very uncharitable thing to say about Spain and its struggling economy. But I felt more at home in Third-World countries than I had felt while in Europe. I smiled through the train window at balconies on high rises with clothes drying on lines. Barefoot people traveled on bicycles between towns. The graffiti on the buildings was very artistic and the colors were beautiful. And there were miles of red poppies on either side of the tracks. I could read and understand most of the signs, but years of limited use had left my Spanish weaker than I thought. Good, this wasn't going to be easy, either. We stopped in Barcelona and I was on my own with no agenda except to rest.

I quickly tired of being without transport in Barcelona and decided to leave. My handy journal told me that David Blakeney and the Acorn Ventures operation was on the Costa Brava at Tossa de Mar. I would be looking for Calle Llevado. These directions seemed straightforward, but it was not to be. Against my better judgement and that of the residents of my new country, I decided to hitchhike. They and I decided that the operative word that Sunday was "try." I spent hours near the entrance to the main road. Traffic was too heavy for anyone to pull over even if they wanted to. I moved a block or two closer to town so that cross-street traffic turning toward the freeway could see me and would be able to get me on board before they picked up speed. *Nada.*

I walked to another entrance and tried again. There was the same congestion problem. I never learned the Spanish word for hitchhike, but I would be willing to bet there wasn't one. I gave up. It was the first time in my life that there had been no ride in response to an outstretched thumb. I took my anger and fatigue and headed for a bus station. It was no easier there. To save money, I was going to try to get far enough out of the city to where traffic would be less frequent and the roads would be wide enough for people to pull over. Then, I would hitchhike again.

The directions for each of the buses seemed straightforward until I got to the one that went to Tossa. It seemed like a very long way. My decision to take the bus for a reasonable distance out of town still seemed like a good one. Value rigidity. I thought about the monkey and the coconut, and I considered that although I might be in slightly less trouble, I might be on the same track.

The coast was beautiful and I was lazily gazing out the window when I realized that the beach patrons on the waterside were wearing very little. It was beyond topless; it seemed to be a thong beach. It was unfortunate that the thong and miniskirt were seldom worn by those who should wear them. Oh great! My American judgment of others' behavior seemed to be reviving. I thought I had left that behind in Malaysia during my first month of travel. Having caught myself, I settled in to observe instead of to judge—a much more difficult proposition. There was certainly a lot of unpressed flesh in the next sixty miles.

In the late afternoon, we arrived in a small town. A very nice Irish gentleman who had been to Spain every year for the last twenty years gave me some helpful hints for getting to Tossa de Mar. We wished each other luck in Spanish and I stepped off the bus. Back to hitchhiking. Now the road was not crowded with anything. A couple of motorcycles went by and I dropped my thumb well before they reached me. One Irish word of advice had been to avoid motorcycles no matter what. Having ridden a cycle since age sixteen, I immediately saw what he meant. It was a hot summer afternoon and those bikers were wearing full leathers. Actually, they were wearing mock-ups of racing team gear. I could have left my thumb up for all the chance I had to see them decelerate. They were heading for the mountainous roads along the coast and didn't need any extra baggage.

An hour passed. The sun was going to set in less than an hour and I knew I had better get moving if I wanted to find a camp before dark. And then I got a ride. A young man was making a delivery of supplies to a hotel in Tossa! It was my lucky day. And he was willing to listen to my halting Spanish as I answered questions and asked some myself. Having just left Barcelona, I could tell him with complete honesty how beautiful the Costa Brava was and how much I enjoyed Spain. He told me about tourism and how the population of this coastal village trebles each summer. Boats, buses, and cars brought people here; they had come to Barcelona from all over the world.

We arrived in Tossa and the sun was minutes above the horizon. Tossa was beautiful and looked like the pictures of the white stucco buildings in Greece. I asked to be dropped off near a service station on the assumption that I could find Acorn Ventures with directions from an attendant. I could not. Three men decided to help me, and we could not. There were a great many tourist places in and around the village, but no one had ever heard of this particular company. I was encouraged to ask at several restaurants. Perhaps someone there would know. An hour later, it was dusk. The sun had gone behind some mountains at sunset. There was more daylight time than I had expected, but not as much as I needed. I was tired.

Tired people make mental errors, and I finally sat down and did what I should have done as soon as I got off the bus. I took out the address David had given me and tried to note any clues about location. All that I had was a number, Calle Llevado, and Tossa de Mar. Then the obvious hit me. I had asked no one where Calle Llevado was. Locals might not recognize a foreign company, but they would be familiar with one of their own streets. At the original service station, I found the directions I had been looking for. It seemed that camp was about four miles back along the road leading to Barcelona. It was uphill, in the dark, but now I knew I was only a few hours from security and rest.

I had to walk the whole distance with my heavy pack. If I had had brains enough at the time, I would have given the entire address to the young man who had given me the ride. I would have been asleep by now after a "slap up" meal. Ah well, I took solace in the fact that the coast of Spain was truly magnificent, and that I wasn't as physically tired as I was mentally tired.

I stopped at a large area with a bar and restaurant on the Calle Llevado about two blocks from the main highway. Sixty or seventy young boys and girls (pre and teen) were playing in the area, but they were Spanish and not English. I asked directions and found myself talking with two instructors from Acorn Ventures. They spoke fluent Spanish but were not from Spain; they were from Chile and had some great travel stories to tell. It was during the fourth story that

David Blakeney and the rest of the staff wandered in. I did all right with the introductions and with the fifteen minutes of small talk about my story and how I came to be there. Then, sensing that I was about three minutes from sleep, David gave me the keys to an empty instructors cabin and told me how to find it. Everything could be sorted out tomorrow.

Tossa del Mar was a sleepy little coastal town, until the summer tourist season. Our camp was just over the hills at Calle Llevado.

The beach at Tossa. The language least frequently heard is Spanish. Boats and buses change the linguistic landscape every summer.

CHAPTER 19
SPAIN

The primary purpose of travel is to be transformed by the experience.
– Overheard in a Spanish bar

Just around the corner from Tossa de Mar in Spain were a series of granite rock formations fronting the Mediterranean. Along the base of these cliffs, about twenty feet separated the crashing waves and gray rock. Within a quarter of a mile there was a beautiful blue inlet—about forty feet wide and extending three hundred feet away from the surf.

This was the Costa Brava and I was rock climbing with David Blakeney. About sixty feet of clear Mediterranean air separated me from a bath, and I smiled the smile of someone who was doing something he shouldn't, and was getting away with it. I had not done any climbing in ten years and nothing serious in twenty. In good shape from my travels, I was now making moves on this cliff that I could have made thirty years ago. It was warm, birds were circling above, and I had absolutely no fear.

That was the case when I was seventeen and was climbing pitches like this, solo. One very important difference between then and now wasn't so much maturity as it was landing surface. First there was the sixty feet of air, and then water that was several hundred feet deep. No rocks stuck out from the all too smooth cliff face—either above or below the water surface. I could swim fairly well; I could only fly briefly. The smooth vertical surface and my climbing skills were made for this sunny day.

Climbing above a belay point usually means that a fall will be the distance above the belay plus an equal distance below it. Dave Blakeney sat on a narrow ledge at water line and payed out rope as I continued up in search of some place to anchor myself. Theoretically, I could then assist him to climb to that height or more. But there had been nothing substantial enough to warrant consideration. The ends of my fingers and the friction from my climbing shoes were all the purchase there had been. That would have been a concern of the first magnitude if there had been anything dangerous below. But on this wall, as long as I pushed away when I fell, I couldn't lose. I could, however, get wet.

As I neared the end of the climb, a likely looking left handhold loomed about eight inches farther than I could stretch. I could see the bottom of it clearly and it looked like the part I couldn't see should be very substantial. Still, to reach it, I had to violate a few climbing rules. One was to not have climbed this high without placing some sort of aid. A second was to not move more than one point at a time (a point being a hand or foot). Three points were supposed to be in contact with the rock at all times; this would be two—with a maybe for a third. If I didn't try it, I would have to jump into the water; climbing down what I'd just come up would be impossible. I knew I couldn't climb down; it was either move up or simulate flight.

About twelve inches above my right hand was the first good handhold in the entire area. My plan was to make the move for the left hand and immediately reach for the right. I rehearsed it a few times and told David exactly what I planned to do. The sixty feet of vertical suddenly looked like a lot more distance than it had when it was only academic. Sixty feet was still a long way down.

A lot happened in the split second following the move. My left hand landed squarely on a very nice knob of rock. However, as my right hand sought its hold, a two-foot section of the left hand's rock broke free because of my sudden additional weight. As my right hand caught, I tried to throw the rock mass away from the cliff face so that David would not be in any danger. There was exactly one "point" between the briny and me. My adrenal cortex worked fine in Spain. I didn't take a bath and with David's help was able to reach the top.

We returned to the camp in fine spirits, but one of us was still shaking while we prepared dinner. Tomorrow, the work would be interesting.

I had come to Spain from Germany. Now I was working for Acorn Ventures because there was a shortage of instructors at the camp for kids. This was about as far away from Asia and Africa as I could imagine. The work was with British kids on holiday in Spain. Most of the activities were associated with the water: kayaking, sailing, snorkeling, and others. It wasn't the same as gymnastics camps in the mountains of Arizona, but children on holiday are much the same everywhere.

Spain wasn't the same at all. Tossa de Mar was a picturesque little coastal town for most of the year. During the summer, it was hard to find the natives for the crowds. Boats, cars, and buses brought huge numbers of tourists and the one language you didn't hear much was Spanish. If any of the Spain described by Hemingway is left, it is on the twisting roads along the coast or on the television sets in the restaurants. Motorcyclists with full racing gear try to coax the absolute maximum out of each corner—and still allow enough room for the frequent tour bus or cornering sports car. Bullfights are commonly covered in great detail on all stations on all televisions.

I was finally in a country where I spoke a lot of the language and understood more than I could say. But as with the rest of my trip, it did me little good. Few people were interested in improving my Spanish; most were concerned with improving their English. I couldn't find much wrong with their English; most of them had seen more recent American movies than I had or had read some of the hundreds of monthly magazines available in most stores. Language was still a problem—but only for me.

There are differences between Spain and Mexico. The first ignorance that I demonstrated in front of others was to ask to change dollars to *pesos. Peso* is pronounced *peseta* in Spain. Perhaps I had been too hard on "James Bond" for his confusion about the Swiss *"shilling,"* and Swiss *franc.*

I noticed that David was fluent in French and in Spanish. Since he had known almost no Nepali after four visits to that country, I was surprised and curious to know about his fluency here. He had not joined the military in England as his friends had. Instead, he had gone to Spain and enlisted in their foreign legion. Knowing none of the language, he was unable to follow orders and spent most of his basic training repairing wounds from various beatings. He told me that he learned rather quickly. The several years he spent training and fighting had left him fluent in Spanish, with some French. I reflected on the nature of nearly all the Westerners I had met on my trip; it seemed that almost everyone had pushed to the limit in many ways. Not surprisingly, there wasn't anyone who watched more than an hour or two of the "telly" per week. They were too busy living. That might be just another judgment of mine, but it seems pretty apt.

Stanching the flow of outgoing money was a good idea and working for David was a lot like working with David. A lot of time was spent preparing the camp for the children and in planning the supervision and extra events for free time. Something was going wrong, however, and I was facing the worst nightmare for a traveler who was not in external danger. About three weeks after I arrived in England, I had a health problem. Something like a boil had developed on one shoulder and on the upper right side of my back. Unlike a typical boil, the inside was not liquid; it was as solid as a rock. There was nothing like an unexplained and painful problem to throw a damper on life. And this was as much pain as I had ever endured. Dr. Green, mad marathoner and dentist, had done a minor surgical procedure, and I was soon feeling much better with only two small scars for souvenirs.

Now, in Spain, I had another one of these mysterious "infections." It had started in France as we drove to several of the Acorn Venture campsites. One of the nurses in the L' Ardeche Valley had been on an across-Africa trip and said that she had seen a lot of these infections. She thought it might be insect-related and recommended a specific type of medication. It hurt in Spain; it was nearly lethal in Spain.

Eventually, the pain was so bad that I could not sleep and had trouble moving one arm above shoulder height. It was time to see a local doctor in Tossa. Without anesthetic, he scraped the area three days in a row. He disinfected the carbuncle-shaped area after each scraping, and I stood outside his office for nearly twenty minutes afterward. Then I would ride a bicycle back up the mountain using just one arm. Each day it was worse.

The doctor did not know that I understood Spanish, and I didn't tell him. In this way I could hear what he and his nurse thought were the causes. Of course, he had never seen anything like this. If it was a *pecho venemoso* (poisonous insect), as he thought at first, it was not responding to treatment. For a while he thought it was cancer, but that also was not conforming to the symptoms. After the fifth visit in seven days, I had come to the end of an increasingly short tether.

One day, while cutting some bamboo for a roof for the kitchen area, I almost passed out from the pain of arm movement. David and the rest of the staff had not seen what was developing because it was bandaged daily. When they removed the bandages that afternoon, my job was terminated. There was unanimous agreement that I needed help and needed it quickly. I was sent back to London with one of the tour groups the next day and instructed to go to a London hospital that had a department specializing in tropical medicine. Spain was over.

CHAPTER 20
<u>HOMEWARD</u>

*It was a far easier matter to begin the journey
than it was to stop it....*
– Bret Varner

I was back across the English Channel. There had been no sleep on the crossing. Because of the problem with my back, I had not slept well for a very long time. There were few positions where I didn't put pressure directly on the swelling. Movement woke me immediately, and it was no use wondering whether it was the movement itself that woke me or fear that the movement would lead to contact with a solid object. For someone who usually fell peacefully asleep, this was a nightmare of the worst kind.

There was a certain irony to the next day's walk to Charing Cross Hospital. As a backpacker, I should have carried my worldly possessions on my back. I used every other position I could imagine. And I soon learned why backs are the area of choice. My arms ached after only a few blocks and my legs were gouged from the effects of the buckles hitting me on each step. I wondered if I would self-destruct before I found out what alien life form had taken hold of me. And that's what it felt like. When the special effects in a movie show an alien life form bursting from a human host's body, people are surprised, shocked, and incredulous. After months of this pain, I would not have been startled in the least. I hoped that the hospital's tropical disease center would have some answers.

The waiting room was very crowded. A wide variety of societal strata were represented. The very poor and the very wealthy were there and so were the old and the young. Everything seemed to be a departure from the typical American waiting room in a clinic of doctors, but I couldn't focus on what the difference was. The clerical work wasn't being done on a computer and a harried staff tried to keep up with the crush of patients. I leaned my good shoulder against a wall and remembered the waves of pain that had washed over me after the Tossa de Mar visits. The same intense pain was now a constant throb across my back and shoulders.

The doctor was exceptionally polite and concerned. He shook my hand, asked me how I liked England, and quizzed me about my problem. He was less calm when he saw the problem. It vindicated my concern when he asked me if they could take some photos for a medical text. I told him that I would agree if they took the pictures just seconds before they cut the heart out of the thing and dissolved it with lye.

They scraped a sample, and then they scraped another. When they asked if it hurt, I just smiled my best España smile and thought of the bike rides up from Tossa de Mar. I was given some medication and a poultice was taped to my back. Extra dressings were provided and I was told that the infected area would have to be cleaned every day and a new poultice applied. As far as I was concerned, anything they wanted was fine with me.

I left the hospital with more hope than I had come in with. The pack rested over my good shoulder, and it seemed almost bearable. I knew that I would be in the United States soon, and I was sure that if this medication didn't work, I would find something there that would.

Penny and Nick were glad to have a last quick visit. Bedford was a nice place to recover for a few days. Now that my departure was so close, I had very mixed feelings about the final leg of my adventure. In Asia and Africa, my skin color and clothing had set me apart immediately, and the people I had met had invariably been friendly. In Europe, my looks didn't matter. Only when I spoke was any measure of foreignness clearly established. Now I was returning to a place where only the content of what I said would alert anyone to my unique perspective, engendered by my travels. The idea that I might be different in some important way was one that Nick didn't share.

Penny and Nick had returned from two years of exciting travel. And almost no one had been more than mildly curious about what they had done or experienced. Even some family members seemed underwhelmed after the first few minutes of welcoming them back. Nick told me to prepare for some of the same. I told him that I was hoping that my situation would be different, but I couldn't be sure. Americans seemed to put more credence into something on television, in the paper, or as part of a lecture. Something experienced by someone they knew was somehow different and less important. I suspected that Nick might be right.

I stepped aboard a plane and turned and waved to my friends. The edge I had been balanced on for so long was now clear in my mind in a way it never had been before. I was less nationalistic than I had been. I had the smatterings of seven languages rolling around in my head with the memory of a hundred people who had greatly influenced me. I had climbed mountains, run races, seen wild animals, and experienced many different societies. And it had gone by much too quickly. Actually, there didn't seem to be an edge any longer, and I knew I would be doing this again. It was time to return and make some money so that I could travel some more. I wanted to see South America very much.

Somewhere over the ocean I reclined my seat and went through a relaxation technique I had learned in Goa, India. I started at the top of my head and gradually worked through each muscle group, and in a half hour I was comfortably at ease. Then I did a similar stress reduction for my mental state. My heart rate dropped, and my breathing slowed. This process was fairly quick. A number of times during my trip this had been the only way to sleep through noise or the pain of muscle aches caused by hard physical work. When it was a mental and physical effort to move my arm, I opened the money belt around my waist.

Out of it I took my passport. Good old number 072727917. My picture stared back at me. I hoped I still looked like that picture so that I could argue that I deserved another trip. I thumbed through the pages of stamps. There were fourteen countries and fifteen stamps. All but that extra stamp brought a flood of memories. The one that didn't? THE SOVEREIGN REPUBLIC OF AMNEISA! Dr. Tom at the medical clinic in Pheriche in Nepal had stamped that one. We had agreed that it would always be the one visa stamp that no one would remember anything about.

I closed the passport and took out the various items given to me by friends. The small black rock that Missy Morrisey had given me was first. All through India I had taken it out of the fanny pack at important times. At the top of Kuari Pass, the sacred shrine of Hemkund Lake, the Ganges River, the Taj Mahal, the Red Fort, and during the sunset in Goa—I had some great associations with that black rock. India had been important to her on a trip she had taken twenty years before. I set it down on the folding tray in front of me and took out the two pennies from the twins in Boise.

I had held these coins in my hand on top of Kala Pattar in Nepal. A small hand-sewn bag had been given to me in India when I had bought some jewelry for some friends back home. I had thought of leaving the coins there at 18,100 feet under the topmost rock. They would be left where they could only be found with directions from me. They might have encouraged two special young women to travel to this far-off land. I had changed my mind when I thought of how long it had taken me to reach that place. Brandi and Bree would be unlikely to make such a time-consuming visit. I brought the coins down the mountain. Now I set them next to the black rock. Black rock? I hadn't thought about that until now. Kala Pattar meant "black rock." And it was the Hindi word, not the Nepali word. The rock and the coins had a connection I couldn't have known until I learned the languages and visited the places.

Sherry's cross was next. Still on a gold chain, it had not gone to Rome. I had not been in a Catholic country until Europe. But I remembered the Catholic Mission in East Africa and the cathedral-like Catholic churches in southern India. It had been blessed in both. It had counted for many hours of conversation with people I had met in foreign lands. No one argued about religion in those hours, they just expressed curiosity about my country and Christianity. I knew Sherry wouldn't be disappointed that the Pope hadn't blessed it. She had written that it was important just to have a reminder of a friend's journey. I curled the chain in my palm and placed it on the tray.

Jelmina's friendship ring was next. I had worn it on the little finger of my left hand for a month, after my arrival in Goa. It was a daily reminder to me that the Philippines would have to be included on another of my trips. "Mina" had been very good about writing to me even though we were almost strangers. Her reactions to my letters invariably led to comments about how her country compared to what I was experiencing at the time. I looked forward to returning her ring and hearing again the things she had told me before I left. Now, they would mean much more. I now spoke the language of travel.

The slip of paper was crumpled and faded from exposure to water in various countries. "Remember Value Rigidity." A half-dozen times on this trip, the paper had reminded me to consider carefully what I thought I knew. Almost everyone I met had demonstrated a different path and a different way of dealing with the same experience I was having. I still hadn't figured out who had written it and slipped it into my passport. Nothing in any of the letters from home had hinted at authorship—not even an oblique reference. It certainly had been an important message.

That wasn't quite all. The Swiss Army knife from Rick was now in the cargo hold. I remembered the breadless onion and tuna sandwiches on the road in Africa, and I remembered dozens of other practical uses in every country. I smiled as each memory unfolded into my relaxed state.

I slipped everything back into the belt. Within a week, I would see each of the people these objects belonged to. Perhaps I would even discover the note writer. Those would be adventures of a different kind. How would I communicate what had happened to me? What had happened to me? I knew these people would care, but would they understand?

I was sure the edge I had once experienced was gone. I could now travel at will and not worry about the process. As I nodded off to sleep over Greenland, I looked beyond the value rigidity of those last two thoughts and saw another adventure—far in the distance, but definitely there. For the first time on any conveyance, I slept soundly.

Paul Quigley celebrated his 50th birthday with some friends atop a Utah mountain peak. His goal to climb Ben Lomond was temporarily halted when an automobile accident left him partially paralyzed. Here, he negotiates the last 100 feet to the summit in a single-wheel "prototype" and with the careful assistance of others.
A single-track trail had taken the group through about 2 miles of easily negotiated area. After a rendition of Happy Birthday *and some pictures, Paul returned home safely. A front-page article in the local paper greeted the group the next day.*
The meaning of life is in the picture—in several ways.
Counterclockwise from right to left: Sam Dean (photographer), Jim Wright (reporter), Liisa Frei, Matt Bickerson, Mike Dennison, Paul Quigley (sitting on the prototype), Jodi Rood, "Skeeter" Chadwick.
Photo by Pat Glassman.

CHAPTER 20
<u>THE MEANING OF LIFE</u>

*Unless a man creates something outside himself, the meaning of life
vanishes at the instant of his death. His gift is his life and how he lives
to move others to reach and live beyond what they thought possible.
Thus, he lives on forever.*
– Jodi Rood

I hadn't realized just how much I had changed until I tried to report back to
Rick on "the meaning of life." We had been pretty flippant about the topic as
I had made hectic plans prior to my flight to Singapore fourteen months earlier.
Now I was back. and he was asking. I tried to write it in a letter:

Dear Rick,

When I started the trip I really did think about "the meaning of
life." I wondered whether it could be found? Certainly, the popularity
of Eastern mysticism in Western society made me think that I might
be starting in the right direction. In my journal I noted everything that
seemed important and I tried to think about how to put it all
together—at least I did when the conditions for relaxed thought were
available.

One part of the answer seemed to be "participation." People
who were actively involved in their own lives seemed to enjoy them
selves more. But Thailand's culture believed the opposite: You make
progress toward enlightenment through non-involvement or passive
involvement—whatever that is.

Sanuk was an excellent concept and I thought that might be the
right idea: Enjoy whatever you are doing, work or play. George Hery,
Stormy Eaton, and you have always exemplified that approach to life.
As I continued to take notes and think about what I was learning, I
tried to take a page out of the Buddha's life. I realized that everything

I had seen could be seen and analyzed much differently. In fact, finding a new point of view emerged as the most common thread in my journal and my trip. I would see something, Americanize it, and then discover that the people of that area didn't see it my way at all. Julie, Bill, and I had been wrong about the *sanuk* of the restaurant staff on Kho Phi Phi. I'd done the same with the Turkana and Samburu people in the African villages and their rites of passage. Again and again, I tried to focus on what was happening around me with my own culture as my guide. The piece of paper warning me about value rigidity constantly reminded me that point of view was crucial to insight. For a while, I thought you might have stuck that note in my passport at our last meeting before I left. Now, I'm not so sure.

And then I found the answer. And as soon as I had it, an avalanche of ideas came crashing down. I spent hours writing as fast as I could and tried to get all of it. I couldn't wait to write to you and tell you what I thought was some very important and good news.

I was in the L' Ardeche Valley in France when it came to me, and I admit that I foolishly tried to explain it to the instructors at the Acorn Ventures camp where I was staying. We were at a pizza parlor and I was being quizzed about what I had been writing for the better part of the day. I told them and as a result discovered something very important about delivering "messages." Be significant. If you think you are going to be heard just because you say you have an important answer, you have committed your first error. Catholics expect the Pope to deliver that kind of news; Buddhists expect that it will come from the leader of their particular sect; atheists expect that a famous scientist or scholar will present their case. Certainly, the British instructors in France didn't think a profound message was going to come from a middle-aged American backpacker. I was reminded of John Denver's character in the movie *Oh God!* He lamented that God hadn't chosen someone more important than a grocery clerk to deliver His message, and he believed that no one would listen to him. The movie was funny; the argument over my pronouncement wasn't.

They debated for a long time and then I sat back and listened, and I watched. That was a pretty significant departure for me and I was surprised. It was a very Buddhist thing to have done. I noticed that antagonism had been the first reaction to my statement. All through Asia and Africa I had replied to questions about my country and culture, and the response to my answers had always been more polite questions. Among the Sikhs at Hemkund Lake, I had welcomed the arrival of my travel companions because the questions had gone on for hours. The various approaches to important pronouncements always seemed to be colored by the culture. That seemed very important.

When I returned to the U.S., I watched debates in the governmental, scientific, and judicial arenas and noted that reasonable men always seemed to disagree—and they did it as often and as strenuously as possible. Their position often left them incapable of seeing their opponent's point of view. Or as I was beginning to understand, any other valid points of view.

I sensed the problem behind the statement "the meaning of life is—" How much of "the truth" is usually just a cultural bias? I looked at the answer I had written on the last page of my journal and the few qualifying phrases that explained what contributed to it; it seemed to be transcultural. And then I got a second part of a new point of view.

If each "meaning of life" answer is specific to a culture, then each culture should have its own solution. And the most devoted and enlightened members of that society should have developed each of those answers. But that didn't seem to be true. The more engrossed people got with finding "the answer," the less enlightened they seemed to be. I didn't hear any great truths coming out of the fundamentalists of any particular group. On the contrary, most fundamentalists seem to become fanatical, and the world is awash in their battles against others. I wondered about that. If you can't get the answer from total immersion in one point of view, can you get it by understanding many points of view? On my last page of my journal, I had my answer. And it seemed to be a good one. Was it time to step back and see how it applied to the world I was traveling around?

I did and I learned that culture does not enable us to understand. Culture is one of the stumbling blocks to understanding. No one is born free of culture, but it is that ability to move beyond the folkways and mores of a society that allows for a freedom of inquiry. I realized that my trip had been my first real experience with this process. As I read my answer over, I could tell that it was a good first attempt. I suspected that I would alter it as I learned to see more and more points of view. If that meant more trips to far-off lands, then I was all for it.

I'll give you the answer and some detailed explanation in the next letter—if you want it.

I gave him the answer in the second letter. In keeping with the idea of cultural points of view, he asked many questions and kept away from the instant antagonism that has become a staple of American media, and therefore American culture. My trip did a lot to me. Each country offered at least one more way to look at the world. My attempts at new languages and new cultural ways of life shifted my ideas enough to make it clear that my assumptions needed examining. I understood, for the first time, why inquiries such as "What is the sound of one hand clapping?" were important. They said more about the state of the listener's enlightenment than the profundity of the speaker. Some cultures would dismiss such a statement, but others would review it with hundreds of hours of thought and speculation. When the student is ready, the teacher will come.

Before my trip, I did not understand that important lessons come to us all of the time. After my trip, that is almost all I can understand.

Did I find the meaning of life? To be very Eastern about it: yes—and no.

To understand it, you have to go beyond the edge.

LOVE

by Angel Shamaya

I quietly Listen to your every thought
as I wrap your soul in warm, soft Light.

By my very nature, I Excite you to your greatest potential.

And, when you found yourself in the throes of struggle,
I remind you to Relax, *for I am Love.*

~ ~

I inspire each note of beautiful music and
every first kiss between Lovers.
I am the loyal Affection of a sprightly young puppy
playfully licking his new human.
I am the bond that ties all Hearts and Spirits though they be
separated by the thin veil you call death.
And, I am much more than this, *for I am Love.*

~ ~

With absolute knowing, I healed the gravest of wounds
this world could inflict.
All who have gone before you have been touched by me
in special Ways.
When they are open, no heart nor life is immune
to my Healing, Guiding Light.
Cascading down through the centuries
has only strengthened my Power, *for I am Love.*

~ ~

Poems and songs are shared in my name
throughout every culture on Earth.
I flow like a quiet, playful brook through the very air you breathe,
filling you with Divinity.
I giggle when you respond to me and tickle you when you least
expect it, *for I am Love.*

~ ~

I am the pulse of creativity on which you soar so freely.

And, late in the night, when the pangs of loneliness
left you swirling in uncertainty, I watched over you as if you were my
only child and I your only safety.

I tucked you into my bosom, warmly blanketing you,
harboring you from distractions so you could heal.

Dreams from my Heart splash through every part of you
like butterflies on a summer breeze,
As I bathe you in that which you need the most.
Such is my nature, *for I am Love.*

~ ~

I am the graceful acceptance of another's ways
and a gentle nudge in the right direction.
I light every path to Higher Ground.
I am timeless certainty that there is more to this life
than meets the eye.
I am the vivifying energy in your Heart,
as you savor the Greatness of Being.
I am knowledge and deeper seeing. I am everybody freeing.
Peace of mind is my signature, *for I am Love.*

~ ~

I am the Power that helps you turn the other cheek, A shield for the
helpless and weak, a Light when it all seems so bleak.

When life lays you bare and vulnerable,
I cry every drop of your sorrow, bleed every drop of your pain.

Your faith pulls me into your Heart,
and there I reside like a Clear, Endless River.

I am The Knower and The Giver,
A Stream of Overflowing Goodness.

I am these things and infinitely more, *for I am Love.*

EPILOGUE

The changes I thought I perceived during the European phase of my trip got worse. Or, from my perspective, they got better. Almost no physical hardship fazed me. I read my journal entries over again and discovered that it was almost like hearing about a stranger. Faced with the past, I discovered that my current choices and attitudes were a rich and varied tapestry. What, I wondered, would this mean for my friendships and my future?

Penny and Nick wrote and called from Bedford, England. They had been right about the mild interest of most acquaintances for my trip. And they had been wrong as well, because some people hadn't been able to hear enough. Some people even wanted to join me on the next trip; they seemed to know before I did that this would happen again.

Ria wrote a number of times while she and her boyfriend, Yves, traveled to South America and suggested places to see. They are married and now have two children, Sebastien and Benoit Hormidas Perreault. I've been invited to be a favored uncle and to sit at their hearth sometime to see how Canadian babies treat old adventurers. E-mail keeps us in touch often and it is a very good thing to hear about their life in the wilderness. Some of that hearth sitting looks like it will involve building a cabin floor.

I called Brad in California and he was back as a pony-tailed accountant and preparing for another trip. He and a friend, Susie, had bicycled from Kathmandu to Lhasa in Tibet—after Africa. He recommended this experience highly, and his description made me homesick for the road. A few months ago, I called him again. He was not at his old address or phone number, and I thought I knew what that meant.

I heard twice from Bill. He sent a Christmas form letter announcing that he and Julie were getting a divorce. During a group counseling session after their return, he had met Carla, and they had decided to marry. I wrote back to the address and got a second note telling me that he was going to do some lecturing and to promote some New Age ideas. He had become affiliated with a group in the Northwest and felt that he had found his calling. His travel experiences, vegetarianism, and other attributes prepared him for this new life. I wished him well, but never heard from him again.

Julie disappeared. I spoke with her mother in Iowa and heard that she had just remarried last year and was going to relocate in Sedona, Arizona. So far, she hasn't activated a published number. While I was curious to hear the other side of what happened, I was sure that it would hold few surprises. Certainly, she should be a happier person now.

Rick was one of those people who seemed enthralled with the trip. He had been in Europe for those two weeks and he was anxious to visit Nepal if I ever elected to return. I opened the trip up to a half-dozen active friends and waited. Rick joined up right away. And we found a third traveling companion from an unusual source. A former girlfriend from a quarter century ago asked if we would take her fourteen-year-old son to Kala Pattar. We agreed and Alex Paulos joined us in what had to be a very early start on epic adventures. The adjustments in responsibility, fitness, and mental toughness are demanding on such a trek. Like Eric in Africa, Alex and Rick hiked themselves into shape and made the Jiri to Namche hike in six days. Eventually, it was the fourteen-year-old who was the only one who made it to the top of Kala Pattar.

In addition to the Nepal trip, Rick had an addition to the family. Bretton Connor was born on February 6, 1998. Anita and Rick had Alexa and Bretton to add to their already hectic lifestyle. They were both delighted, as was I. By the time young Alexa and Bretton are old enough to bike and run seriously, I will be old enough to confine my exploits to stories of the good old days.

Prior to my trip, six of my friends had died, reminding me how fragile life can be. When I returned it was to more unwanted lessons. In 1995, Stormy Eaton died in a small plane crash in Arizona. One of the U.S. gymnastics coaches, he was a close friend for twenty-five years; his death tore a hole in the hearts of thousands of people. We had coached together and had made the annual gymnastics camp and a Lake Powell vacation an integral part of our lives. I started him on a running career and he pushed that from marathons to triathlons. He hadn't traveled in the same way I had, but he had always had one of the best concepts of the meaning of life of anyone I had ever known.

And then my mom died.

Thankfully, she passed away while taking a nap. She had worked the *New York Times* crossword that morning, and I found it and her pen on the kitchen table. Her music was still open on the grand piano. She had practiced that morning because she only put the music away after the last practice session in the evening. And her work gloves and muddy shoes were outside the back door; she had tended her garden in the early afternoon. A friend of mine called her about three in the afternoon to leave a message to be passed on to me. She had gone to her room for her afternoon nap and had died about four o'clock. The diabetes and heart condition she had hidden from everyone had finally taken the ultimate toll. I immediately understood that hers had been a "good" death. The more stories I heard from friends about the lingering deaths of their loved ones, the more that was reaffirmed. My trip had meant the most to her. She had kept the more than four dozen letters I had written in a special file box; she re-read them often. In many ways it was the trip she had always wanted to take but had never found time for.

I found out what was beyond the edge. It was the best view, of course. The sound of one hand clapping.

With Mom

With Jodi Rood on a winter bike ride at Mueller Park above Bountiful, Utah.
(Photo by Robert Craven)